U.S. Court Cases

U.S. Court Cases

Volume 2

Court Cases:

Korematsu v. United States —
Zablocki v. Redhail
Index

Edited by
THE EDITORS OF SALEM PRESS

SALEM PRESS, INC.
Pasadena, California   Hackensack, New Jersey

Essays originally appeared in *American Justice*, 1996;
American Indians, 1995; *Censorship*, 1997; *Women's Issues*,
1997; *Encyclopedia of Family Life*, 1998; *Ethics*, 1994; *Great
Events from History II: Human Rights Series*, 1992; *Great
Events from History: North American Series*, rev. 1997; and
Survey of Social Science: Government and Politics, 1995; new
material has been added.

∞ The paper used in these volumes conforms to the
American National Standard for Permanence of Paper for
Printed Library Materials, Z39.48-1992(R1997).

Library of Congress Cataloging-in-Publication Data
U.S. Court Cases / edited by the editors of Salem Press.
    p.   cm. — (Magill's choice)
Includes bibliographical references and index.
    ISBN 0-89356-422-2 (set: alk. paper). — ISBN 0-89356-
423-0 (vol. 1: alk. paper). — ISBN 0-89356-424-9 (vol. 2:
alk. paper)
    1. Law—United States—Cases. 2. Courts—United States.
I. Salem Press. II. Title: US court cases. III. Series.
KF385.A4U15   1999
347.73'1—dc21   99-19926
                                      CIP

First Printing

PRINTED IN THE UNITED STATES OF AMERICA

Contents

Appendices

Court Cases
(continued)

Korematsu v. United States

U.S. SUPREME COURT
RULING ISSUED DECEMBER 18, 1944

- In this case, the Supreme Court refused to rule in favor of the privacy rights of an American citizen of Japanese ancestry who was detained in a relocation camp during World War II.

In 1942, American military authorities arrested Fred Toyosaburo Korematsu, an American citizen of Japanese ancestry, for remaining in San Leandro, California, a restricted region, in violation of a military order. The military acted under authority of President Franklin Roosevelt's Executive Order 9066, which authorized the secretary of war and appropriate military commanders to establish military areas from which persons might be excluded. The president issued this order on his authority as commander in chief of the army and navy. After being found guilty of violating the military order, Korematsu appealed his case to the U.S. Supreme Court.

In December, 1944, the U.S. Supreme Court ruled 6 to 3 in favor of the United States and in support of Korematsu's arrest. The majority opinion, written by Justice Hugo L. Black, sustained Korematsu's removal because "the properly constituted military authorities" feared an invasion of the West Coast and had decided that military urgency required the removal of persons of Japanese origin from the area.

Black admitted that the exclusion order worked hardship on the Japanese American population, "but hardships are a part of war and war is an aggregation of hardships." Furthermore, the exclusion program did not constitute racial discrimination as such; Korematsu had not been excluded because of his race but because of the requirements of national security. As to the question of loyalty, Black stated that there was insufficient time to separate the loyal from the disloyal Japanese. The only recourse, then, was for the military leaders to take such action as they deemed necessary to protect the country and its citizens from possible aggression. The section of Black's opinion that has most often been cited, however, states that "all legal restrictions which curtail the civil rights of a single racial group are immediately suspect" and must be given "the most rigid scrutiny."

Three justices differed from the majority and registered vigorous dissents. Justice Owen J. Roberts objected on the grounds of both loyalty and race. This was a "case of convicting a citizen as punishment for not submitting to imprisonment in a concentration camp, solely because of his ancestry," without evidence concerning his loyalty to the United States. Justice Frank Mur-

Japanese American families awaiting relocation after President Franklin D. Roosevelt issued Executive Order 9066 in early 1942. *(National Archives)*

phy was equally adamant in his dissent. He denounced the removal of Japanese citizens as "one of the most sweeping and complete deprivations of constitutional rights in the history of this nation in the absence of martial law." He concluded that the exclusion program itself "goes over the 'very brink of constitutional power' and falls into the very ugly abyss of racism."

The importance of *Korematsu v. United States* lies in the difficulty that the Court had in determining the dividing line between the constitutional rights of the citizen and the nation's power to defend itself. In this case, the Court did not rule on the constitutionality of the internment of someone on the basis of race, only that the presidential executive order and the subsequent military orders were deemed necessary for the defense of the nation and its citizens. While it took the United States more than forty years officially to rectify and repudiate the internment of Japanese Americans (reparations payments were authorized by Congress in 1988), many commentators have long believed that the United States acted improperly and in violation of the civil rights of American citizens by its use of the internment camp program.

Kevin F. Sims

Lau v. Nichols

U.S. SUPREME COURT
DECIDED JANUARY 21, 1974

• Landmark Supreme Court ruling that failure to supply adequate education to non-English-speaking students violates the Constitution. The opinion declares that some form of bilingual education must be reserved for these individuals.

In 1954, the Supreme Court ruled in *Brown v. Board of Education of Topeka, Kansas* that the Fourteenth Amendment to the U.S. Constitution forbade school systems from segregating students into separate schools for only whites or African Americans. The decision effectively overturned a previous Court ruling, in *Plessy v. Ferguson* (1896), that such facilities could be "separate but equal." Instead of desegregating, however, Southern school systems engaged in massive resistance to the Court's order during the next decade. Congress then passed the Civil Rights Act of 1964, which prohibits many types of discrimination. Title VI of the law bans discrimination by recipients of federal financial assistance, including school systems.

In 1965, Congress adopted the Immigration and Nationality Act, under which larger numbers of Asian immigrants arrived in the United States than ever before, and their non-English-speaking children enrolled in public schools. In the San Francisco Unified School District, students were required to attend school until sixteen years of age, but in 1967, 2,856 students could not adequately comprehend instruction in English.

Although 433 students were given supplemental courses in English on a full-time basis and 633 on a part-time basis, the remaining 1,790 students received no additional language instruction. Nevertheless, the state of California required all students to graduate with proficiency in English and permitted school districts to provide bilingual education, if needed. Except for the 433 students in the full-time bilingual education program, Chinese-speaking students were integrated in the same classrooms with English-speaking students but lacked sufficient language ability to derive benefit from the instruction. Of the 1,066 students taking bilingual courses, only 260 had bilingual teachers.

Some parents of the Chinese-speaking children, concerned that their children would drop out of school and experience pressure to join criminal youth gangs, launched protests. Various organizations formed in the Chinese American community, which in turn made studies, issued proposals, circulated leaflets, and tried to negotiate with the San Francisco Board of Education. When the board refused to respond adequately, a suit was filed in federal district court in San Francisco on March 25, 1970. The plaintiffs were Kinney Kinmon Lau and eleven other non-English-speaking students, mostly U.S. citizens born of Chinese parents. The defendants were Alan H.

Nichols, president of the San Francisco Board of Education, the rest of the Board of Education, and the San Francisco Board of Supervisors.

On May 25, 1970, the Office for Civil Rights (OCR) of the U.S. Department of Health, Education, and Welfare issued the following regulation pursuant to its responsibility to monitor Title VI compliance: "Where inability to speak and understand the English language excludes national-origin minority group children from effective participation in the educational program offered by a school district, the district must take affirmative steps to rectify the language deficiency in order to open its instructional program to these students." OCR had sided with the Chinese-speaking students.

One day later, the court ruled that the school system was violating neither Title VI nor the Fourteenth Amendment; instead, the plaintiffs were characterized as asking for "special rights above those granted other children." Lawyers representing the Chinese Americans then appealed, this time supported by a friend-of-the-court brief filed by the U.S. Department of Justice. On January 8, 1973, the Court of Appeals also ruled adversely, stating that there was no duty "to rectify appellants' special deficiencies, as long as they provided these students with access to the same educational system made available to all other students." The appeals court claimed that the children's problems were "not the result of law enacted by the state . . . but the result of deficiency created by themselves in failing to learn the English language."

On June 12, 1973, the Supreme Court agreed to hear the case. Oral argument was heard on December 10, 1973. On January 21, 1974, the Supreme Court unanimously overturned the lower courts. Justice William O. Douglas delivered the majority opinion, which included the memorable statement that "There is no equality of treatment merely by providing students with the same facilities, textbooks, teachers, and curriculum; for students who do not understand English are effectively foreclosed from any meaningful education." The Court returned the case to the district court so that the school system could design a plan of language-needs assessments and programs for addressing those needs. In a concurring opinion, Chief Justice

Warren E. Burger and Justice Harry A. Blackmun observed that the number of underserved non-English-speaking, particularly Chinese-speaking, students was substantial in this case, but they would not order bilingual education for "just a single child who speaks only German or Polish or Spanish or any language other than English."

The Supreme Court's decision in *Lau* ultimately resulted in changes to enable Chinese-speaking students to obtain equal educational opportunity in San Francisco's public schools, although it was more than a year before such changes began to be implemented. The greatest impact has been among Spanish-speaking students, members of the largest language-minority group in the United States.

Subsequently, Congress passed the Equal Educational Opportunities Act in 1974, a provision of which superseded *Lau* by requiring "appropriate action to overcome language barriers that impede equal participation," which a federal district court later applied to the need for new methods to deal with speakers of "Black English" in *Martin Luther King, Jr., Elementary School Children v. Michigan Board of Education* (1979). Also in 1974, the Bilingual Education Act of 1968 was amended to provide more federal funds for second-language instruction so that school districts could be brought into compliance with *Lau*. Bilingualism was further recognized when Congress passed the Voting Rights Act of 1975, which established guidelines for providing ballots in the languages of certain minority groups.

In 1975, OCR established informal guidelines for four bilingual programs that would enable school districts to come into compliance with the Supreme Court ruling. The main requirement was first to test students to determine language proficiency. Students with no English proficiency at all were to be exposed to bilingual/bicultural programs or transitional bilingual education programs; secondary schools also had the option of providing "English as a second language" or "high intensive language training" programs. If a student had some familiarity with English, these four programs would be required only if testing revealed that the student had low achievement test scores.

Because the OCR guidelines were not published in the *Federal Register* for public comment and later modification, they were challenged on September 29, 1978, in the federal district court of Alaska (*Northwest Arctic School District v. Califano*). The case was settled by a consent decree in 1980, when the federal agency agreed to publish a "Notice of Proposed Rulemaking"; however, soon after Ronald Reagan took office as president, that notice was withdrawn.

By 1985, a manual to identify types of language discrimination was compiled to supersede the 1975 guidelines, but it also was not published in the *Federal Register* for public comment. Meanwhile, methods for educating limited-English-speaking students evolved beyond the OCR's original conceptions, and further litigation followed. In 1981, a U.S. circuit court ruled in *Castañeda v. Pickard* that bilingual educational programs are lawful when they satisfy three tests: (1) the program is recognized by professionals as sound in educational theory; (2) the program is designed to implement that theory; and (3) the program actually results in overcoming language barriers.

During the presidency of Ronald Reagan, civil rights monitoring focused more on "reverse discrimination" than on violations of equal educational opportunities. Congressional hearings were held to goad OCR into action. Although in 1991 OCR's top priority was equal educational opportunities for national-origin minority and Native American students with limited-English proficiency (LEP) or non-English proficiency (NEP), results were difficult to discern, and a movement to make English the official language of the United States (the "English-only" movement) threatened to overturn *Lau* and related legislation.

Michael Haas

Bibliography

Biegel, Stuart. "The Parameters of the Bilingual Education Debate in California Twenty Years After *Lau v. Nichols*." *Chicano-Latino Law Review* 14 (Winter, 1994). The status of *Lau* in light of the 1990's English-only movement.

Bull, Barry L., Royal T. Fruehling, and Virgie Chattergy. *The Ethics of Multicultural and Bilingual Education*. New York:

Columbia University Teachers College Press, 1992. Contrasts how liberal, democratic, and communitarian approaches to education relate to bilingual and multicultural education.

Fineberg, Elliot M., et al. "The Problems of Segregation and Inequality of Educational Opportunity." In *One Nation Indivisible: The Civil Rights Challenge for the 1990's*, edited by Reginald C. Govan and William L. Taylor. Washington, D.C.: Citizens' Commission on Civil Rights, 1989. Reviews under-enforcement of laws dealing with language-minority students during the Reagan years.

Moran, Rachel F. "Of Democracy, Devaluation, and Bilingual Education." *Creighton Law Review* 26 (February, 1993). Contrasts special-interest bargaining and bureaucratic rule-making methods for dealing with needs for bilingual education.

Newman, Terri Lunn. "Proposal: Bilingual Education Guidelines for the Courts and the Schools." *Emory Law Journal* 33 (Spring, 1984). Legal requirements of *Lau* presented as guidelines for school systems in establishing bilingual programs.

Orlando, Carlos J., and Virginia P. Collier. *Bilingual and ESL Classrooms: Teaching in Multicultural Contexts*. New York: McGraw-Hill, 1985. Discusses the need for bilingual education, alternative approaches available, and resources required.

United States Commission on Civil Rights. *A Better Chance to Learn: Bilingual-Bicultural Education*. Washington, D.C.: Author, 1975. Assesses the national impact of *Lau*; contains the text of the Supreme Court decision and related documents.

Wang, L. Ling-chi. "*Lau v. Nichols*: History of Struggle for Equal and Quality Education." In *Asian-Americans: Social and Psychological Perspectives*, edited by Russell Endo, Stanley Sue, and Nathaniel N. Wagner. Palo Alto, Calif.: Science & Behavior Books, 1980. Describes how the Lau case was pursued, especially the resistance to implementation.

Lemon v. Kurtzman

U.S. SUPREME COURT
DECIDED JUNE 28, 1971

- The Court established a three-part test to determine when governmental assistance to religious institutions violated the establishment clause of the First Amendment.

After *Everson v. Board of Education* (1947) applied the establishment clause to the states while allowing states to reimburse students' costs for attending parochial schools, the U.S. Supreme Court found it difficult to arrive at standards for deciding which kinds of assistance were consistent with the "wall of separation" between church and state. In *Board of Education v. Allen* (1968), the Court upheld a New York law that provided secular textbooks to religious schools, ruling that the law had both "a secular legislative purpose and a primary effect that neither advances nor inhibits religion." In *Walz v. Tax Commission* (1970), the Court upheld property-tax exemptions for religious organizations but added that governments must not foster "excessive governmental entanglement with religion."

A Pennsylvania law of 1968, going beyond the New York program, directly reimbursed parochial schools for the costs of secular instruction, including teacher salaries, textbooks, and various instructional materials. Alton Lemon, a Pennsylvania taxpayer, challenged the law in a suit against David Kurtzman, state superintendent of education. A federal district court dismissed Lemon's complaint, but about the same time another district court ruled that a similar Rhode Island law violated the establishment clause. Granting review for both cases, the Supreme Court consolidated them into a single decision.

The Court unanimously decided that the Pennsylvania law was unconstitutional and voted 8 to 1 against the Rhode Island law. Writing the opinion, Chief Justice Warren Burger noted that the establishment clause was "at best opaque," but he interpreted it to forbid "a step that could lead to" the establishment of religion. Combining earlier precedents, he formulated a three-pronged test for evaluating the constitutionality of such laws. First, a law must have "a secular legislative purpose"; second, its primary effect must not be to advance or to inhibit religion; third, it must not lead to an "excessive entanglement" between church and state. Burger emphasized the danger that subsidies for teachers' salaries might be used in part for religious instruction. He argued that in order to certify that government funds were used only for secular purposes, the two laws required the kind of inspection and evaluation of religious content that fostered an impermissible degree of entanglement.

The *Lemon* decision was very important because of its three-pronged test, which provided a frame of reference for judging whether laws violated the establishment clause. In subsequent cases, the Court would disagree about whether the "Lemon test" was a strict standard or simply a loose guideline. The real question was whether the Court would allow governmental accommodation of religion or insist upon a strict separation between the two spheres, and the *Lemon* framework, while helpful, could be interpreted from either perspective.

Thomas T. Lewis

Lochner v. New York

U.S. SUPREME COURT
DECIDED APRIL 17, 1905

• Reflecting laissez-faire economics and emphasizing freedom of contract, this decision invoked the Fourteenth Amendment to negate a state labor law, thus by implication minimizing the effects of state and federal social legislation upon business.

Between 1890 and 1937, the U.S. Supreme Court attempted to introduce the era's popular laissez-faire economic philosophy into constitutional law. Consequently, the Supreme Court's conservative justices delivered a series of decisions invalidating state legislation establishing minimum wages and maximum hours of employment, mandating workers' compensation, setting prices, and otherwise regulating business activities. The Court's authority for such decisions was drawn chiefly from the due process and equal protection clauses of the Fourteenth Amendment.

Ratified in 1868 during Reconstruction, the Fourteenth Amendment was drafted primarily to protect the extension of certain legal and civil rights to newly freed blacks. Its due process clause was then interpreted as guaranteeing individuals' procedural rights: the right to counsel, to *habeas corpus*, and to trial by jury in criminal and civil cases, among other procedural safeguards. The predominantly conservative Supreme Court of the late nineteenth century and early twentieth, however, began interpreting due process in a substantive manner, construing the due process clause as a device for protecting businesses and vested interests against "unreasonable" state and federal social legislation.

Substantive interpretation was brought to bear in *Lochner v. New York*. In 1897, New York State enacted a law limiting the hours of employment in bakeries and confectionery establishments to ten hours a day and sixty hours a week. New York justified this and similar laws as exercises of its police power: the obligation to protect public health, welfare, safety, and morals. Joseph Lochner, the proprietor of a Utica, New York, bakery, accordingly, was fined fifty dollars for violating this hours law—a conviction sustained by a New York appeals court. On a writ of error, Lochner's case then landed before the U.S. Supreme Court.

Justice Rufus W. Peckham, a lifelong opponent of social and economic legislation and a champion of laissez-faire policies, delivered the Court's opinion in 1905. The Court, he asserted, previously had been liberal in viewing the states' use of the police power. Since nearly any legislation, Peckham argued, could be justified as protective of the public's health, welfare, safety, and morals—thus leaving the states with "unbounded power"—the Fourteenth Amendment had to be invoked to set limits. The question at issue in *Lochner*, he reasoned, was whether New York's law represented a fair and appropriate employment of the police power, or whether it was an "arbitrary interference" with an individual's personal liberty and right to enter freely into contracts.

Peckham held for Lochner and invalidated New York's hours law, a victory for due process over the police power, by declaring that rights to personal liberty and freedom of contract should prevail when they clashed with the states' right to legislate. Justice Oliver Wendell Holmes, Jr., filed a brilliant dissent. By implication the *Lochner* decision was modified in *Muller v. Oregon* (1908) and was silently overturned in *Bunting v. Oregon* (1917).

Clifton K. Yearley

Lone Wolf v. Hitchcock

U.S. SUPREME COURT
ARGUED OCTOBER 23, 1902; DECIDED JANUARY 5, 1903

• This case established the precedent that congressional plenary power over tribal property was virtually unlimited and that Indian treaties were subject to unilateral abrogation.

In this litigation, Lone Wolf, a principal chief of the Kiowa Nation, sought a perpetual injunction against congressional ratification of a 1900 agreement that allotted tribal lands and led to a direct loss of more than 2 million acres of Indian territory. The tribes contended that the forced allotment of their lands violated Article Twelve of the 1867 Treaty of Medicine Lodge. This article explicitly stated that no cession of tribal lands would be valid without the consent of "three-fourths of all the adult male Indians."

In 1892 the Jerome Commission concluded an allotment agreement with certain representatives of the Kiowa, Comanche, and Apache (KCA) tribes. Although the commission-

Kiowa paramount chief Lone Wolf in 1869. *(National Archives)*

ers secured a number of Indian signatures, the three-fourths
provision was unfulfilled. Nevertheless, the agreement was
rushed to Washington, D.C., for congressional ratification. Almost immediately upon hearing about the allotment agreement, more than three hundred KCA tribal members urged the
Senate to disapprove the 1892 agreement because "misrepre-

sentations, threats, and fraudulent" means had been used by the government's commissioners to secure Indian signatures. Tribal consent, in other words, had not been legitimately secured.

More important, as the 1892 agreement wound its way through the ratification process, Congress substantially revised the agreement. These revisions were never submitted to the KCA tribes for their approval. Nevertheless, on June 6, 1900, and despite the protestations of the tribes concerned, Congress ratified the amended agreement.

Justice Edward D. White wrote the opinion, which was, shortly after its pronouncement in 1903, called the "Dred Scott decision number two" because it inculcated the doctrine that Indian treaty rights, although the "supreme law of the land," could be disregarded with the passage of virtually any federal law. White stated that the 1867 treaty provision had been abrogated by the 1900 agreement even though the later statute contradicted the treaty provision and lacked tribal consent. This, White said, was in keeping with "perfect good faith" toward the Indians.

White inaccurately stated that Congress had exercised plenary authority over tribes "from the beginning" and that such power was "political" and therefore not subject to judicial review. These statements were legal rationalizations, yet they were also in line with the reigning policy view of Indians at the time held by the federal government: Indians were dependent wards, subject to their sovereign guardian—the United States.

Lone Wolf v. Hitchcock was a devastating blow to tribal sovereignty. The Court's brazen refusal to examine congressional acts that abrogated treaty-acknowledged property rights was particularly oppressive because the lion's share of tribal sovereign, political, and property rights was defined by the hundreds of ratified treaties and agreements tribes negotiated with the United States. Indian rights, in short, were not created by or included in the federal Constitution. As a result of this decision, treaties as legal contracts were no longer enforceable if Congress decided to act in a manner that violated their provisions.

C. B. Clark

Lorance v. AT&T Technologies

U.S. SUPREME COURT
OPINION RENDERED ON JUNE 12, 1989

• This U.S. Supreme Court opinion strictly interprets federal legislation limiting the time an individual has to file an Equal Employment Opportunity Commission (EEOC) complaint regarding unfair employment practices.

In a 1979 collective bargaining agreement, Local 1942 of the International Brotherhood of Electrical Workers and AT&T Technologies, Inc., changed the way in which the seniority of employees was calculated. Prior to that time, hourly employees were ranked solely by number of years employed in the plant. Individuals promoted to higher-paying "tester" positions were allowed to keep their seniority. A tester's seniority after 1979, however, was not based on length of plantwide service but on time as a tester, although one could regain plantwide seniority after five years.

Patricia Lorance, a tester when the new agreement became policy, was demoted in 1982 when her employer cut its workforce. Lorance and other female employees filed charges with the EEOC in 1983, followed by action in a district court alleging that the seniority system implemented in 1979 violated Title VII of the Civil Rights Act of 1964. The women claimed that the system in place protected male employees and discriminated against female employees, who had only recently become testers in increasing numbers.

The Supreme Court held that Lorance had no claim because she had not filed a charge with the EEOC within 180 days of the alleged unfair employment practice, as required by law. Critics of the decision say this opinion harms victims of discrimination: Because some of the claimants were not employed in the division when the policy was adopted, they would have to anticipate discrimination before it occurred.

Donald C. Simmons, Jr.

Loving v. Virginia

U.S. SUPREME COURT
RULING ISSUED JUNE 12, 1967

• In this decision the Supreme Court struck down the antimiscegenation laws of several states that prohibited interracial couples from marrying or living together while not married.

In 1958 Virginia and several other states outlawed interracial marriage and sex between unmarried interracial partners. All such laws prohibited whites and African Americans from intermarrying; some also applied to members of other races.

Richard Loving, a white man, and Mildred Jeter, an African American woman, lived in Virginia and wanted to be married. They went to the District of Columbia, where they were married legally. When they returned to their home in Virginia, however, they were arrested. The circuit court of Caroline County, Virginia, found them guilty and sentenced them to one year in jail, a sentence which would be suspended if they agreed to leave the state.

The Lovings moved to Washington, D.C., and filed an appeal against the Virginia court decision. In 1967 the case reached the U.S. Supreme Court. The Court's justices unanimously sided with the Lovings, overturning the Virginia statute and those similar to it. By denying interracial couples the right to do something that other couples were allowed to do, antimiscegenation laws violated these citizens' right to the equal protection of the laws as guaranteed by the Fourteenth Amendment of the U.S. Constitution. This decision removed the legal stigma some states had attached to interracial unions, and it prohibited states from punishing people as criminals for loving someone of a different race.

Roger D. Hardaway

Lucas v. South Carolina Coastal Council

U.S. SUPREME COURT
DECIDED JUNE 29, 1992

- In this case, the Court held for the first time that a state land-use regulation violated the Fifth Amendment's prohibition against taking private property without "just compensation" because, although it did not physically take property or transfer title, it reduced the land's value without compensation to the owner.

In 1986, David Lucas, a South Carolina real estate developer, paid almost a million dollars for two oceanfront lots zoned for single-family residential construction. Two years later, before Lucas built, the state legislature changed its coastal regulations, moving the construction line inland. Lucas' lots, on each of which he had planned to build a house, were stranded seaward of that line.

Lucas sued, alleging that the Beachfront Management Act of 1988 (BMA), the legislation that revised the regulations, had effected a taking of the value of his property without just compensation. The trial court agreed that Lucas had suffered a total loss of the value of his property and concluded that a regulatory taking had occurred. On appeal, the South Carolina Supreme Court reversed the decision, on the grounds that the BMA had been passed to prevent serious public harm. Lucas petitioned the U.S. Supreme Court to review the matter, and the Court sided with Lucas in a 6-2 opinion. Justices Harry Blackmun and John Paul Stevens dissented, and a separate statement was written by Justice David Souter.

Writing for the majority, Justice Antonin Scalia stated that it was impossible to ascertain whether the BMA had been designed to prevent harm or to obtain a free public benefit. Instead, he turned to the common-law principle that the right to use one's property is limited by the equal right of one's neighbor to an equivalent freedom of use. If a neighbor can bar a landowner's plan to put a nuclear plant on an earthquake fault, for example, the legislature may also act without compensation. Yet if a use is one permitted between private landholders—such as the construction of a private residence—the legislature cannot bar such a use without compensating the owner for its loss, at least when the loss is total. The use Lucas sought to make of his property fell into the category of such an "essential use" and hence could not be barred without compensation. The Court's opinion thus endorsed the proposition that the common law of private nuisance is the appropriate guide to the constitutionality of land-use regulation.

The Supreme Court's holding in *Lucas* applies only to total loss of value, an uncommon situation. The logic of the *Lucas* opinion, however, is not limited to the case of total loss. If the difference between a regulation that prevents harm and one that confers a benefit is indeterminate, it is so whether or not the loss caused by the regulation is total. Indeed, Justice Scalia, challenged by Justice Stevens to explain why a total loss would be compensated but a 95 percent loss would not, could give no principled reason for restricting the scope of the opinion. Such uncertainty suggests that a later court may further restrict the legislative power to enact incompensable land use and environmental regulation.

Louise A. Halper

Lynch v. Donnelly

U.S. SUPREME COURT
DECIDED MARCH 5, 1984

- The Court ruled that the inclusion of a Christian symbol in a city-sponsored display did not violate the Constitution's prohibition of religious establishment.

For at least four decades, the city of Pawtucket, Rhode Island, had used public funds to erect and maintain a nativity scene, or crèche, as part of the Christmas exhibit in its shopping district. In addition to the crèche, which contained figures of Jesus, Mary, Joseph, shepherds, and angels, the display included figures and symbols of a secular nature, including a reindeer pulling Santa's sleigh, a clown, and a Christmas tree. A local resident, Daniel Donnelly, joined with the American Civil Liberties Union to bring suit against Pawtucket mayor Dennis Lynch in federal court. The challengers argued that the nativity scene created both the appearance and the reality of a governmental endorsement of a particular religion, contrary to the establishment clause of the First Amendment. Both the district court and the court of appeals ruled in favor of the challengers, and the city of Pawtucket appealed the case to the Supreme Court.

A sharply divided court voted 5 to 4 to reverse the lower court's ruling and to allow Pawtucket to continue its Christmas display. Writing for the majority, Chief Justice Warren Burger began with the argument that rather than requiring a complete separation of church and state, the First Amendment "affirmatively mandates accommodation, not merely tolerance, of all religions, and forbids hostility toward any." He observed that the first Congress of 1789 employed members of the clergy as official legislative chaplains and that historically the three branches of the federal government had not hesitated to acknowledge the role of religion in American life. Burger found that the display had the secular motive of encouraging community spirit, promoting downtown business, and depicting the historical origins of a national holiday, and that any benefit to religion was "indirect, remote, and incidental."

In a vigorous dissent, Justice William J. Brennan answered that the crèche retained a specifically Christian meaning and that Pawtucket's action was an unconstitutional endorsement of a particular faith. He quoted from the city leaders to show that their intent was to "keep Christ in Christmas."

In the *Lynch* decision, the Court allowed governments much discretion to accommodate the majority's religious culture by allowing governmental acts that appeared to encourage that culture. A few years later, however, the Court narrowed the importance of the decision in *Allegheny County v. American Civil Liberties Union, Greater Pittsburgh Chapter* (1989), a case involving a county-sponsored nativity scene that was not diluted with secular symbols and that proclaimed, "Glory to God in the Highest." In the *Allegheny County* case, the majority found the more pious crèche to be an unconstitutional endorsement of religion. The idea that a religious display is considered constitutional if it is accompanied by secular images is sometimes referred to as the "reindeer rule."

Thomas T. Lewis

McCleskey v. Kemp

U.S. Supreme Court
Decided April 22, 1987

- In this case, the Supreme Court rejected a death row inmate's claim that Georgia's system of sentencing people to death was unconstitutional because it discriminated on the basis of race.

In 1978, Warren McCleskey, a black man, was convicted of killing a white police officer during an armed robbery of a store in Atlanta, Georgia. McCleskey's jury—which consisted of eleven whites and one black—sentenced him to die in Georgia's electric chair. McCleskey sought a writ of *habeas corpus*, arguing, among other things, that the Georgia capital sentencing process was administered in a racially discriminatory manner and violated the U.S. Constitution. According to McCleskey, the jury's decision to execute him violated the Eighth Amendment because racial bias rendered the decision arbitrary and capricious. Also, the equal protection clause of the Fourteenth Amendment was violated because McCleskey, a black man, was treated differently than white defendants in the same position.

To support his claim of racial discrimination, McCleskey offered as evidence a sophisticated statistical study performed by Professor David B. Baldus and his colleagues at the University of Iowa (the Baldus study). The Baldus study showed that race played a dual role in deciding whether convicted murderers in Georgia would be sentenced to death. First, the race of the murder victim played a large role in whether a defendant would be sentenced to die. According to the study, defendants charged with killing whites received the death penalty in 11 percent of the cases. Defendants charged with killing blacks received the death penalty in only 1 percent of the cases. After taking account of thirty-nine variables that could have explained the disparities on nonracial grounds, the Baldus study concluded that, in Georgia, defendants charged with killing white victims were 4.3 times as likely to receive a death sentence as defendants charged with killing blacks.

Second, the race of the defendant played an important role during capital sentencing. According to the Baldus study, black defendants were 1.1 times as likely to receive a death sentence as other defendants. Thus, the study showed that black defendants such as McCleskey who had killed white victims had the greatest likelihood of receiving the death penalty.

By a 5-4 vote, the Supreme Court ruled against McCleskey. The Supreme Court accepted the validity of the Baldus study but held that McCleskey failed to prove "that decisionmakers in his case acted with discriminatory purpose." In other words, McCleskey failed to show that his constitutional rights were violated because he did not prove that anyone involved in his particular case intentionally discriminated against him based on his race. Justice Lewis Powell's opinion for the majority expressed special concern that if the Court accepted McCleskey's argument—that racial bias impermissibly tainted capital sentencing proceedings—all criminal sentences would be subject to attack based on allegations of racial discrimination. The *McCleskey* decision is a landmark ruling in the modern era of capital punishment.

Warren McCleskey died in Georgia's electric chair on September 25, 1991. That same year Justice Powell, whose 5-4 majority opinion sealed Warren McCleskey's fate, told a biographer that he would change his vote in that case (thus sparing McCleskey's life) if he could. Also, although executions had resumed in the United States in 1977, 1991 marked the first time in the modern era of American capital punishment that a white defendant (Donald "Pee Wee" Gaskins) was actually executed for killing a black person.

Randall Coyne

Maher v. Roe

U.S. SUPREME COURT
RULING ISSUED JUNE 20, 1977

- The Court ruled that while a woman's right to abortion is constitutionally protected, states are not required to provide Medicaid funding for abortions that are not "medically necessary".

Connecticut adopted a law which refused Medicaid support for abortions for poor women which were not "medically necessary"—necessary to protect the life or health of the mother. To receive state funding, the hospital or clinic performing the abortion had to submit physician certification that the abortion was medically necessary. A case was filed on behalf of indigent women in U.S. district court against Edward Maher, the Connecticut commissioner of social services. The suit argued that the law violated Title XIX of the Social Security Act (Medicaid) and violated the constitutional rights of poor women, including the Fourteenth Amendment guarantees of due process and equal protection under the law. It further argued that by providing Medicaid support for childbirth but not abortion the state was favoring some procedures pertaining to pregnancy over others, thus limiting poor women's free choice. The district court found in favor of Roe, and the case was appealed to the Supreme Court.

In a 6-3 decision, the Court found in favor of Maher and the state of Connecticut. The majority argued that while *Roe v. Wade* (1973) guaranteed a woman's right to abortion, the Constitution does not require state funding of pregnancy-related medical procedures for indigent women. It ruled that states have the right to decide what will be covered under Title XIX. Additionally, it qualified *Roe v. Wade* by stating that it did not affirm an unconditional right to abortion but only required that states not impose undue burdens on women attempting to obtain an abortion. The majority argued that poverty may constitute a burden, but it is not caused by the state and so the state is not required to alleviate the hardships pertaining to access to abortion that poverty causes.

In response to the objection that Connecticut favored childbirth over abortion, the Court cited the trimester provision of *Roe v. Wade*, arguing that states do, indeed, have a vested interest in potential (fetal) life and may enact policies that encourage childbirth over abortion. Finally, the majority held that a statement from the attending physician attesting the medical necessity of a Medicaid-funded abortion was appropriate. The minority opinion objected that failure to fund elective abortions for the poor makes it almost "impossible" for many of them to obtain safe abortions and so violates their constitutional rights. The case is one of many which has qualified the right to abortion first affirmed in the *Roe v. Wade* decision.

Charles L. Kammer

Malloy v. Hogan

U.S. SUPREME COURT
DECIDED JUNE 15, 1964

• The Supreme Court reversed prior decisions by holding that the privilege against self-incrimination is safeguarded by the due process clause of the Fourteenth Amendment.

William Malloy was arrested during a gambling raid in Connecticut in 1959. After pleading guilty to a gambling misdemeanor he received a light jail sentence, was fined $500, and was placed on probation. Sixteen months later he was summoned to testify before a state court referee—a procedure similar to a grand jury investigation—on his gambling activities.

Several questions were asked regarding the events surrounding his arrest and conviction. He refused to answer any question on the ground that to answer "may tend to incriminate me." The Superior Court held him in contempt and sentenced him to prison until he was willing to answer the questions. Malloy appealed to Connecticut's Supreme Court of Errors, which held that the Fifth Amendment's privilege against self-incrimination did not apply to state proceedings and that the Fourteenth Amendment's due process clause did not confer such a privilege. Malloy petitioned the Supreme Court for a hearing on the issue.

The Supreme Court reversed the state court's decision. Justice William J. Brennan, Jr., wrote the opinion for the majority. In it he argued that the right not to incriminate oneself is fundamental to an adversary system of justice. Therefore it is one of the rights which operate against state governments through the due process clause of the Fourteenth Amendment. Brennan held that the Fifth Amendment self-incrimination clause in its entirety limits state governments.

The question in the case then became whether Malloy had in fact been asked to incriminate himself. The questions he had been asked had to do with the identity of the person or persons who employed him at the time of his gambling convictions. Connecticut was trying to find out who was in charge of the gambling operation. The state argued that Malloy was in no danger of incriminating himself: He had already been convicted and could not be tried again for the same crime. Justice Brennan's opinion argued that Malloy's answers might furnish a link in a chain of evidence which might convict him of some new crime or more recent crime, particularly if he were still connected to the person who was running the gambling operation. Because "injurious disclosure" might result, Malloy was protected by the privilege against self-incrimination.

Four members of the Court dissented in two separate dissenting opinions. Justice John M. Harlan's dissent begins by pointing out that this issue was first encountered by the Supreme Court in 1908 in *Twining v. New Jersey*. *Twining*, and all the Court's subsequent cases regarding the privilege against self-incrimination, left it to the states to decide the extent of the self-incrimination privilege. Harlan argued that the Court should adhere to the precedents. First, it is not absolutely clear that the right is "fundamental." It is not necessarily unfair to ask a person to give an accounting of himself or even to compel an answer by legal means. Second, the decision fastens federal criminal procedure to the states, depriving them of the ability to experiment or to establish procedures that their own citizens wish to have. Finally, Harlan argued, Malloy's commitment for contempt would have been proper even under the federal standard espoused by the majority. Even if Malloy had answered the questions he would not have incriminated himself.

Malloy v. Hogan has had an immense impact on state legal procedures. As a result of this case, states have far less power to compel witnesses to testify in grand jury or other investigatory proceedings.

Robert Jacobs

Mapp v. Ohio

U.S. SUPREME COURT
DECIDED JUNE 19, 1961

• The Court required that illegally obtained evidence must be excluded from criminal trials in state courts, a rule that previously had been applied to federal trials in 1914.

In 1957, Cleveland police officers went to the home of Dollree Mapp, acting on information that a suspect in a recent bombing and related paraphernalia were located in her home. After Mapp refused to admit them, the officers forcibly entered, conducted a widespread search of the house, and discovered some illegal pornography. Mapp was arrested and convicted of violating Ohio's antiobscenity statute. Unable to demonstrate that the officers had possessed a valid search warrant, the state of Ohio argued that even if the search had been illegal, precedents of the U.S. Supreme Court did not forbid the admission of the resulting evidence in a state trial.

For many years the Supreme Court had been debating the issue of the so-called exclusionary rule. Earlier in the century, in *Weeks v. United States* (1914), the Court had required that illegally obtained evidence be excluded from federal prosecutions. Thirty-five years later, in *Wolf v. Colorado* (1949), the Supreme Court applied the Fourth Amendment right of privacy to the states through the due process clause of the Fourteenth Amendment, but the Court decided against imposing the exclusionary rule as an essential element of that right. By 1961, nevertheless, about half the states had adopted the *Weeks* rule.

In *Mapp v. Ohio*, the Court ruled 5-3 to make the exclusionary rule binding on the states. In the majority opinion, Justice Tom Clark declared that the rule was "an essential part" of the constitutional rights of individuals, but he also pointed to the rule's deterrence as a justification for the decision. Experience demonstrated, he wrote, that other remedies were "worthless and futile" in preventing officials from disobeying the prohibition against unreasonable searches and seizures.

Three members of the Court were opposed to overruling the *Wolf* precedent. They objected that the briefs and oral arguments of the case had dealt more with the obscenity issue than with the exclusionary rule, but even more, they insisted that the principle of federalism should allow states to have flexibility in devising alternative remedies to deter unreasonable searches and seizures. Justice Potter Stewart wanted to decide the case on the basis of the First Amendment and refused to join with either the majority or the minority.

The *Mapp* decision, a landmark of the Warren Court years, has been one of the most controversial opinions ever rendered by the Supreme Court. Since most criminal prosecutions take place in state courts, the decision's impact was much greater than that of *Weeks*. Many state officials resented *Mapp* as an intrusion into the traditional prerogatives of the states, and members of the public had difficulty understanding why there were not other means to enforce the right to privacy implicit in the Fourth Amendment. In later cases such as *Massachusetts v. Sheppard* (1984), the majority of justices of the Court have accepted the deterrent rationale for the exclusionary rule, and this has resulted in flexibility in its application.

Thomas T. Lewis

Marbury v. Madison

DECIDED FEBRUARY 24, 1803

• In this case, the Supreme Court for the first time exercised the power of judicial review to invalidate an act of Congress.

This case evolved out of the political conflict between the Federalist Party, which had controlled the government since the Constitution had been ratified, and the new Democratic-Republican party headed by Thomas Jefferson. The Federalists favored a strong national government, including the power of the federal courts to interpret the Constitution, while Jefferson and his party supported the idea that state legislatures, not the courts, should have the final say in disputes centering on the meaning of the Constitution.

In the elections of 1800, Jefferson not only defeated President John Adams but also carried a Democratic-Republican majority into Congress on his electoral coattails. Adams and his fellow Federalists were horrified; they considered Jefferson and his political followers dangerous radicals. Adams was still president, however, and the Federalists still controlled Congress, so they decided to take advantage of the time prior to Jefferson's inauguration to place as many judges in the federal court system as possible.

Since Article III, section 1 of the Constitution says that federal judges "shall hold their Offices during good Behavior," they had every reason to believe that these would be lifelong appointments. When the new justices were in place, the Federalists hoped they could be relied upon to check the worst consequences of the Democratic-Republican takeover until the Federalists made a political comeback.

Adams immediately began to appoint dozens of new justices. On March 3, 1803, the day before Jefferson was to take the oath of office, he worked into the night signing the last of what became known as his "midnight appointments." He then handed them over to his secretary of state, John Marshall, for delivery. The more important of the commissions were delivered without mishap. Possibly because Marshall, whom on January 27 Adams had appointed chief justice of the United States, was preoccupied preparing for the events of the next day when he would administer the oath of office to the new president, or perhaps because of an oversight on the part of a clerk, seventeen minor commissions were left for the incoming secretary of state, James Madison, to deliver. Upon assuming office, however, Jefferson, angered by the last-minute attempt to "pack" the federal judiciary with Federalist justices, ordered Madison not to deliver the commissions.

One of the midnight appointees who did not receive a commission was William Marbury. Adams had appointed Marbury justice of the peace for the District of Columbia. The forty-one-year-old Marbury, a little-known aide to the first secretary of the navy, was a staunch Federalist. In an attempt to acquire his commission and, at the same time, strike a blow at Jefferson and the Democratic-Republicans, he sought redress before the Supreme Court. Specifically, Marbury asked the Court to issue a writ of *mandamus* to force Madison to deliver his appointment. A writ of *mandamus* is a court order directing a government official to perform an act required by law, and it was Marbury's contention that Section 13 of the Judiciary Act of 1789 granted the Supreme Court the authority to issue such writs. The stage was set for one of the most momentous Supreme Court decisions of all time.

Marshall, the man who had failed to deliver Marbury's appointment and was now chief justice, seemed to be faced with two equally unpalatable alternatives. The Supreme Court, at that time, had nowhere near the power and prestige that it would later acquire, and Marshall had every reason to believe that Jefferson would defy an order to deliver Marbury's commission. He also knew that with no military or police at its disposal, the Court would be helpless in the face of such noncompliance. On the other hand, if he failed to issue the writ, the damage to the Court's prestige could be irrevocable. It would appear as if he was caving in to the Democratic-Republicans and would add credence to their belief that the courts had no power to intrude on the executive branch.

To no one's astonishment, the Court's unanimous decision, written by Marshall, held that Congress had authorized the Supreme Court to issue writs of *mandamus* in Section 13 of the Judiciary Act of 1789. Therefore, Marshall declared, under this provision of the law Marbury was entitled to his commission. Then he shocked both his Federalist allies and their political opponents by declaring Section 13 unconstitutional.

When Congress passed Section 13, according to Marshall, it had overreached its constitutional authority by adding to the Court's original jurisdiction, which Article III, section 2 of the Constitution specifically restricts to cases involving ambassadors, foreign ministers, and states. In one bold stroke, he avoided weakening the Court by rendering a decision that Jefferson would in all likelihood ignore and, at the same time, chastised the Democratic-Republicans by establishing the power of the Court to declare a federal law invalid. Judicial review—the power of the Court to declare a congressional act unconstitutional—is not mentioned anywhere in the Constitution, but by declaring Section 13 unconstitutional Marshall set the precedent for judicial review and established the Supreme Court as a coequal branch of government.

Thomas J. Mortillaro

Bibliography

An accessible overview of *Marbury* is John A. Garraty, "The Case of the Missing Commissions," in John A. Garraty, ed.,

Quarrels That Have Shaped the Constitution (rev. ed. New York: Harper & Row, 1987). Albert J. Beveridge, *The Life of John Marshall* (Boston: Houghton Mifflin, 1916), provides historical context. Concerning judicial review, Charles A. Beard, *The Supreme Court and the Constitution* (Englewood Cliffs, N.J.: Prentice-Hall, 1938), explains its origins; John Hart Ely, *Democracy and Distrust: A Theory of Judicial Review* (Cambridge, Mass.: Harvard University Press, 1980), discusses its modern applications; and Jesse H. Choper, *Judicial Review and the National Political Process* (Chicago: University of Chicago Press, 1980), examines its pros and cons.

Maryland v. Craig

U.S. SUPREME COURT

DECIDED JUNE 27, 1990

• In this case, which upheld a Maryland statute permitting a child to testify via one-way, closed-circuit television, the Supreme Court determined that the witness-confrontation rights of defendants guaranteed by the Sixth Amendment are neither absolute nor an indispensable part of criminal hearings.

In 1986, Sandra Ann Craig, an operator of a Maryland child-care center and kindergarten, was indicted for sexually abusing a six-year-old child in her care and was subsequently convicted. Under a state statute, the victim and other children were allowed to testify on a closed-circuit television without directly confronting the defendant. On the grounds that the law violated a defendant's right to face an accuser, guaranteed by the Sixth Amendment, Craig appealed the conviction. Although the Maryland Court of Special Appeals upheld the conviction, the next higher court, the Court of Appeals of Maryland, ordered a new trial, finding that the state prosecutors had not sufficiently justified their use of the closed-circuit television procedure. It also questioned the statute's constitutionality but did not determine it per se.

On *certiorari*, the U.S. Supreme Court vacated the lower court's order and remanded, holding that the confrontation clause of the Sixth Amendment did not invalidate the Maryland statute's procedure. Justice Sandra Day O'Connor, writing the 5-4 majority opinion, argued that under "narrow circumstances," when there are "competing interests," dispensing with witness-confrontation rights is warranted. Further, the Court stated that the term "confront" as used in the Sixth Amendment cannot be defined simply as "face-to-face." A state's concern for the psychological and physical well-being of a child abuse victim, as reflected in the Maryland statute, was deemed important enough to supersede a defendant's right to face an accuser. The majority also argued that in previous cases other Sixth Amendment rights had been interpreted "in the context of the necessities of trial and the adversary process."

A vigorous dissenting opinion, presented by Justice Antonin Scalia, argued that "confront" as used in the Sixth Amendment clearly means "face-to-face," whatever else it may also mean. The majority was also chided for distorting explicit constitutional text to suit "currently favored public policy." Although granting that the procedure authorized by the Maryland statute may be fair, the dissenters maintained that it violated the constitutional protection afforded defendants in the confrontation clause of the Sixth Amendment.

A controversial case, *Maryland v. Craig* left in its wake the likelihood of additional problems of interpretation precisely because it held a constitutional guarantee to be less than absolute and incontrovertible. Determining which "narrow circumstances" will validate a suspension of a defendant's right to a face-to-face confrontation with an accuser will be an ongoing issue in jurisprudence, because it must be decided virtually on a case-by-case basis.

John W. Fiero

Massachusetts Board of Retirement v. Murgia

U.S. SUPREME COURT
DECIDED JUNE 25, 1976

- In this age discrimination case, the Court restrained extensions of previously expanded categories of discrimination and the applicability of the equal protection clause to them.

Robert Murgia was a fifty-year-old uniformed officer with the Massachusetts State Police. Annual medical examinations required by the state had consistently shown him to be in excellent physical and mental health. Health notwithstanding, Murgia, like all uniformed officers, was subject to a state statute that mandated retirement on his fiftieth birthday. Murgia challenged the law, arguing that his compulsory retirement by Massachusetts discriminated against him on the basis of his age and therefore violated the equal protection clause of the U.S. Constitution's Fourteenth Amendment.

A three-judge federal district court upheld Murgia's challenge, concluding that the Massachusetts statute "lacked a rational basis in furthering any substantial state interest." The Massachusetts Board of Retirement, however, appealed to the U.S. Supreme Court, then headed by President Richard Nixon's appointee, Chief Justice Warren Burger, who had succeeded Chief Justice Earl Warren. Unlike Warren, Burger was a moderate conservative who advocated judicial restraint, in which he often was supported by Justices William Rehnquist, Lewis Powell, Byron R. White, and Harry Blackmun. By the mid-1970's, however, the Burger Court was in a difficult position. Through the 1960's, the Warren Court's antidiscrimination rulings had lent a literal interpretation to the equal protection clause, namely that no state should deny to any person within its jurisdiction equal protection of the laws. The clause was therefore applied to an increasing number of alleged civil rights discriminations.

This represented a significant shift for the Court. Previously the equal protection clause had been invoked almost exclusively in cases involving the civil rights of blacks. Thus the Warren Court launched so-called substantive due process and substantive equal protection. Under the Fourteenth Amendment, people's federally protected rights were also applied to violations of those rights by the states. Under Burger, the Court sought rational grounds to restrain this process by "strict judicial scrutiny." It was in this context that the Murgia appeal came before the Court.

In a 7-1 decision, the Court ruled against Murgia. It did not deny the adverse effects that premature retirement can have on individuals, nor did it suggest that the Massachusetts statute was well drafted or wise. Rather, it decided that drawing lines that created distinctions—age, in this case—was a legislative task, that the statute was rational, and that the Massachusetts legislature had not denied Murgia equal protection of the laws. Determining the appropriate applications of substantive equal protection has continued to trouble the Supreme Court.

Clifton K. Yearley

Massachusetts v. Sheppard

U.S. SUPREME COURT
DECIDED JULY 5, 1984

- The Court ruled that, the Fourth Amendment notwithstanding, a search authorized by a defective warrant was proper because the police had acted in good faith in executing what they thought was a valid warrant.

Osborne Sheppard was convicted in a Massachusetts state court of first-degree murder. Sheppard appealed his conviction to the Massachusetts Supreme Judicial Court on the basis that the police had knowingly searched his residence with a defective search warrant.

Boston police detective Peter O'Malley had drafted an affidavit to support an application for an arrest warrant and a search warrant authorizing the search of Sheppard's residence. The affidavit stated that the police wanted to search for such items as the victim's clothing and a blunt instrument that might have been used on the victim. The affidavit was reviewed and approved by the district attorney.

Unable to find a proper warrant application form, O'Malley found a previously used warrant form used in another district to search for controlled substances. After making some changes on the form, it and the affidavit were presented to a judge at his residence. The judge was made aware of the defective warrant form, and he made further changes before he signed it. He did not change the substantive portion, however, which continued to authorize a search for controlled substances, nor did the judge alter the form to incorporate the affidavit.

The police believed that the warrant authorized the search, and they proceeded to act in good faith. The trial judge ruled that the exclusionary rule did not apply in this case because the conduct of the officers was objectively reasonable and largely error free. On appeal, Sheppard argued that the evidence obtained pursuant to the defective warrant should have been suppressed. The Supreme Judicial Court of Massachusetts agreed and reversed the lower court's conviction of Sheppard. The court held that it did not recognize a good-faith exception to the exclusionary rule.

Massachusetts filed a petition for writ of *certiorari*. Speaking for the U.S. Supreme Court, Justice Byron White stated that the police officers who conducted the search should not be punished. They acted in good faith in executing what they reasonably thought was a valid warrant—one that was subsequently determined invalid—issued by a detached and neutral magistrate (*United States v. Leon*, 1984). The exclusionary rule, White said, did not apply because it was adopted to deter unlawful searches by police, not to punish the errors of judges. He stated that an error of constitutional dimension may have been committed by the judge who did not make the necessary changes, but not the police. Judgment of the Supreme Judicial Court was therefore reversed and remanded for further proceedings consistent with the U.S. Supreme Court's opinion.

Bill Manikas

Meritor Savings Bank v. Vinson

U.S. SUPREME COURT
DECIDED NOVEMBER 17, 1986

• This case found the U.S. Supreme Court holding that sexual harassment was discrimination and that a hostile working environment constituted harassment.

Mechelle Vinson was hired by Meritor Savings Bank in 1974 and proceeded up the ladder from teller-trainee to teller to head teller to assistant branch manager. In September, 1978, she took an indefinite sick leave and was discharged on November 1, 1978, for excessive use of that leave. Vinson sued, claiming sexual harassment in violation of Title VII of the Civil Rights Act of 1964, which bars discrimination in the workplace based on several factors, including sex. Vinson described the cause of her leave: She said that her supervisor had invited her out to dinner, then suggested they go to a motel to have sexual relations. At first, she had refused, but then for fear of losing her job, she agreed. Afterward, her supervisor made repeated demands for sexual favors, and they had intercourse forty or fifty times over the next several years. She also accused him of other forms of sexual harassment.

The position of the bank was that the law was only concerned with tangible loss of an economic character, not purely psychological aspects of the workplace environment, but Justice William Rehnquist, for a unanimous Court, disagreed. He said that the Equal Employment Opportunity Commission (EEOC) issued guidelines in 1980 holding that sexual harassment is a form of discrimination, and it includes a hostile or abusive work environment. If the sex-related conduct was unwelcome, the law was broken.

The implications of *Meritor Savings Bank v. Vinson* were that sexual harassment is illegal and that a hostile environment is harassment. Also, the voluntary nature of the act was not the issue, but whether it was unwelcome.

Robert W. Langran

Merryman, Ex parte

U.S. CIRCUIT COURT, BALTIMORE
ISSUANCE OF CHIEF JUSTICE TANEY'S WRIT, MAY 26, 1861;
TANEY'S RULING, MAY 28, 1861

• President Abraham Lincoln's suspension of the writ of *habeas corpus* as an executive emergency act at the outbreak of the Civil War provoked a clash with the chief justice of the United States and became the first of several celebrated wartime civil liberties cases.

For centuries, wherever Anglo-American law prevails, a citizen's right to a writ of *habeas corpus*—that is, the right not to be arrested and held by government authorities without being charged—has been regarded a basic civil liberty. As secession continued and fighting that signaled the opening of the Civil War erupted, President Lincoln authorized Union military commanders to suspend the privilege of *habeas corpus*. Article I, section 9 of the U.S. Constitution stipulates that this privilege "shall not be suspended" unless "in cases of rebellion or invasion the public safety may require it."

Of particular concern to Lincoln were the border states which teetered on the brink of secession. Maryland, adjoining Washington, D.C., was one of these states and, indeed, hostile actions against Union forces were already under way there. John Merryman was a wealthy and well-born Maryland landowner—in fact, a descendant of Francis Scott Key, who had written the national anthem. Merryman was also a lieutenant in a secessionist cavalry unit that had destroyed bridges and telegraph lines during April, 1861. Along with other suspected traitors, Merryman's arrest was ordered by a Union general, William H. Keim. Merryman's lawyer promptly petitioned a federal circuit court in Baltimore for a writ of *habeas corpus*. Merryman, meantime, was imprisoned at Fort McHenry.

In 1861, justices of the U.S. Supreme Court still were assigned individually to preside over one of nine federal circuit courts. In this instance, Chief Justice Roger B. Taney, a Marylander, was presiding over the federal court in Baltimore when Merryman's petition reached him. Taney denied the president's right to suspend the writ. The chief justice reasoned that the Constitu-

Ex parte Merryman was a circuit court ruling; however, Chief Justice Roger Taney presided over the court at that time, under an old system in which each Supreme Court justice was responsible for a specified circuit. *(Mathew Brady/Collection of the Supreme Court of the United States)*

tion placed the right of suspension in the Congress and that Congress had not exercised that power. Further, Taney argued that the Constitution neither sanctioned the arrest of civilians by army officers without prior authorization by civil courts nor allowed citizens to be imprisoned indefinitely without trial. Lincoln refused to obey Taney's ruling, declaring before a special session of Congress on July 4, 1861, that suspension was necessary in order to quell the rebellion and preserve the nation.

Opinions concerning both Lincoln's action and Taney's ruling were divided. As had been true of earlier clashes between presidents and the Supreme Court, the president could enforce his view, and without his acquiescence the Court could not. Nevertheless, in a few weeks Merryman was released. Although he was indicted by a U.S. circuit court, he was never brought to trial. Passage of the Habeas Corpus Act of 1863 represented an effort to respect authority of the courts while not seriously restricting executive and military decisions.

Clifton K. Yearley

Miller v. California

U.S. SUPREME COURT
DECIDED JUNE 21, 1973

- In this landmark obscenity case, a relatively unified Supreme Court, under Chief Justice Warren Burger, formulated specific guidelines for regulating "hard-core" sexually explicit material.

In this case, the defendant, Marvin Miller, was convicted by a California jury of violating a state statute prohibiting the distribution of obscene materials. Miller had conducted an aggressive mass mailing campaign to advertise sale of "adult materials." A pamphlet, sent to California residents who had not necessarily requested the information, included explicit pictures and drawings of sexual acts with genitalia prominently displayed. Miller's conviction was upheld by the California Superior Court. In *Miller v. California*, the U.S. Supreme Court by a vote of 5 to 4, remanded, or sent back, the decision of the lower courts for further deliberations consistent with its revised obscenity standards.

The Court had struggled with the issue of obscenity for nearly two decades prior to the *Miller* ruling. In *Roth v. United States* (1957), the Court obtained majority agreement for the following obscenity standard: whether to the average person applying contemporary community standards, the dominant theme of the material, taken as a whole, appeals to prurient interests. *Roth* was also important because in it the Court explicitly stated that obscenity was not protected speech under the First Amendment.

In *Roth* and subsequent decisions leading up to *Miller*, the Court's standards became increasingly more liberal. In *Jacobellis v. Ohio* (1964), a Supreme Court opinion by Justice William J. Brennan clarified that contemporary "community" standards are national standards, those of the "society at large." National standards are likely to be more permissive than those of local communities. Further definitional clarification by the Court in *Jacobellis* held that the material must be "utterly without redeeming social importance" to meet the criteria for obscenity. The standard made obscenity convictions difficult.

In the 1960's, the Supreme Court was internally divided on the obscenity issue. For example, in *Jacobellis*, Justice Brennan was assigned to write the majority opinion, but all eight of the other justices wrote either concurring or dissenting opinions, indicating their factiousness. The task of writing clear guidelines for determining what is obscene is daunting, as a result of the value-laden nature of "obscenity." Justice Potter Stewart suggested this when he declared in his opinion in *Jacobellis* that he found it difficult to articulate a definition of obscenity, but "I know it when I see it." A lack of consensus and firm principles on the part of the justices resulted in a case-by-case examination of materials in obscenity cases. Case-by-case determination left lower federal and state courts perplexed about what standards to use.

The *Miller* Court, led by Chief Justice Warren Burger, reformulated obscenity standards, building on the doctrine established in *Roth*. These standards were intended to provide clearer guidance to lower courts and to prevent the need for the U.S. Supreme Court to review allegedly obscene materials. The standards established were:

> (a) whether the average person, applying contemporary community standards, would find that the work, taken as a whole, appeals to the prurient interest; (b) whether the work depicts or describes, in a patently offensive way, sexual conduct specifically defined by the applicable state law; and (c) whether the work, taken as a whole, lacks serious literary, artistic, political, or scientific value.

The *Miller* standards eliminated the "utterly without redeeming social value" test. In addition, the new standards placed emphasis on local community standards rather than national standards, recognizing the differences in values that exist in different parts of the country. Despite clearer standards in *Miller*, debate about the meaning of obscenity continues, with significant challenges from libertarians, who support broader free expression rights, from some conservatives, who support stronger regulation of obscenity, and from some feminists, who believe that the emphasis in *Miller* on offensiveness is misplaced and should be refocused on the harms of pornography to women.

Mary A. Hendrickson

Miller et al. v. Civil City of South Bend

U.S. COURT OF APPEALS FOR THE SEVENTH CIRCUIT
DECIDED MAY 25, 1990

• This decision held that nonobscene barroom nude dancing constituted "expressive activity," as opposed to "mere conduct," and thus deserved First Amendment protection.

This case represents an attempt to navigate the First Amendment's often elusive boundary between expression and conduct. The suit was originally brought in 1985 by several adult-entertainment entrepreneurs and dancers in an effort to prevent the state of Indiana from enforcing its public indecency law, which banned nudity in public places, against them. The plaintiffs challenged the statute as an unconstitutional infringement on their First Amendment rights of expression. In rebuttal, the state justified its law as an attempt to protect the public morality and family structure.

In an earlier case, the same statute had been challenged before the Indiana Supreme Court on overbreadth grounds. In that 1979 suit, the plaintiffs claimed that in addition to its permissible restrictions, Indiana's statute restricted constitutionally protected rights of free speech and expression. The Indiana Supreme Court had rejected this contention and interpreted the statute to apply to conduct alone and not to forms of expressive activity. Moreover, the court held that barroom dancing was "mere conduct," which could be constitutionally prohibited by the state.

In this later case, the district court for the Northern District of Indiana was asked to consider the statute as applied to nonobscene nude dancing. The court was able to skirt the definition of "obscenity" because the state conceded that the activity in question was not obscene. Instead, the state argued that the activity in question was "mere conduct," outside the realm of First Amendment protection. After viewing a videotape of the challenged activity, the district court agreed and held that nude barroom dancing was not expressive activity and thus could be prohibited by the state. *Miller et al. v. Civil City of South Bend* marked an appeal from that ruling.

The U.S. Court of Appeals for the Seventh Circuit reversed the Indiana district court to find that nude barroom dancing, when performed for entertainment, was a form of expression deserving of First Amendment protection. The appeals court reached this result by relying on several strands of U.S. Supreme Court precedent. Most important, in its 1981 decision, *Schad v. Mt. Ephraim*, the Supreme Court had invalidated a zoning ordinance that prohibited all live entertainment and confirmed the First Amendment's protection of live entertainment. The Supreme Court clarified that nudity, or sexual content, does not automatically remove an activity or material from the ambit of First Amendment protection, although nudity alone, when not combined with some form of expressive conduct, was not protected.

In its invalidation of Indiana's public nudity statute as applied to nude barroom dancing, the appeals court rejected the dissent's suggestion that courts should distinguish between "high" and "low" art, on the grounds that such a determination risks affording unpopular forms of expression no constitutional protection at all. Instead, the court reiterated the principles at the heart of First Amendment protection: All expression is presumptively protected against government interference and restraint, and the government cannot prohibit the expression of an idea simply because the idea is offensive or distasteful.

Elizabeth Van Schaack

Milligan, Ex parte

U.S. SUPREME COURT
RULING ISSUED APRIL 3, 1866; OPINIONS RELEASED DECEMBER 17, 1866

- In this case, which began during the Civil War, the Supreme Court for the first time limited the authority of military courts acting under presidential authority to try civilians for acts subverting a war effort.

In October, 1864, Union military authorities in Indiana arrested Lambdin P. Milligan, a civilian, and several other Confederate sympathizers for conspiring to attack federal arsenals and free

Confederate prisoners. The military acted under authority of President Abraham Lincoln's order stipulating that military courts could try and punish persons "guilty of any disloyal practice affording aid and comfort to the rebels." After a military commission found Milligan and two others guilty and sentenced them to be hanged, Milligan disputed the commission's jurisdiction and sought a writ of *habeas corpus* asserting his constitutional right to a trial by jury.

In 1866 the U.S. Supreme Court ruled 9 to 0 in Milligan's favor and ordered that he be released. Though unanimous in its holding, the Court split, 5 to 4, in its reasoning. The majority opinion, written by Justice David Davis, held that "it is the birthright of every American citizen, when charged with crime, to be tried and punished according to law." Military authority could thus not lawfully supersede civilian authority "where the courts are open and their process unobstructed"—as was the case in Indiana. In what became a famous statement of a fundamental principle of American constitutionalism, Davis wrote: "The Constitution of the United States is a law for rulers and people, equally in war and peace, and covers with the shield of its protection all classes of men, at all times, and under all circumstances. No doctrine, involving more pernicious consequences, was ever intended by the wit of man than that any

The Court of Chief Justice Salmon Chase (center) around the time it issued the *Milligan* decision in 1866. *(M. P. Rice/Collection of the Supreme Court of the United States)*

of its provisions can be suspended during any of the great exigencies of government."

While such sweeping language appears to deny martial law any trace of legitimacy, Davis argued in the same opinion that if "courts are actually closed" because of foreign invasion or civil war, then within a "theater of active military operations" the military may "govern by martial law until the laws can have their free course." Four justices differed from the majority in maintaining that the military's actions in the Milligan case would have been legal had Congress expressly authorized them; however, the majority held that even Congress lacks power to establish a system of military rule where civil courts are open and functioning.

The importance of *Ex parte Milligan* is twofold. While it establishes the legitimacy of martial law when invasion or rebellion makes normal law enforcement impossible, it also prohibits such martial law if the civil courts are functioning, even during wartime. *Milligan* has stood as a landmark for more than a century. Although the Court has never expressly repudiated it, some commentators believe that its principles were violated by the internment of Japanese Americans in World War II—an action that the Supreme Court upheld in *Korematsu v. United States* (1944).

Joseph M. Bessette

Milliken v. Bradley

U.S. Supreme Court
Decided July 25, 1974

• In this case, the U.S. Supreme Court decided that courts did not have the authority to order school desegregation plans that required moving schoolchildren across school district lines unless it could be shown that school district lines had been constructed in a manner designed to preserve segregation.

By the early 1970's, many urban school districts continued to operate schools with a majority black population because of the dearth of white students in those school districts. In 1971, the U.S. Supreme Court in *Swann v. Charlotte-Mecklenburg Board of Education* had held that urban school boards could be required to engage in extensive school busing to integrate their schools. The *Swann* decision, however, did not address the issue of how to integrate urban school districts that had few white students.

In the early 1970's, a group of black parents, with the assistance of the National Association for the Advancement of Colored People (NAACP) Legal Defense and Educational Fund, brought suit seeking to desegregate the Detroit school system. In 1972, federal district court judge Stephen Roth ruled that the Detroit schools were in fact illegally segregated and ordered a multidistrict desegregation plan involving the Detroit city school district along with fifty-three surrounding suburban school districts. One year later, the U.S. Court of Appeals for the Sixth Circuit affirmed, holding that the Detroit schools could not be adequately desegregated without such a multidistrict plan. Shortly thereafter, the U.S. Supreme Court agreed to hear the case.

In 1973, the Supreme Court had considered a similar multidistrict desegregation plan involving the Richmond, Virginia, schools. In that case, the Court had divided 4 to 4, with Justice Lewis Powell recusing himself because of his prior membership on the Richmond School Board. The Court took the Detroit case to decide the question whether multidistrict desegregation plans were required when inner-city school districts could not otherwise be desegregated. In the meantime, the specter of multidistrict desegregation prompted a firestorm of activity in Congress, as many members of Congress backed both legislation and amendments to the Constitution restricting the ability of federal courts to order extensive desegregation plans.

The Supreme Court held in the *Milliken v. Bradley* decision, with a 5-4 vote, that a district court should not order an interdistrict remedy unless it could be shown that the school district lines had been constructed in a manner to preserve segregation or unless state government officials had taken other action that contributed to the interdistrict segregation. This was a burden of proof that would prove difficult to meet. The *Milliken* decision marked the first time that the Supreme Court had declined to refine existing school desegregation jurisprudence to further integrationist goals.

In the wake of the *Milliken* decision a few metropolitan areas did adopt interdistrict desegregation remedies, but for the most part, the decision undermined desegregation efforts in America's cities. Unable to utilize an assignment plan that included children from surrounding suburban school districts, inner-city school boards were greatly restricted in their efforts to desegregate their schools.

Davison M. Douglas

Minnick v. Mississippi

U.S. SUPREME COURT
DECIDED DECEMBER 3, 1990

- The Supreme Court found that a reinitiated interrogation of a murder suspect who had been advised of his Miranda rights and received counsel still violated the suspect's Fifth Amendment rights because it was conducted without counsel being present.

Robert S. Minnick, the petitioner, sought reversal of his conviction for murder in the circuit court of Lowndes County, Mississippi, on the grounds that his constitutional rights against self-incrimination had been violated when his confession was taken during an interrogation conducted without counsel present. Minnick, a fugitive from prison, had been arrested and held in a California jail, where two federal agents, after reading the Miranda warnings to him, began an interrogation on a Friday. He requested that they return on the following Monday, when he would have counsel present. The agents complied, breaking off their questioning.

An appointed attorney then advised Minnick to speak to no

one about the charges against him. After an interview with the agents on Monday, Minnick was questioned by a deputy sheriff from Mississippi. The deputy advised Minnick of his Miranda rights, and the accused, who refused to sign a waiver of those rights, confessed to the murder for which he was subsequently tried and sentenced to death.

At Minnick's murder trial in Mississippi, he filed a motion to suppress the confession, but his request was denied. The conviction was then upheld by the Supreme Court of Mississippi, which ruled that Minnick's right to counsel, as set forth in the Fifth Amendment, had been granted in accordance with the guidelines established in *Edwards v. Arizona* (1981), which stipulates that a defendant who requests counsel during questioning cannot be subjected to further interrogation until the counsel is "made available" to the defendant. According to the Mississippi Supreme Court, that condition had been met when Minnick consulted with his appointed attorney.

The U.S. Supreme Court, on *certiorari*, reversed and remanded in a 6-2 decision. In the majority opinion, written by Justice Anthony Kennedy, the justices ruled that in a custodial interrogation, once counsel is provided, questioning cannot be resumed without counsel being present. It stipulated that the *Edwards v. Arizona* ruling regarding protection against self-incrimination is not met, nor is that protection terminated or suspended, by the mere provision of counsel outside the interrogation process. The majority found that Minnick's confession to the Mississippi deputy sheriff should have been inadmissible at his murder trial. In a dissenting opinion, Justice Antonin Scalia argued the contrary, holding that the *Edwards v. Arizona* rule excluding self-incrimination without counsel was not applicable after Minnick's first interview with his appointed attorney.

The Court's relatively narrow interpretation of what constitutes right to counsel leaves a legacy of stringent procedural requirements on law enforcement agencies, which must comply with a suspect's right to have counsel present during custodial interrogations that had been broken off and later resumed. From the point of view of such agencies, its practical effect is to inhibit an expeditious interrogation of suspects.

John W. Fiero

Minor v. Happersett

U.S. SUPREME COURT

DECIDED MARCH 9, 1875

• This Supreme Court case produced the first voting rights decision concerning women.

Virginia Louise Minor, an advocate of women's rights, was denied the right to register to vote in Missouri. A judgment against her in the state's lower courts was affirmed by the Missouri Supreme Court. In her appeal to the U.S. Supreme Court, Minor invoked the citizenship and privileges and immunities clauses of the recently ratified Fourteenth Amendment. Defining citizenship extremely narrowly "as conveying the idea of membership of a nation, nothing more," and finding that the right to vote is not among the privileges and immunities granted under the Fourteenth Amendment, the Court unanimously rejected Minor's claim in 1875. The Fourteenth Amendment was thus found to ensure neither a federal suffrage right nor a federal limitation on voting procedures controlled, by tradition, by the states.

The first woman suffrage amendment had been introduced in Congress in 1868 and defeated. A decade later, another amendment, modeled on the Fifteenth Amendment granting suffrage to African American men, was proposed. By this time, suffragists had reason to be concerned about the fate of such an amendment, and *Minor v. Happersett* was clearly a test case intended to force Congress' hand. It would take forty-five more years and yet another constitutional amendment, the Nineteenth Amendment, before women were granted the franchise.

Lisa Paddock

Miranda v. Arizona

U.S. SUPREME COURT
DECIDED JUNE 13, 1966

- In this case the Supreme Court decided that arrested persons must be informed of their rights to remain silent and to counsel before police interrogation may begin.

Miranda v. Arizona was one of a series of landmark Supreme Court cases of the mid-1960's establishing new guarantees of procedural fairness for defendants in criminal cases. The Court's decision in *Miranda* sprang from two different lines of precedents under the Fourteenth Amendment.

One of these lines was the right-to-counsel cases: *Powell v. Alabama* (1932), in which the Court held that indigent defendants had to be afforded counsel in capital cases; *Gideon v. Wainwright* (1963), which extended the right to counsel for indigent defendants to all felony cases; and *Escobedo v. Illinois* (1964), in which the Court held that a confession obtained from a defendant who had asked for and been denied permission to speak to an attorney was inadmissible. By 1964, the right to counsel had expanded to include mandatory representation for indigents at trial in all felonies and also gave potential defendants the right to representation during questioning while in custody if they requested it.

The second line of cases culminated with *Malloy v. Hogan* (1964), in which the Court had held that the privilege against self-incrimination applied to the states. Moreover, prior to the *Miranda* case, a long series of Supreme Court decisions had established that neither physical coercion nor certain forms of psychological coercion could be used by police to obtain confessions from accused persons. Thus, on the eve of *Miranda*, constitutional rules barred the admission of confessions which had been coerced through either physical or psychological pressures or which had been obtained from an in-custody defendant who had requested the attendance of an attorney.

Chief justice Earl Warren in 1966, at the time he wrote the majority opinion in *Miranda*. *(Library of Congress)*

By then it was also clear that the entire body of the Fifth Amendment's self-incrimination clause was to be applied to the states through the due process clause of the Fourteenth Amendment. Like the other cases mentioned, *Miranda* rests on the due process clause of the Fourteenth Amendment, which requires that criminal procedure in state courts be fundamentally fair.

Ernesto Miranda's case involved a confession to rape and kidnapping which was elicited from him in a police interrogation room after his arrest. In addition to his oral admissions to the investigating officers, Miranda wrote out by hand a short statement, which he signed. The questioning, by two Phoenix detectives, involved neither physical nor psychological coercion as these had been defined in the earlier cases. The transcript of Miranda's interview showed that he answered the officers' questions freely, and that after an initial denial, he readily admitted abducting the victim and raping her. The entire interrogation and the preparation of Miranda's written statement took less than two hours.

At trial, Miranda's oral admissions and his written statement were admitted into evidence over his objection; the victim testified against him as well. The jury found Miranda guilty of rape in the first degree and kidnapping, and he was sentenced to prison for a term of twenty to thirty years. He appealed to the Supreme Court of Arizona. After losing in that court, he appealed to the U.S. Supreme Court, which decided to hear the case in 1965. *Miranda* and three companion cases were argued February 28-March 2, 1966. On June 13, 1966, the Court decided in Miranda's favor by a 5-4 vote.

Chief Justice Earl Warren wrote for the majority, which consisted additionally of Justices Hugo Black, William O. Douglas, William J. Brennan, Jr., and Abe Fortas. Warren's opinion focused on the coercive elements present in any custodial interrogation. He argued that an accused person is isolated from friends, family, and his or her attorney and is often fearful of the police. The police, as contemporary text-books on interrogation showed, were schooled in a variety of tricks and techniques which are designed to overbear the will of an arrested person and induce confession.

These techniques, according to Chief Justice Warren's opinion, skirt the edge of improper physical or psychological coercion and demonstrate that custodial interrogation is inherently coercive. Consequently, an accused person does not have a free opportunity to use the Fifth Amendment right not to incriminate himself or herself or the Sixth Amendment right to counsel. Accordingly, the Court held that before any custodial interrogation can take place, an arrested person must be given a four-fold warning—what has become known as the "Miranda warning." Under this rule, a suspect in custody has to be informed of the right to remain silent, of the potential use of his or her words in evidence against him or her, of the right to consult an attorney before questioning, and of the right to an assigned attorney if he or she is indigent.

Any statement elicited by the authorities is inadmissible at trial unless the defendant has been given the warning and has freely and knowingly waived these rights. Moreover, if during questioning the defendant has asked at any point that interrogation cease or that he or she be allowed to consult an attorney, any subsequent statements obtained by the police are also inadmissible.

Justice John Marshall Harlan's dissenting opinion in this case argued that the Court was searching for a kind of "utopian" voluntariness. The dissenters believed that Miranda's statement had been voluntarily given. No physical brutality or discomfort had been visited upon him, nor did the investigating officers use any special psychological tricks or deceptions. The record showed that Miranda freely gave a statement about the crimes of which he was accused. By the standards of 1963, the Phoenix police had acted properly. Harlan argued that the admissibility of Miranda's confession was supported by precedent; moreover, in Miranda's brief interrogation, there was "a legitimate purpose, no perceptible unfairness, and certainly little risk of injustice." Justices Byron White and Potter Stewart adhered to Harlan's opinion; Justice Tom Clark submitted a separate dissenting opinion.

The immediate result of *Miranda v. Arizona* was to reverse Miranda's conviction for kidnapping and rape. The Arizona authorities persevered in the prosecution, and in 1969, at his second trial, Miranda was again convicted. Although the confession was not introduced against him this time, the victim's testimony alone was enough to persuade the jury of his guilt. In consequence of this conviction he served a prison term from which he was paroled in 1972.

Ernesto Miranda was killed in a barroom fight in 1976; ironically, the man who stabbed him to death was given the Miranda warning when arrested.

The larger consequence of this controversial case was to require police officers all over the United States to provide themselves with "Miranda cards" which embodied the warning required by the Supreme Court. Once a person has been detained, no questioning may take place unless the detainee has been given the warning and has waived the 'rights to silence and to consult counsel before responding to questions. If a detainee does request the assistance of an attorney, interrogation must stop until he or she has had the opportunity to consult with a lawyer. Treatment of arrested persons changed significantly after *Miranda v. Arizona*. Because the Court's decision placed on the state the burden of demonstrating knowing and voluntary waiver of the right to silence, police must persuade the defendant to agree if they wish to elicit a statement. The atmosphere in which an arrested person finds himself or herself in the crucial moments after arrest has changed substantially as a result of the Court's decision.

There has been much discussion of the impact of this rule on American law enforcement. In most criminal cases, the defendant's words constitute a significant part of the case against him or her. Police and prosecutors feared that the Court's holding in *Miranda* would cripple their efforts; they argued that the new rule would make it impossible for investigators to get the kinds of inculpatory statements necessary to obtain criminal convictions. Once a defendant had consulted counsel, they believed, no further statements of any kind would be forthcoming, since any competent lawyer would immediately urge silence on the client.

Despite these fears, which were shared by large portions of the public, *Miranda* does not seem to have crippled the work of the police and criminal courts. There have been a number of empirical studies of the behavior of arrested persons. Most criminal defendants do give statements—often incriminating statements—even after receiving the Miranda warning. Moreover, there have been as many successful prosecutions in relation to the number of arrests after the Miranda case as before.

Miranda also accomplished something else very important to the protection of the rights of arrested persons. There are signs that since *Miranda* the incidence of brutal or abusive police practices has diminished. Most observers of law enforcement practices in the United States believe police brutality is much less common than before this case. One strong indication is the rarity of claims of coerced confession in trials where the "coercion" involves police practices more abusive than violations of the Miranda rule itself.

In the largest sense this is the real significance of *Miranda*: By forcing the police to attend to a rigid technical requirement which respects the defendant's rights, the opportunity for abusive behavior is lessened. Moreover, the increased professionalism of police that has resulted from *Miranda* and the other cases of the 1960's has benefited both police and prosecutors in preparing good cases. In this light, *Miranda* represents an important step toward actualizing the rights of accused persons regardless of whether it achieves Chief Justice Warren's stated aim, which was "to assure that the individual's right to choose between silence and speech remains unfettered throughout the interrogation process."

Robert Jacobs

Bibliography

Baker, Liva. *Miranda: The Crime, the Law, and the Politics.* New York: Atheneum, 1983. Excellent essays about the *Miranda* case, blending the legal and political issues raised.

Hook, Sidney. *Common Sense and the Fifth Amendment.* New York: Criterion, 1959. Argument *against* the privilege against self-incrimination. Hook argues that one can correctly infer guilt from a defendant's silence most of the time. Written in the context of the red scare of the 1950's.

Israel, Jerold, and Wayne LaFave. *Criminal Procedure.* 3d ed. St. Paul, Minn.: West Publishing, 1980. Good discussion of the rules for police interrogation and a summary of empirical evidence regarding the efficacy of the Miranda rule in giving potential defendants a free choice whether or not to speak.

Jacobs, Robert. "*Miranda*: The Right to Silence." *Trial* 11 (March/April, 1975): 69-76. An analysis and critique of the logic underlying the Court's decision in *Miranda* as well as a discussion of the psychology of confession.

Kamisar, Yale. *Police Interrogation and Confessions: Essays in Law and Policy.* Ann Arbor: University of Michigan Press, 1980. Kamisar, a professor of law, presents this series of essays which emphasize the actualities of police questioning.

Levy, Leonard. *Origins of the Fifth Amendment: The Right Against Self-Incrimination.* New York: Oxford University Press, 1968. Discussion of the historical purposes and original meaning of the Fifth Amendment.

Lewis, Anthony. *Gideon's Trumpet.* New York: Random House, 1964. A study of the case of Clarence Earl Gideon, whose handwritten appeal to the Supreme Court resulted in the decision entitling all indigent defendants to assigned counsel. This book is particularly strong on Supreme Court procedure and on the issues raised by Gideon's appeal.

Medalie, Richard, Leonard Zeitz, and Paul Alexander. "Custodial Interrogation in Our Nation's Capital: The Attempt to Implement *Miranda.*" *Michigan Law Review* 66 (1968): 1347. Empirical study of interrogations in Washington, D.C., subsequent to the Court's decision in *Miranda.*

Mendelson, Wallace. *The American Constitution and Civil Liberties.* Homewood, Ill.: Dorsey Press, 1981. This text has a strong chapter on constitutional theory and practice as applied to criminal procedure.

United States. Supreme Court. "*Miranda v. Arizona.*" *United States Reports* 384 (1966): 436. Any study of this landmark case begins with the arguments made by the justices of the Supreme Court of the United States. Chief Justice Warren's opinion for the majority and John Marshall Harlan's dissent are both cogent and powerful.

Moose Lodge No. 107 v. Irvis

U.S. SUPREME COURT
DECIDED JUNE 12, 1972

• The Court ruled that a state did not deny the equal protection of the law when it granted a license to serve alcohol to a racially discriminatory private club.

Moose Lodge No. 107 was a private club in Harrisburg, Pennsylvania, that served both food and alcohol, the latter under a license granted by the Pennsylvania Liquor Control Board. The club was often used by members of the state legislature for lunch breaks and after-hours relaxation. A white member of the lodge brought an African American fellow legislator, K. Leroy Irvis, into the club's dining room and bar, where the pair were refused service on the grounds of Irvis' race.

The Fourteenth Amendment to the Constitution forbids state action in furtherance of racial discrimination. Since the lodge's refusal to serve Irvis amounted to racial discrimination, the Supreme Court was asked to determine whether Pennsylvania's granting of a liquor license constituted state action in furtherance of that discrimination.

The Court ruled in a 6-3 vote that mere state licensing of a private club on private land did not make every action of the club an action of the state. The majority noted that the impetus for discrimination did not have to originate with the state in order for there to be state action, so long as the state was involved in enforcing private discrimination in a significant way.

If the lodge had been a tenant in a state-owned building and had opened its facilities to all members of the pubic except African Americans, the state would have been engaged in a joint venture with the club, and the club's discrimination would have been state action. Here, however, the building was privately owned, it rested on privately owned land, and its facilities were open not to the public in general, but to members only. The Court observed that the state provided many services, among them water, electricity, licensing, and police and fire protection. The mere provision of such services was not enough to convert every action of the beneficiary into state action.

The dissenters argued that there was state action, since the liquor regulatory scheme was pervasive, regulating "virtually every detail of the operation of the licensee's business." They also observed that since the quota for liquor licenses had been exceeded in Harrisburg, the state's renewal of the Moose Lodge's license prevented a different facility with nondiscriminatory policies from opening.

This important case limited the reach of the Fourteenth Amendment by defining state action narrowly. It remains possible for victims of discrimination to find recourse in federal and state antidiscrimination statutes. Leroy Irvis was able to do just that when he brought suit against Moose Lodge No. 107 under Pennsylvania's public accommodations law. He eventually gained admission to the club's facilities and was later elected speaker of the Pennsylvania House of Representatives.

William H. Coogan

Mueller v. Allen

U.S. SUPREME COURT

DECIDED JUNE 29, 1983

• The Supreme Court upheld a state law that allowed taxpayers to deduct educational expenses that mostly benefited parents of children in private religious schools.

A Minnesota statute authorized state taxpayers to deduct up to seven hundred dollars from their gross income for expenses incurred in school tuition, textbooks, and transportation for dependents who attended elementary or secondary schools in the state. Although the law extended the benefits to parents of children attending both public and private schools, more than 95 percent of the benefits went to those whose children were in religious schools. Several Minnesota taxpayers contested the law in federal court, arguing that it violated the separation of church and state required by the establishment clause of the First Amendment. After the trial and appellate courts ruled that the law was constitutional, the plaintiffs took their case to the U.S. Supreme Court.

The precedents of the Court appeared to suggest that the

statute would be ruled unconstitutional. In *Committee for Public Education and Religious Liberty v. Nyquist* (1975), the Court had struck down a New York law that had provided tuition grants and tax credits for parents of children in church-related institutions. *Nyquist* and other precedents had established that a state may not aid parochial schools either by direct grants or by indirect tax credits to the parents.

In *Mueller*, however, the Court voted 5 to 4 to uphold the Minnesota law. Writing for the majority, Chief Justice William Rehnquist argued that the law was consistent with the three-pronged test of *Lemon v. Kurtzman* (1971). First, the law had the secular purpose of educating children and promoting diversity of educational institutions; second, it was religiously neutral, because it was designed to benefit parents of children in both public and private schools; third, it did not result in "excessive entanglement" between church and state, since there was no program for monitoring instructional materials.

The three dissenters argued that the Minnesota law was unconstitutional because it had the effect of providing financial assistance to sectarian schools. They emphasized that parents of public school children were unable to claim large deductions for tuition and textbooks, and that 95 percent of the law's financial benefits went to parents with children in reli gious schools. Also, they observed that the statute did not restrict private schools to books approved for the public schools, with the result that the state became entangled in religious questions when deciding which books might qualify for tax exemption.

The *Mueller* decision was important because the majority of the Court went further than in perhaps any other case toward allowing an indirect subsidy for religious education. In *Aguilar v. Felton* (1985), however, the Court appeared to return to the idea of strict separation. Few observers expected that future cases would consistently defend either the state's right to accommodate religion or the duty to maintain a high wall of separation.

Thomas T. Lewis

Muller v. Oregon

U.S. SUPREME COURT

DECIDED FEBRUARY 24, 1908

- For the first time in an important case, the Supreme Court sanctioned the use of sociological jurisprudence and adopted the position that the meaning given to law should evolve in relation to social needs.

In 1908 attorney Louis D. Brandeis defended before the Supreme Court an Oregon law prohibiting the employment of women in factories and laundries for more than ten hours a day. That statute had been challenged by employers who argued that it impaired women's freedom of contract and violated their rights under the due process clause of the Fourteenth Amendment.

In his now famous 104-page brief, in which only two pages dealt with abstract logic and legal precedents, Brandeis argued that existing law acknowledged that the right to purchase or sell labor was part of the "liberty" protected by the Constitution and that such liberty was subject to such reasonable restraints as a state government might impose, in the exercise of its police power, to protect the health, safety, morals, or general welfare. The question at issue, argued Brandeis, was whether Oregon's maximum-hour law was a necessary restraint. The answer to that question, said Brandeis, could not be answered by legal logic, only by facts.

In his defense Brandeis argued that a woman's special role (her child bearing and maternal functions) and her lack of physical strength relative to men required restricting her hours of work to ten per day. Armed with data from reports of factory inspectors, physicians, experts in hygiene, and special industrial commissions that had been gathered for his use by the National Consumers' League, Brandeis submitted seventy-five thousand words of facts to prove that long hours of work are dangerous to the health and safety of women. In a unanimous decision, the Supreme Court agreed and affirmed Oregon's ten-hour law. "Woman's physical structure, and the [maternal] functions she performs in consequence thereof," said the Court, "justify special legislation restraining or qualifying the conditions under which she should be permitted to toil."

Muller v. Oregon is important for several reasons. Although the decision related solely to the number of hours worked by women and could not be taken as a reversal of the Court's earlier ruling in *Lochner v. New York* (1905) that restricting the hours that men worked in a bakery was not a legitimate use of a state's police power, it did suggest a change in the Court's thinking. As a result, the *Muller* decision revived the entire field of protective labor legislation. Over the next eight years, forty-one states enacted new or revised hour laws for working women. In a broader sense, however, and for the first time in an important case, the Supreme Court allowed a new means of legal argumentation and accepted the position that the meaning given to the law should evolve in relation to social needs. The decision, in effect, sanctioned what came to be known as "sociological jurisprudence"—presenting factual data to establish the need for social legislation.

Thomas T. Lewis

Mutual Film Corporation v. Industrial Commission of Ohio

U.S. SUPREME COURT

FEBRUARY 23, 1915

• This Supreme Court decision—and *Mutual Film Corporation v. Kansas*, which the Court decided at the same time—upheld the constitutionality of 1913 Ohio and Kansas laws allowing the states to censor films on the grounds that motion picture films were not protected forms of speech under the First Amendment; these decisions opened the door to decades of government censorship of films.

At stake in Mutual's suits against Ohio and Kansas was the right of states to allow public officials to review films for their moral content before permitting them to be shown to the general public. Under Ohio's and Kansas' laws, films found to be "sacrilegious, obscene, indecent, or immoral," or that might "corrupt the morals," could be banned from being shown in public. In appealing an earlier decision against it to the Supreme Court, the Mutual Film Corporation claimed that state review of films was a violation of "the freedom to say, write or publish whatever one will on any subject." In defense of their right to act as censors, the states of Ohio and Kansas argued that film censorship was a legitimate exercise of the authority of the state to protect public morality.

In deciding in the states' favor, the Court reflected for the first time on the question of just what a motion picture was. Possibly influenced by the popular press, which reported on the infant film industry as though it were primarily a source of cheap mass entertainment, the Court determined that films fell into the category of entertainment designed to make a profit. Although films certainly contain ideas, the Court explained, they are not a means of communicating them. With that distinction in mind, the Court decided for Ohio on the grounds that state censorship of films did not violate any personal liberties covered by the First Amendment. Using the same line of reasoning, it also ruled in Kansas' favor.

Coming at a time when films were new, these decisions had a powerful impact. They made film censorship possible, allowing for state and local governments to control what films were shown in theaters. They also opened up a wide latitude for the censorship of films, which could be banned as "immoral" for many different reasons. The decisions enabled private pressure groups, particularly religious organizations such as the Legion of Decency, to bring pressure and influence to bear on the decisions of public censorship boards. It took more than thirty-five years for the Supreme Court, ruling on a case relating to the film *The Miracle*, to overturn this decision by ruling that films did indeed communicate ideas and thus were entitled to constitutional protection.

Diane P. Michelfelder

National Treasury Employees Union v. Von Raab

U.S. SUPREME COURT

DECIDED MARCH 21, 1989

- In this case the Supreme Court expanded the scope and discretion of public employers to utilize mandatory drug testing in their efforts to promote a drug-free work environment.

The rules of the drug-testing program of the U.S. Customs Service required a very closely monitored urine test for employees seeking transfers or promotions to specified job classifications. Positions covered included those involved with classified materials, drug interdiction, and the carrying of firearms. The National Treasury Employees Union (NTEU) challenged these rules in federal district court on the grounds that they called for an unlawful search, a violation of employees' Fourth Amendment rights.

The court agreed, arguing that the drug testing was an overly intrusive violation of the employees' privacy and an unlawful search, given the lack of any actual evidence of drug abuse. An injunction was issued to keep the Customs Service from implementing the rules.

This injunction was later vacated by the circuit court of appeals, which, while it agreed that the testing did represent a "search," in the meaning of the Fourth Amendment, concluded that the Customs Service rules were "reasonable." This conclusion was based on the Customs Service's strong law enforcement function and its related need to maintain public confidence that key employees were drug free.

The U.S. Supreme Court, in a 5-4 decision, upheld the majority of the testing program, based largely on the rationale of *Skinner v. Railway Labor Executives' Association* (1989). The Court ruled that there must be a balance between an employee's legitimate expectation of privacy and the government's legitimate public policy interest, a balance that must be evaluated on a case-by-case basis. Thus, for example, the Court excluded the drug-testing procedures for Customs Service positions dealing with "classified materials," concluding that the term was too vaguely defined.

The ongoing need to strike a balance was further demonstrated by the dissenting opinion of Justice Antonin Scalia. Though he had voted with the majority in *Skinner*, Scalia argued that in this instance the Customs Service did not adequately demonstrate a potential for great harm in the absence of drug testing and thus the government's interest in this case should not supersede the employees' Fourth Amendment protection.

NTEU v. Von Raab, in conjunction with *Skinner*, established that the Fourth Amendment does not exclude all drug testing of employees. Rather, some searches are "reasonable" and are therefore lawful. On the other hand, the government employer does not have an unfettered right to impose drug testing. The government must, in each instance, demonstrate that there is a rational connection between drug testing and the broader public interest. Properly and reasonably crafted drug-testing procedures are legal, and thus *NTEU v. Von Raab* both expanded and defined the scope of public sector drug testing.

David Carleton

Neagle, In re

U.S. SUPREME COURT
DECIDED APRIL 14, 1890

- This case, involving an attack on Supreme Court Justice Stephen J. Field, expanded federal power by making certain acts committed under color of federal law subject to the jurisdiction of federal law rather than state criminal law.

While sitting as a circuit court judge in his native California in 1888, Justice Stephen J. Field delivered an opinion invalidating the purported marriage between William Sharon, a wealthy Nevada mine owner, and Sarah Althea Hill. During Sharon's federal action to nullify a state court award to Hill of a judgment of divorce and alimony, he died, and Hill married David S. Terry, one of Field's former colleagues on the California Supreme Court. Hill and Terry were outraged by Field's ruling, precipitating a courtroom brawl that resulted in Field citing them for contempt and sentencing them to jail.

Terry began a campaign of public vilification of Field, going so far as to threaten to kill him. Against all warnings, in 1889 Field returned to California for circuit duties. He traveled with David Neagle, a federal marshal who had been assigned to protect him. While eating breakfast on his way to Los Angeles, where he was to hold court, Field was attacked by Terry, who struck him twice. Neagle, who believed Terry to be reaching for a weapon, drew his own gun and shot Terry dead.

Neagle was arrested by state officials and charged with murder under California law. He appealed to the federal circuit court for a writ of *habeas corpus*, which federal law authorized if a person was being held against federal law. California then appealed the grant of the writ, and the release of Neagle, to the U.S. Supreme Court.

Justice Field did not participate in the case, which by a 6-2 vote upheld the lower court's grant of the writ. While the majority interpreted the authority under which the writ was granted to mean that federal "law" included Neagle's perform-ance of his assigned duties as a federal marshal, the minority objected that this was a strained interpretation formulated solely to justify the intrusion of the federal government into the jurisdiction of state criminal law.

To be sure, the Court wanted to save Neagle—who had possibly saved the life of one of their own in the course of doing his job—from the vagaries of California law. In effect, however, the Supreme Court decided that the federal circuit court had the authority, on the basis of a petition for a writ of *habeas corpus*

Melville W. Fuller (1833-1910) was chief justice at the time of the *Neagle* decision. *(Albert Rosenthal/Collection of the Supreme Court of the United States)*

and without benefit of the fact-finding process afforded by a trial, to make a determination that Terry's murder had been justifiable homicide. The majority of laws governing criminal behavior are promulgated by individual states, and when criminal matters come before federal courts, customarily it is state law that applies. *In re Neagle* thus expanded federal judicial and executive power into a realm normally reserved for the states.

Lisa Paddock

Near v. Minnesota

U.S. SUPREME COURT
DECIDED JUNE 1, 1931

• In this case the Supreme Court held for the first time that injunctions on the press to prevent publication are presumptively unconstitutional "prior restraints" and that the parties seeking them have a heavy burden to overcome; however, it also suggested that prior restraints could be acceptable under certain circumstances.

Based on a statute that allowed a court to enjoin (prohibit) the publication of a newspaper if it was detrimental to public morals and general welfare, a Minnesota district attorney requested an injunction against the *Saturday Press* because of its anti-Semitic and racist remarks. The trial court concluded that the publication was chiefly devoted to malicious, scandalous, and defamatory articles and enjoined the editors from publishing, editing, producing, and circulating their publication. The Supreme Court of Minnesota affirmed this decision, but the Supreme Court of the United States reversed it.

The Court held that the statute amounted to a prior restraint in violation of the First Amendment. Since the effect of the application of the statute was the suppression of information, the Court held that it operated as a system of censorship. The

Court suggested that prior restraints are the most dangerous infringement on freedom of the press because their effect is to suppress speech totally and because of the inability of the press to challenge the constitutionality of the order by disobeying it. The Court suggested, however, that prior restraints could be acceptable in limited circumstances, including cases of obscene material, cases of fighting words and incitement to violence or to overthrow the government, and cases of national security during war where the information to be published could endanger U.S. troops or the success of a mission. The Court offered no explanation for these exceptions.

Justice Pierce Butler wrote a dissenting opinion joined by three other justices. They argued that the original court order did not have the effect of a prior restraint but of punishment imposed after publication to preserve law and order. They also emphasized the fact that the statute did not authorize administrative, licensing, or censorship control by the government. Therefore, they suggested, the statute did not amount to censorship.

The decision of the Court stated clearly for the first time that by issuing an injunction against the media prior to publication the state would be abridging freedom of the press. In reaching this conclusion, the Court gave the concept of prior restraint a much broader meaning than it had been afforded before. Traditionally, the phrase "prior restraint" was used to describe an administrative licensing system which allowed the state to determine in advance what could be published.

The Minnesota statute did not create a licensing system; the decision to enjoin a publication was made by a court after a hearing and not by an administrative licenser or censor prior to publication. Yet the Court declared that the primary purpose of the First Amendment is to protect against governmental actions that have the ultimate effect of a prior restraint, whatever their character might be. Since *Near v. Minnesota*, therefore, the doctrine against prior restraints on the media has been related to the effects on speech notwithstanding the method used by the government in regulating it.

Alberto Bernabe-Riefkohl

New Jersey v. T.L.O.

U.S. SUPREME COURT

DECIDED JANUARY 15, 1985

- This decision established the standards by which the protections of the Fourth Amendment apply to searches of students by school officials.

A teacher at Piscataway High School in New Jersey found two students smoking cigarettes in a school restroom in violation of the school's rules. After being sent to the school office, one of the students, "T.L.O.," a fourteen-year-old freshman, denied smoking. Based on the report he had received from the teacher, the assistant vice principal searched T.L.O.'s purse and discovered a pack of cigarettes. As he reached for the cigarette pack, he then noticed other items, including cigarette rolling papers, which he associated with marijuana use. He then searched the purse more thoroughly and discovered marijuana, a pipe, plastic bags, a large sum of money in single dollar bills, a list of students who owed T.L.O. money, and two letters which suggested T.L.O. was involved in marijuana sales. School officials notified T.L.O.'s mother and the police.

On the basis of this evidence and a later confession, the state brought delinquency charges against T.L.O. T.L.O. appealed the charges, arguing that because the search of her purse was improper under the Fourth Amendment, the evidence was inadmissible. The U.S. Supreme Court, however, ruled that the search was conducted within the constitutional standards of the Fourth Amendment. In its opinion, the Court established standards to be used by school officials in searches of students' pockets, purses, and other items associated with the student's person. The Court specifically did not address searches of school lockers.

Until this case, public school officials had typically relied on the doctrine of in loco parentis, whereby school officials had broad search powers akin to those of a student's parents. The U.S. Supreme Court rejected this argument and held that when public school officials conduct a search of a student, they may be held to the same Fourth Amendment standards as government officials. In its analysis, the Court recognized that public school students maintain an expectation of privacy in their personal effects even on a public school campus, but the Court did not go so far as to hold school officials to exactly the same standards as police officers in conducting searches.

While police officers are usually required to show they had probable cause to believe the person has violated the law, the Court allowed that school officials may need to show only that they had a reasonable suspicion that a search would produce evidence that the student had violated a school code. The Court justified this relaxed standard for school officials by citing the major social problems evident in schools nationwide and a school's need to maintain an educational environment.

Paul Albert Bateman

New York v. Ferber

U.S. Supreme Court

Decided July 2, 1982

- The Court ruled that pornography depicting sexual performances by children was a category of material not protected by the First Amendment.

The state of New York, like nineteen other states, had a statute that criminalized the dissemination of material depicting sexual conduct of children under the age of sixteen, regardless of whether the material satisfied the legal definition of obscenity. The owner of a Manhattan adult bookstore, Paul Ferber, was tried and convicted under the statute for selling films that depicted young boys masturbating. The New York Court of Appeals, however, reversed the conviction, holding that the statute violated the First Amendment because it was inconsistent with the recognized legal standard of obscenity. The state then appealed the case to the U.S. Supreme Court.

The Court voted unanimously to uphold the conviction of Ferber under the New York statute. Justice Byron White, writing for the Court, proclaimed that child pornography was "a category of material outside the protection of the First Amendment." He emphasized five points. First, the state had a compelling interest in safeguarding minor children from sexual exploitation and abuse. Second, the distribution of materials depicting the sexual activity of juveniles was intrinsically related to their sexual abuse. Third, the advertising and selling of child pornography provided an economic motive for an activity that was everywhere illegal. Fourth, child pornography was of very modest literary, scientific, or educational value. Finally, the recognition of a category of material outside the protection of the First Amendment was compatible with earlier decisions of the Court. White concluded that the test for child pornography was much less demanding than the three-part test in *Miller v. California* (1973), but he also wrote that the prohibited conduct must be adequately defined in state law.

The most important aspect of the *Ferber* decision was that all the justices agreed that the state's interest in protecting children was sufficiently compelling to justify more discretion in criminalizing child pornography than when dealing with other forms of pornography. The majority of the Court was unwilling to consider the possibility of constitutional protection of any material depicting juveniles engaged in sexual conduct. A liberal minority cautioned, however, that such material would be protected by the First Amendment if its depictions were found to contain serious literary, artistic, scientific, or medical value.

Thomas T. Lewis

New York Times Co. v. Sullivan

U.S. Supreme Court
Decided March 9, 1964

- In this case, the Supreme Court ruled that the press and public have wide latitude against claims of libel when commenting on the official conduct of public officials.

On March 29, 1960, *The New York Times* ran a full-page advertisement sponsored by the "Committee to Defend Martin Luther King and the Struggle for Freedom in the South." The advertisement appealed for financial support for the Civil Rights movement in the South. In the ad, various incidents of discriminatory action in southern cities, including Montgomery, Alabama, were described. The ad was ostensibly endorsed by sixty-four well-known persons in the fields of religion, trade unions, public affairs, and performing arts. (Later, many proclaimed that they had never been contacted before the ad was released.)

The description of events in the advertisement relating to Montgomery, Alabama, was contested by L. B. Sullivan, an elected Montgomery commissioner with supervisory responsibility for the police department. The ad made several references to wrongdoing by police, which, Sullivan maintained, implicated him and defamed his reputation. Sullivan himself was not mentioned by name.

Sullivan pointed to several erroneous factual statements in the description of events. For example, the ad described an incident in which students were expelled following a protest on the Montgomery capitol steps, at which they had recited "My Country 'Tis of Thee," and it stated that truckloads of police had surrounded the Alabama State College campus with shotguns and tear gas. In reality, Sullivan said, the police had not surrounded the campus, as claimed, but had been on campus several times in response to events; the protesting students had sung the National Anthem, not "My Country 'Tis of Thee"; and the students were expelled for a demonstration at which they had demanded service at a courthouse lunch counter, not for a capitol demonstration.

The Montgomery County Circuit Court found that Sullivan had been defamed and awarded him $500,000, an unprecedented amount in a libel trial. Sullivan effectively convinced the Court that *The New York Times* had been irresponsible in printing the ad with the factual errors, since its own files contained articles with conflicting information. The Supreme Court of Alabama affirmed the lower court judgment.

The U.S. Supreme Court reversed the judgment, holding that the Alabama courts had failed to place sufficient weight on First and Fourteenth Amendment claims. The Supreme Court determined that constitutional free press guarantees extend to an advertisement with political content, especially since members of the public without access to the press may need to buy space to publicize their ideas. The Court further pointed to a potential chilling effect on freedom of press by damage awards for criticism of public officials' conduct, even if factual errors are involved. In an opinion authored by Justice William J. Brennan, the majority held that "erroneous statement is inevitable in free debate" and that it "must be protected if the freedoms of expression are to have the breathing space they 'need to survive.' " Brennan argued that forcing critics of government action to guarantee the truth of their assertions could bring about self-censorship as a result of fear of potential libel suits.

The Court's opinion pointed out that the Constitution's framers believed in debate which is robust and uninhibited, even if it includes "vehement, caustic, and sometimes unpleasantly sharp attacks on government and public officials."

In *New York Times Co. v. Sullivan*, the Court fashioned a federal standard for libel cases involving public officials. The standard prohibits public officials from recovering damages for defamatory falsehoods relating to official conduct unless an official "proves that the statement was made with 'actual malice'—that is, with knowledge that it was false or with reckless disregard of whether it was false or not."

New York Times Co. v. Sullivan recognized the importance of allowing the public and press to criticize freely the official conduct of public officials without the crippling fear of libel suits in retaliation for that criticism. While the decision has been refined and clarified in subsequent cases, the principle of encouraging free debate of public officials' conduct and actions has been strongly preserved.

Mary A. Hendrickson

New York Times Co. v. United States

U.S. SUPREME COURT
DECIDED JUNE 30, 1971

- This was the first Supreme Court decision involving a restraint directly on the media under the national security exception to the prior restraint doctrine.

During 1971, Daniel Ellsberg, one of the original writers of a secret government study of U.S. involvement in Vietnam, leaked a copy to *The New York Times.* Two days after the newspaper published some sections of it, the government filed a petition for a restraining order, arguing that further publication would threaten national security. This petition was originally denied, but the denial was later reversed by a court of appeals. Meanwhile, the government also filed a petition for an injunction against the *Washington Post*, which had also begun to publish the report. Eventually, this petition was denied. Both cases were then appealed to the Supreme Court. The issue before the Court was whether the media could be enjoined from publishing truthful information of public interest because it would allegedly endanger the nation's security. The media argued that such injunction would constitute censorship in violation of the First Amendment.

A total of ten separate opinions were published by the Supreme Court. The opinion of the Court was very short and

unsigned. It merely reiterated that any order prohibiting publication has a heavy presumption against constitutional validity, and that the petitioner has a heavy burden of showing that
such a remedy is justified. It then held that the government had
not met the burden that would justify the restraining order.
Therefore, it was implied that the state could have enjoined the
media had it been able to produce better evidence of the danger
to national security.

Each justice filed a separate opinion. Seven of them accepted
the idea that there could be a national security exception to the
prior restraint doctrine, as had been suggested in passing in the
1931 decision *Near v. Minnesota*. Suggesting that the Court had
not provided clear standards for future decisions, Justice Harry
Blackmun called for the creation of clear standards to be used
in prior restraint cases. Only Justices William Brennan and
Potter Stewart suggested such standards. Brennan suggested
that only in cases where the petitioner could prove that the
publication would "inevitably, directly and immediately cause
the occurrence of an event kindred to imperiling the safety of a
transport already at sea" can a prior restraint be issued. Stewart
suggested the standard should be proof that the publication
would "surely result in direct, immediate and irreparable damage to our Nation or its people."

Even though the Supreme Court was dealing for the first
time with the national security exception mentioned in *Near*,
it did not explain the meaning of the burden needed to justify the order. The Court did not create any standards to determine the constitutionality of restraining orders. It is also
nearly impossible to get an accurate idea of what standards
would have been acceptable to a majority of the justices. The
Court did not provide any discussion on the restraining
order itself and did not discuss the evidence used by the government to support its claim. In essence, the Court failed to
provide any guidelines for future litigants as to what would
constitute sufficient evidence to overcome the presumption of
invalidity of a petition for an order banning publication by
the press.

Alberto Bernabe-Riefkohl

Newberry v. United States

U.S. SUPREME COURT
DECIDED MAY 2, 1921

- The Supreme Court concluded that the federal government lacked the constitutional authority to regulate party primaries, a ruling that had the unintended consequence of disfranchising black citizens in the single-party South.

In 1918, Truman H. Newberry, Republican candidate for the U.S. Senate, was tried in Michigan, along with more than one hundred associates, for conspiring to violate the Federal Corrupt Practices Act of 1910. The statute violated had set a limit on campaign financing, and the indictment claimed that Newberry had exceeded this limit in primary and general election expenditures. Newberry and his associates were found guilty in the U.S. District Court for the Western District of Michigan.

The U.S. Supreme Court reversed the conviction and sent the case back to the lower court, finding that the statute on which Newberry's conviction rested had no constitutional authority. The Court argued that prior to the Seventeenth Amendment, the only part of the Constitution empowering Congress to regulate the election process was to be found in Article I, section 4, which pertained only to the time, place, and manner of holding general elections and failed to address such matters as party primaries and conventions, additions to the election process unforeseen by the Framers of the Constitution. Consequently, the Court ruled that in the relevant section of the Corrupt Practices Act, Congress had exceeded its authority.

The Court also maintained that because the statute antedated the ratification of the Seventeenth Amendment, which extended congressional authority, it was invalid at the time of its enactment. The Court held that a power later acquired could not, *ex proprio*, validate a law that was unconstitutional at the time of its passing. The Court did not question a state's right to regulate primaries and campaign financing, claiming that "the state may suppress whatever evils may be incident to primary or convention."

The *Newberry* ruling imposed an important barrier to the enfranchisement of black Americans in the single-party South. Although the Court would strike down laws expressly prohibiting African Americans from voting in primaries, as late as 1935, in *Grovey v. Townsend*, it upheld legal measures taken in Texas to bar blacks from participating in the state Democratic convention, arguing that such "private" discrimination did not come under constitutional purview. *Grovey* and *Newberry* were finally successfully challenged in *United States v. Classic* (1941), which held that Congress had the authority to regulate both primary and general elections for federal offices.

Three years later a final legal blow to *de jure* disfranchisement of African Americans was dealt in *Smith v. Allwright* (1944), which held that laws governing all elections—local, state, and federal—could be invalidated if they violated Article I, section 4 of the Constitution. Sponsored by the National Association for the Advancement of Colored People, the plaintiff argued that Texas Democratic Party officials had denied him a primary ballot because of his race. The Supreme Court concurred, noting that state laws regulated both primary and general elections and were therefore responsible for barriers to the ballot box erected on racial grounds.

John W. Fiero

Nixon v. Herndon

U.S. SUPREME COURT
DECIDED MARCH 7, 1927

• The Supreme Court voided an attempt by the Texas legislature to restrict black participation in primary elections.

In 1921, the U.S. Supreme Court ruled in *Newberry v. United States* that Congress lacked authority to regulate primary elections. Southern state legislatures immediately took advantage of this decision to prohibit black participation in state primary elections. "White primaries" were quickly adopted throughout the South. Texas, during the first half of the twentieth century, was part of the Democrat-dominated South. The only competition that mattered was within the Democratic Party, so if blacks were not allowed to participate in the Democratic primary they would effectively be denied any meaningful choice in the electoral process.

In 1924, the Texas legislature passed a law barring blacks from voting in the Democratic primary. L. A. Nixon, a black resident of El Paso, attempted to vote in the primary and was refused by Herndon, an election judge. Nixon and the National Association for the Advancement of Colored People (NAACP) claimed that the Texas law violated the Fourteenth and Fifteenth Amendments. The Supreme Court did not deal with the issue of the Fifteenth Amendment, but a unanimous Court found that the Texas white primary law violated the "equal protection clause" of the Fourteenth Amendment.

The NAACP won the battle but temporarily lost the war. Texas responded to the Court's decision by engaging in the strategy of "legislate and litigate." By passing a different white primary law after their defeat in *Nixon v. Herndon*, the Texas legislature forced the NAACP to institute another attack on the white primary. When the second law was declared unconstitutional in *Nixon v. Condon* in 1932, Texas came up with a third variation of the white primary. This time, in *Grovey v. Townsend* (1935), the U.S. Supreme Court upheld the Texas white primary, arguing that no state discrimination was present. According to the Court, the Texas Democratic Party, a private voluntary association, decided to exclude blacks from voting in the primary elections. It was not until *Smith v. Allwright* (1944) that a unanimous Supreme Court declared that the Fifteenth Amendment could be used as a shield to protect the right to vote in primary elections.

From the passage of the first white primary law in 1924 until the final abolition of white primaries in the *Smith* case in 1944, blacks were denied the right to vote in Democratic Party primaries, the only election of significance at that time. The white primary cases illustrate one of the dilemmas in using the federal courts—the fact that justice delayed is justice denied.

Darryl Paulson

Nollan v. California Coastal Commission

U.S. SUPREME COURT
DECIDED JUNE 26, 1987

• In this case, the Supreme Court substantially expanded the protection of property rights by limiting the power of states to force land owners to consent to physical occupations of their property by third parties as a precondition to obtaining government permission to develop the property.

James and Marilyn Nollan planned to demolish a dilapidated bungalow and replace it with a three-bedroom house on a beachfront lot in California located between two public beaches to the north and south. Pursuant to state law, the Nollans sought a development permit from the California Coastal Commission to enable them to proceed. The Coastal Commission conditioned the granting of the permit on the Nollans' agreeing to create an easement that would allow the public to cross their beachfront to gain better access to the adjacent public beaches. The Nollans challenged this condition in state court on the grounds that it violated the Fourteenth Amendment by "taking" their property without the payment of just compensation. When the state court of appeal ruled against them, the Nollans sought review from the U.S. Supreme Court.

In a 5-4 decision, the Supreme Court held that the Coastal Commission had violated the Constitution and reversed the ruling of the court of appeal. Justice Antonin Scalia, writing for the majority, argued that the commission could not directly require property owners to grant an easement to the public to cross their land unless the state paid the owners just compensation as the Constitution required. The issue before the Court in *Nollan* was whether the state could avoid the constitutional obligation of paying for this property interest by denying the owners the right to develop their property unless they agreed to grant the sought-after easement to the public without receiving compensation in return.

The Court conceded that a state agency might impose lawful conditions on the development of property even to the point of requiring owners to dedicate easements to the public. Such conditions would comply with the takings clause of the Fifth Amendment, made applicable to the states by incorporation into the Fourteenth Amendment, if the condition mitigated or offset some externality caused by the proposed development. Thus, if the anticipated use of private property resulted in a burden to the community in which the property was located, the state could refuse to allow the development of the property to protect the public from the anticipated externality, or it could condition the development on the owners taking appropriate steps to reduce or eliminate the problems their development would cause.

Without this "essential nexus" between the conditions placed on development permits and some legitimate state interest in avoiding harms caused by the development, however, the state's demand for concessions from the property owner amounted to a constitutionally impermissible use of the state's regulatory power to take property interests without paying for them.

The majority did not find the required "nexus" in the facts before it. There seemed to be no connection whatsoever between any burden to the public that might result from the construction of the house and the public easement the Coastal Commission was requiring. The Nollans' house would not interfere with the public's rightful access to any public beach. Therefore, the easement could not be upheld as a legitimate regulatory response. If the Coastal Commission still wanted a public easement on the Nollans' land, it would have to acquire it through the power of eminent domain and pay for it.

Nollan is an important land use decision because many states and cities throughout the United States regularly impose land dedication conditions on property owners as a way of offsetting the burden on municipal services and infrastructure created by new land development in a community. *Nollan* is the first case in which the Supreme Court indicated that this "dealmaking" form of land use regulation is limited by constitutional constraints. Subsequent cases, particularly *Dolan v. City of Tigard* (1994), expanded on this foundation and further limited the state's ability to regulate land use by placing conditions on development permits.

Alan E. Brownstein

Ogden v. Saunders

U.S. SUPREME COURT
DECIDED FEBRUARY 19, 1827

• The Supreme Court took a first important step in restricting the operation of the contract clause of the U.S. Constitution.

A New York State law, passed in 1801, gave relief to people who could not pay their debts. The Constitution forbids the states to "pass any . . . Law impairing the Obligation of Contracts." Therefore the New York law could not constitutionally be applied to contracts made prior to the passage of the law. *Ogden v. Saunders* tested whether the New York law could be applied to contracts made after the law's passage. It was argued that all contracts carry with them the state laws which prescribe the rules for the enforcement of contracts—including debtor relief provisions.

After elaborate and protracted argument in 1824, in which Daniel Webster and Henry Clay participated, the Supreme Court decided 4 to 3 that a state bankruptcy law such as the New York law does not impair the obligation of contracts which are entered into after passage of the law. The decision was accompanied by six separate extensive opinions by the justices, which revealed deep disagreements within the Court. Chief Justice John Marshall was in the minority in this case for the only time in his judicial career. Marshall's conservative view was that the constitutional grant of power to Congress to establish uniform bankruptcy rules necessarily excluded the operation of all state bankruptcy laws.

A second issue settled by *Ogden v. Saunders* was whether a debtor discharged under the New York State law could claim that discharge for a contract or debt owed to a citizen of another state. On this issue the Court split differently. Chief Justice Marshall and the other conservatives on the Court held that the debt was still collectible in a federal court. To hold otherwise would produce "a conflict of sovereign power and a collision with the judicial powers."

In sum, then, the Court decided that state bankruptcy and debtor relief laws are unconstitutional when applied to contracts entered into before passage of the law and constitutional with respect to contracts made after passage of the law. Second, such laws are unconstitutional if they attempt to invalidate a debt owed to a citizen of another state.

This decision began the restoration of state powers which had been restricted by the contract clause as the Court had previously interpreted it. *Ogden v. Saunders* presaged a broader view of the state's police powers which soon became dominant and has prevailed in the United States ever since.

Robert Jacobs

Olmstead v. United States

U.S. Supreme Court
Decided June 4, 1928

• Although a majority of justices rejected the argument that government wiretaps on telephones constituted illegal searches and compelled self-incrimination, Justice Louis D. Brandeis' famous dissenting opinion laid the groundwork for the later development of a constitutional right to privacy.

During the Prohibition era, Roy Olmstead was convicted of being the general manager of a significant illegal smuggling operation that brought liquor to the United States from Canada in violation of federal law. Olmstead's illegal business had fifty employees and reportedly earned more than two million dollars each year. The evidence that produced the convictions of Olmstead and his associates was gathered through the use of wiretaps. Law enforcement officials had attached wires to the telephone lines leading from Olmstead's residence and office. Officials had listened to and had stenographers take notes on the conversations secretly overheard through the telephone lines.

Olmstead and his codefendants challenged the use of such investigative techniques and evidence. They claimed that the wiretaps constituted an illegal search and seizure in violation of the Fourth Amendment and that the use of private conversations as evidence violated the Fifth Amendment's prohibition on compelled self-incrimination.

In an opinion by Chief Justice William Howard Taft, the Supreme Court rejected Olmstead's arguments. Taft concluded that the Fourth Amendment protected only against unreasonable searches of material things and that telephone lines running between two people's property could not be considered protected against intrusion by government. Taft also declared that the defendants' conversations were voluntary and therefore could not be regarded as compelled self-incrimination.

In a famous dissenting opinion, Justice Louis D. Brandeis made an eloquent plea for the recognition of a constitutional right to privacy. According to Brandeis, the authors of the Constitution "sought to protect Americans in their beliefs, their thoughts, their emotions, and their sensations. They conferred, as against the government, the right to be let alone—the most comprehensive of rights and the right most valued by civilized men."

Brandeis was not the lone dissenter in the case; Justices

THE SUPREME COURT OF THE UNITED STATES

Justice Edward Terry Sanford
Tennessee; appointed January 29, 1923

Justice George Sutherland
Utah; appointed September 18, 1922

Justice Pierce Butler
Minnesota; appointed December 21, 1922

Justice Harlan Fiske Stone
New York; appointed February 5, 1925

Justice James Clark McReynolds
Tennessee; appointed August 29, 1914

Justice Oliver Wendell Holmes
Massachusetts; appointed December 4, 1902

Chief Justice William Howard Taft
Connecticut; appointed June 30, 1921

Justice Willis Van Devanter
Wyoming; appointed December 16, 1910

Justice Louis D. Brandeis
Massachusetts; appointed June 1, 1916

William Howard Taft (center) and his court a few years before it issued its *Olmstead* decision. *(Harris and Ewing/Collection of the Supreme Court of the United States)*

Oliver Wendell Holmes, Jr., Pierce Butler, and Harlan F. Stone also found fault with Taft's conclusions. Brandeis, however, was the lone justice to place great emphasis on a general right of privacy. The other justices were also concerned about the definition of a search under the Fourth Amendment or the legality of police methods.

Brandeis could not manage to gain majority support for his ideas during his lifetime. Instead, his eloquent defense of a right to privacy stood for more than thirty years as the primary argument against government intrusions into citizens' private lives. Beginning in the 1960's, when the Supreme Court's composition had changed significantly, Brandeis' words were used by a generation of justices who followed his ideals and established the existence of a constitutional right to privacy in *Griswold v. Connecticut* (1965).

Christopher E. Smith

Osborne v. Ohio

U.S. Supreme Court
Ruling issued April 18, 1990

- In this case, the Supreme Court upheld the states' rights to prohibit the possession and viewing of child pornography.

Clyde Osborne was convicted of possessing child pornography after police found sexually explicit photographs of a nude minor male in his home. Ohio law prohibited any person from possessing or viewing materials that include a nude minor who is not their child unless they have a "bona fide purpose" or written consent from the minor's parents for such materials. Sentenced to six months in prison, Osborne appealed on the contention that the First Amendment protected his right to possess and view the photographs. In 1990, the Supreme Court ruled 6 to 3 to uphold Ohio's law, although Osborne's conviction was reversed and a new trial ordered. Essentially, the case contained three elements: whether Ohio's law was constitutional; whether Ohio's law was overbroad; and whether Osborne was denied due process.

In appealing the constitutionality of Ohio's child pornography law, Osborne relied on the Supreme Court's 1969 ruling in *Stanley v. Georgia* in which the court struck down the state's right to prohibit obscene materials. Justice Byron White, however, writing for the majority, pointed to the different underlying motivations for the Georgia and Ohio laws. In the case of *Georgia*, the state wished to prevent the "poisoning of the viewer's mind," while in Ohio's law, the motivation was to protect the victims of child pornography and to destroy the market for such materials. The Court ruled that the state's interest in this case was sufficiently compelling and deemed the law constitutional.

Osborne's second contention, that the Ohio law was overbroad, was also struck down by the Court. The Ohio statute prohibited only "lewd exhibition" or "graphic focus of the genitals" of a child who was not the child of the person charged. The court ruled that this interpretation was specific in its intentions and therefore denied Osborne's overbroad arguments. Osborne's due process arguments were noted, however, and the Court ruled that he should receive a new trial.

Justice William Brennan wrote the dissenting opinion, with Justices Thurgood Marshall and John Paul Stevens concurring. Brennan saw the Ohio law as overbroad, especially concerning its definition of "nudity." While the photographs were "distasteful," Brennan contended that Osborne had the right to possess the photographs under the protection of the First Amendment. The dissenting opinion also suggested that the state's interest was better served through other laws prohibiting the "creation, sale and distribution of child pornography."

Although somewhat weak in its ruling, the *Osborne* case is significant in its upholding of the states' rights to prohibit the possession of child pornography. As the dissenting opinion reveals, however, to stand up to further Supreme Court scrutiny, such laws need to be carefully worded to avoid overbroad interpretation.

Jennifer Davis

Palko v. Connecticut

U.S. SUPREME COURT
RULING ISSUED DECEMBER 6, 1937

- In this case, while refusing to apply the Fifth Amendment right against double jeopardy to the states, the Supreme Court established an influential test for determining which fundamental rights contained within the Bill of Rights are incorporated into the Fourteenth Amendment's due process clause.

On the night of September 29, 1935, Bridgeport, Connecticut, police officers Wilfred Walker and Thomas J. Kearney were shot and killed. Frank Palko was charged with first-degree murder, a charge which carried a death sentence. On January 24, 1936, a trial jury found Palko guilty of only second-degree murder because the killings were not sufficiently premeditated. Palko received a sentence of life imprisonment.

On July 30, 1936, the Supreme Court of Errors of Connecticut ordered a new trial by finding that the trial judge gave improper instructions to the jury. On October 15, 1936, a second jury found Palko guilty of first-degree murder, and he was sentenced to death. Palko's case came to the U.S. Supreme Court with the claim that the second trial violated his Fifth Amendment right to not "be subject for the same offense to be twice put in jeopardy of life or limb." At the time, however, the Supreme Court had applied the Fifth Amendment right against double jeopardy only to criminal cases in federal, rather than state, courts.

For most of American history, the provisions of the Bill of Rights protected individuals only against actions by the federal government. The ratification of the Fourteenth Amendment in 1868 applied constitutional rights to protection against the states, but those rights were vaguely worded protections involving "due process" and "equal protection." People repeatedly brought cases to the Supreme Court asserting that the provisions of the Bill of Rights should apply against state as well as federal government officials. Beginning in 1925, the Supreme Court gradually incorporated a few rights—speech, press, and religion—into the Fourteenth Amendment's due process clause and thereby made those rights applicable to the states.

Unfortunately for Palko, the Court was unwilling to incorporate the Fifth Amendment's protection against double jeopardy in 1937. Thus Palko's conviction was affirmed, and he was subsequently executed for the murders. Justice Benjamin Cardozo's majority opinion, however, established a test for determining which rights to incorporate by declaring that only rights which are "fundamental" and "essential" to liberty are contained in the right to due process in the Fourteenth Amendment.

In analyzing Palko's case, Cardozo decided that many criminal justice rights contained in the Bill of Rights, such as trial by jury and protection against double jeopardy and self-incrimination, are not fundamental and essential because it is possible to have fair trials without them.

The importance of *Palko v. Connecticut* is that Cardozo's test established an influential standard for determining which provisions of the Bill of Rights apply against the states. Although justices in later decades disagreed with Cardozo's specific conclusions and subsequently incorporated double jeopardy and other rights for criminal defendants, most justices continued to use Cardozo's basic approach of evaluating whether each specific right was fundamental and essential to liberty.

Christopher E. Smith

Pasadena City Board of Education v. Spangler

U.S. SUPREME COURT
DECIDED JUNE 28, 1976

- In this school desegregation case, the Supreme Court held that a federal district court exceeded its authority in ordering annual reassignments of students to facilitate changes in the racial makeup of schools caused by demographic shifts.

In 1968, several students and their parents filed suit against the Pasadena Unified School District in California, alleging that the district's schools were segregated as a result of official action on the part of the district. In 1970, the federal district court found for these plaintiffs, concluding that the district had engaged in segregation and ordering the district to adopt a plan to cure the racial imbalances in its schools. The federal court's order provided that no school was to have a majority of minority students. The district thereafter presented the court with a plan to eliminate segregation in the Pasadena schools; the court approved the plan, and the district subsequently implemented it.

Approximately four years later, the Pasadena Unified School District asked the district court to modify its original order and eliminate the requirement that no school have a majority of minority students. The district contended that though it had abandoned its racially segregative practices, changing racial demographics had created new racial imbalances in the district's schools. The federal district court refused to modify its original order, however, and the Ninth Circuit Court of Appeals upheld the district court's ruling.

Reviewing this decision, Justice William H. Rehnquist, joined by five other justices, concluded that the district court had abused its authority in refusing to remove the requirement that no district school have a majority of minority students. According to the Court, there had been no showing that changes in the racial mix of the Pasadena schools had been caused by the school district's policies. Since the school district had implemented a racially neutral attendance policy, the federal district court was not entitled to require a continual reshuffling of attendance zones to maintain an optimal racial mix. Justices Thurgood Marshall and William J. Brennan dissented from this holding, emphasizing the breadth of discretion normally allotted to federal district courts to remedy school segregation once a constitutional violation had been shown.

The majority's decision signaled that the broad discretion with which the Court previously had seemed to have invested federal district courts was not without limits. It had been widely thought that once officially sanctioned or *de jure* segregation had been shown, a federal court had great latitude in eliminating not only such *de jure* segregation but also *de facto* segregation—that is, segregation not necessarily tied to official conduct. The majority's decision in this case, however, signified otherwise.

Timothy L. Hall

Payne v. Tennessee

U.S. SUPREME COURT

DECIDED JUNE 27, 1991

- In a dramatic departure from *stare decisis* (the practice of basing decisions on precedents of previous cases) the Supreme Court overruled two cases it had decided within the past four years and held that victim impact evidence would be permitted in capital sentencing hearings.

In 1987, the Supreme Court in *Booth v. Maryland* had held that prosecutors in capital cases would not be permitted to use victim impact evidence to persuade the jury that the defendant deserved to be executed. The five members of the *Booth* majority held that evidence about the personal characteristics of the murdered person and evidence about the impact of the crime on surviving family members was irrelevant to the jury's decision whether the character of the defendant and the circumstances of the crime called for the death penalty or for some lesser punishment.

Because victim impact evidence focused the jury's attention on the victim and surviving family members, it diverted the jury's attention from the defendant. Most important, it created a risk that a death sentence might be based on arbitrary and capricious reasons, such as the willingness and ability of surviving family members to articulate their grief, or the relative worth of the murder victim to the community.

Four justices had sharply dissented. In their view, victim impact evidence was relevant to the defendant's moral blameworthiness because it gave the jury important information about the extent of the harm caused by the defendant.

The *Booth* decision was reaffirmed two years later in *South Carolina v. Gathers*, when another bare majority of the Court held that prosecutors could not present victim impact evidence to the jury during closing arguments in death penalty cases. By 1991, however, two members of the *Booth* majority had retired from the Court and had been replaced by more conservative justices. That same year, the Court agreed to reconsider its recent decisions and granted *certiorari* in *Payne v. Tennessee.*

Pervis Tyrone Payne had stabbed to death twenty-eight-year-old Charisse Christopher and her two-year-old daughter, Lacie. Payne also stabbed and left for dead Charisse's three-year-old son, Nicholas. Nicholas survived his stab wounds, several of which passed completely through his body. During Payne's trial, Nicholas' grandmother testified emotionally as to the effect of the murders on Nicholas. In addition, during closing arguments to the jury, the prosecutor strongly implied that returning a death sentence would somehow help Nicholas. The jury sentenced Payne to die.

In the Supreme Court, Payne argued that the grandmother's testimony and the prosecutor's argument to the jury constituted victim impact evidence and thereby violated *Booth* and *Gathers*. In a radical departure from past practice, the Supreme Court discarded those recent decisions and announced a new rule: Victim impact evidence would be permitted in capital sentencing proceedings. According to the majority, victim impact evidence gave the jury important information about the extent of the harm caused by the defendant.

Justice Thurgood Marshall, who voted with the majority in *Booth* and *Gathers*, was enraged and disheartened. Breaking tradition, Justice Marshall read his dissent from the bench on the last day of the Court's 1991 term. He said: "Neither the law nor the facts supporting *Booth* and *Gathers* underwent any change in the last four years. Only the personnel of this Court did." Within two hours of reading his dissent, Justice Marshall announced his resignation from the Court.

Randall Coyne

Personnel Administrator of Massachusetts v. Feeney

U.S. SUPREME COURT

DECIDED JUNE 5, 1979

- This case found the Supreme Court upholding a law that affected women adversely.

Under a Massachusetts law, all military veterans were given an absolute lifetime preference, which meant that as long as they passed the examination for classified civil service jobs, they were ranked above all other candidates. Since 98 percent of the veterans were male, the law was challenged as a violation of the Fourteenth Amendment's equal protection clause, which requires states to treat persons equally. In a 7-2 opinion, however, the U.S. Supreme Court upheld the law.

Justice Potter Stewart argued that veteran status is not uniquely male and that the nonveteran class is not substantially all-female. In fact, there are significant numbers of nonveterans who are men, and all nonveterans were placed at a disadvantage by the law. Since so many men were affected, the statute was not a pretext for preferring men over women. Nevertheless, since most veterans are men, there are adverse consequences of the law for women, but the law was not enacted to keep women in a stereotypic and predefined place in the Massachusetts civil service.

The impact of *Personnel Administrator of Massachusetts v. Feeney* was the formulation of a basic rule that a law adversely affecting women but not specifically classifying on the basis of sex does not fall within equal protection analysis.

Robert W. Langran

Phillips v. Martin Marietta Corporation

U.S. SUPREME COURT
DECIDED JANUARY 25, 1971

- This was the first Title VII case to reach the Supreme Court, and the outcome was a victory for women.

Title VII of the Civil Rights Act of 1964 prohibits discrimination in the workplace on the basis of a number of factors, including sex. The first Title VII case to reach the Supreme Court was the one in which Ida Phillips sued Martin Marietta Corporation over its refusal to hire her as an assembly trainee because she had preschool-aged children although the company hired men with preschool-aged children for the same position. Both lower courts had rejected her complaint, holding that she was not refused the job because of her sex alone.

The Supreme Court, however, in a unanimous unsigned per curiam (by the Court) opinion, disagreed with the lower courts and in so doing rejected this "sex plus" reasoning. The Court held that discrimination on the basis of sex plus another characteristic does violate Title VII. The law does not allow a company to have one hiring policy for men and another for women.

Nevertheless, the Court then sent the case back to the lower court to determine whether sex was a bona fide occupational qualification (BFOQ) for the job, as the law does allow that exception. The company would have the chance to show that having preschool-aged children might significantly hamper a woman's job performance. If it could so prove, the company could refuse to hire women with small children.

The impact of *Phillips v. Martin Marietta Corporation* was that the Court did accept the argument that sex discrimination, even though accompanied by another factor, is a violation of the law.

Robert W. Langran

Pierce v. Society of Sisters

U.S. SUPREME COURT

DECIDED JUNE 1, 1925

• This case, which struck down state legislation requiring parents to send their children to public rather than private schools on grounds that such legislation violated the liberty clause of the Fourteenth Amendment, has provided important authority in Supreme Court cases in the areas of contraceptive, abortion, and homosexual rights.

In 1922, the state of Oregon adopted the Compulsory Education Act, which compelled general attendance at public schools by normal children between the ages of eight and sixteen. The Society of the Sisters of the Holy Names of Jesus and Mary, a private parochial school, challenged this legislation on the grounds that it conflicted with the right and liberty of parents to send their children to schools of their own choosing and violated the right of private schools and teachers therein to engage in a useful business and profession.

In a unanimous decision, the U.S. Supreme Court held that "the Act of 1922 unreasonably interferes with the liberty of the parents and guardians to direct the upbringing and education of children under their control." Justice James C. McReynolds, writing for the Court, explained that "rights guaranteed by the Constitution may not be abridged by legislation which has no reasonable relation to some purpose within the competency of the state."

This decision has since become a focal point for vigorous judicial debate over the application of the Ninth Amendment as authority for the invalidation of state legislation in such areas as contraceptive, abortion, and homosexual rights. That amendment states: "The enumeration in the Constitution, of certain rights, shall not be construed to deny or disparage others retained by the people." One judicial view, espoused by Justices Arthur Goldberg and William Brennan, is that the Ninth Amendment clearly implies that there are other rights, not specifically set forth in the Bill of Rights, which are protected from government infringement and that the Court may therefore strike down state legislation deemed to infringe upon such other rights as might be subsumed under the liberty clause.

An opposing view expresses alarm that the Ninth Amendment, adopted by the states as a means of ensuring that the federal government did not exceed its limited and enumerated powers, might be used in a way to expand federal veto power over state legislation. As Justice Potter Stewart stated in his dissenting opinion in *Griswold v. Connecticut* (1965), "The Ninth Amendment was passed, not to broaden the powers of this Court . . . but . . . to limit the federal government."

The former view has prevailed in cases such as *Roe v. Wade* (1973), in which the Court, upholding a woman's right to an abortion, cited *Pierce v. Society of Sisters* for the proposition that personal rights that can be deemed "implicit in the concept of ordered liberty" are guaranteed by the Constitution. In *Bowers v. Hardwick* (1986), however, the Court narrowly declined to find the freedom to engage in homosexual conduct as a right subsumed under the Fourteenth Amendment.

Robert M. Hardaway

Planned Parenthood v. Casey

U.S. SUPREME COURT

DECIDED JUNE 29, 1992

• The Supreme Court reaffirmed its holding in *Roe v. Wade* (1973) that the constitutional right of privacy pro-

tects a woman's right to choose to have an abortion before the fetus she is carrying becomes viable; a controlling plurality of the Court also determined that regulations making it more difficult for a woman to obtain
an abortion will be upheld as long as they do not unduly burden the woman's decision to terminate her pregnancy.

Five medical clinics and one physician challenged the constitutionality of certain provisions of the Pennsylvania Abortion
Control Act, which restricted access to abortion services. The
Supreme Court, however, could not reach a consensus on the
appropriate standard of review to apply to these regulations.
Three justices wrote a joint opinion upholding all but one of the
challenged provisions on the grounds that they did not unduly
burden the right to have an abortion. Four other justices, arguing that the Constitution does not recognize a right to have an
abortion, concurred in that result. Thus, seven justices voted to
uphold the following abortion regulations. Prior to obtaining
her informed consent to surgery, physicians must provide a
woman seeking to have an abortion with specific information
about the nature of an abortion, the risks associated with this
medical procedure, and the gestational age of the fetus. A
woman must wait twenty-four hours after receiving this information before she can obtain an abortion. A woman under
the age of eighteen may not obtain an abortion without either
the informed consent of one of her parents or the determination
by a court that the woman is mature enough to make this
decision for herself or that having an abortion is in her best
interests.

The three-justice plurality struck down as unduly burden-
some a regulation prohibiting a married woman from obtaining
an abortion unless she first notifies her spouse of her decision
to terminate her pregnancy. Two other justices, who argued that
all abortion regulations should be strictly scrutinized, concurred in declaring this provision unconstitutional.

The Court's decision in *Casey*, particularly the plurality opinion of Justices David Souter, Anthony Kennedy, and Sandra
Day O'Connor, appeared to reflect a constitutional compromise

on the abortion issue. On the one hand, the right to have an abortion was explicitly affirmed by a majority of the Court out of respect for *stare decisis*, the obligation of judges to respect past precedent, if for no other reason. Under the authority of *Casey*, any law attempting to criminalize abortion, as many state laws did prior to the Court's decision in *Roe v. Wade* in 1973, would be declared unconstitutional on its face.

On the other hand, the "undue burden" standard applied by the plurality to determine the constitutionality of abortion regulations in *Casey* represented a significant retreat from the trimester framework and rigorous review the Court had applied during the twenty-year period after *Roe* was decided. Unlike the old approach, under which virtually any regulation of abortion during the first two trimesters of the gestation period would be struck down, regulations that increased the cost of having an abortion after *Casey* would be upheld unless plaintiffs challenging their constitutionality could demonstrate the severity of the resulting burden on a woman's right to choose to terminate her pregnancy.

This new standard of review not only was more lenient than its predecessor, but also seemed more ambiguous in its meaning and less predictable in its application. The plurality opinion in *Casey* defined an undue burden as "shorthand for the conclusion that a state regulation has the purpose or effect of placing a substantial obstacle in the path of a woman seeking an abortion of a nonviable fetus." Exactly what constituted a substantial enough burden to justify a court invalidating an abortion regulation remained unclear. The plurality's language left unanswered many important questions that could only be resolved by further litigation and additional judicial decisions.

Notwithstanding this criticism, the Court's decision in *Casey* did resolve one important constitutional question in unambiguous terms. The core holding of *Roe v. Wade* was not overruled. As the plurality stated emphatically, "a State may not prohibit any woman from making the ultimate decision to terminate her pregnancy before viability."

Alan E. Brownstein

Planned Parenthood of Central Missouri v. Danforth

U.S. SUPREME COURT
DECIDED JULY 1, 1976

- The Court ruled that states cannot require a spouse's consent for an abortion and upheld the right of minors to receive abortions without parental consent.

In June of 1974, the Missouri Abortion Act was passed. It required a woman to sign a consent form prior to abortion, spousal consent for abortions, and parental consent for abortions for minors. It also required that physicians make every effort to preserve the life of viable fetuses and prohibited the use of saline amniocentesis as a method of abortion. Planned Parenthood of Central Missouri filed a suit on behalf of itself, women seeking abortions, and physicians who perform abortions. The defendant was John Danforth, attorney general of Missouri. The U.S. District Court, Eastern Missouri, upheld most of the provisions of the law, leading to the case's appeal to the Supreme Court.

The Supreme Court, in a 5-4 decision, overturned the law's central provisions. It ruled that the law did not provide adequate definition of viability and further that the restrictions on physicians placed improper legal constraints in an area that was a matter of medical judgment. Drawing on its *Roe v. Wade* (1973) decision, the Court struck down the prohibition of saline amniocentesis as a method of abortion, for its earlier ruling permitted restriction on abortion methods during the second trimester only on the grounds of health risks to the mother. It found no serious health threats to maternal life from this procedure.

The court also ruled that requiring parental consent for minors was improper, since such consent was not legally required for other medical procedures. Significantly, it argued that rights do not emerge at a certain age but that competent minors already have a "right to privacy" that assures them access to abortion. Its most far-reaching decision involved the denial of a right of spousal consent for abortion. The Court ruled that the woman's right to privacy takes precedence over any claims that others may have.

The minority opinion objected that the state's interest in developing fetal life, as articulated in *Roe v. Wade*, permitted states to require physicians to attempt to save viable fetal life. It also argued that the *Roe* decision did not establish an absolute right to abortion. Consequently, they supported provisions for spousal consent in cases where the spouse was willing to assume the burden of care for the child. Similarly, they indicated that parental consent for minors would be acceptable if there was provision for court intervention in the case of conflict or for court permission in lieu of parental consent in potentially abusive family situations. This last provision has been enacted in a number of subsequent state laws and upheld by the Court.

Charles L. Kammer

Plessy v. Ferguson

U.S. SUPREME COURT
DECIDED MAY 18, 1896

- In this case, the U.S. Supreme Court ruled that Louisiana's requirement of segregation on railroad passenger cars was constitutional; this ruling set the stage for the creation of the "separate but equal" policies that shaped U.S. race relations until the mid-1950's.

Ultraconservative white Democrats in the Louisiana legislature approved the Separate Car Act in 1890, which required that railroads provide segregated seating accommodations for white and African American passengers. The railroads could provide either separate cars or separate sections of a car. Homer

Plessy, an African American, deliberately violated the law in 1892 in order to test its constitutionality. Critics maintained that the measure violated the "equal protection of the law" guarantee of the Fourteenth Amendment to the U.S. Constitution.

The Supreme Court ruled in its hearing of Plessy's appeal that the Separate Car Act was a constitutional exercise of the state's power to promote the common good, peace, and order. The Court held that the Fourteenth Amendment "could not have been intended to abolish distinctions based upon color, or to enforce social . . . equality." The majority opinion approving Louisiana's required segregation formed the constitutional basis for the "separate but equal" doctrine that permeated American race relations for nearly sixty years: As long as accommodations for people of the two races were equal, then it was constitutional for them to be separate.

Even though the ruling technically applied only to railroad passenger cars, the "separate but equal" doctrine allowed many states to impose "Jim Crow" laws upon their black citizens,

John Marshall Harlan (first row, second from right) was the only member of Chief Justice Fuller's court to dissent in *Plessy. (C. M. Bell/Collection of the Supreme Court of the United States)*

segregating almost all aspects of public intermingling. The resulting segregated facilities were most often unequal, with those provided for the majority clearly superior to those provided for the minority.

Only Justice John M. Harlan dissented from the opinion of the other eight justices in the *Plessy* decision. His dissent established an interpretation of constitutional equality that would wait nearly sixty years before it became the guiding principle for American race relations: "[I]n view of the Constitution . . . there is in this country no superior, dominant, ruling class of citizens. . . . Our constitution is color-blind and neither knows nor tolerates classes among its citizens."

The Supreme Court began signaling during the late 1930's that it might be reconsidering the constitutionality of the "separate but equal" doctrine. Beginning with *Gaines v. Canada* in 1938 and including *Morgan v. Virginia* in 1946 and *Shelley v. Kraemer* in 1948, the court chipped away at the doctrine. It finally overturned "separate but equal" in the *Brown v. Board of Education* case in 1954. "Separate educational facilities are inherently unequal," the justices ruled unanimously. "Therefore, we hold that the plaintiffs . . . are, by reason of the segregation complained of, deprived of the equal protection of the law guaranteed by the Fourteenth Amendment." The influence of the *Plessy v. Ferguson* decision had ended at last.

Jerry Purvis Sanson

Plyler v. Doe

U.S. SUPREME COURT
DECIDED JUNE 15, 1982

• This case, which held that Texas' refusal to provide free public education to illegal aliens was unconstitutional, provided a basis for injunctions against implementation of laws seeking to deny certain public benefits to illegal aliens.

In May, 1975, the Texas legislature enacted a law that denied financial support for the public education of the children of undocumented aliens. The state's local school districts, accordingly, were allowed to exclude such children from public school enrollment. The children of noncitizen aliens who henceforth paid for their public school education still were permitted to enroll. Despite the statute, Texas public school districts continued enrolling the children of undocumented aliens until 1977-1978, when, amid a continuing economic recession and accompanying budget tightening, the law was enforced. An initial challenge to the 1975 law arose in the Tyler Independent School District in Smith County, located in northeastern Texas, but similar challenges in other school districts soon produced a class-action suit.

The problem that had inspired the state law was the massive influx—principally of Mexicans but also of persons from other Central American countries—into Texas, as well as into New Mexico, Arizona, and California. Some of these people entered the United States for seasonal agricultural jobs, while others, undocumented, remained. Most were poor and seeking economic opportunities unavailable to them in Mexico and Central America. Figures released by the U.S. Immigration and Naturalization Service estimated that when the *Plyler* case arose, between two and three million undocumented aliens resided in Texas and other southwestern portions of the United States.

Texas claimed that 5 percent of its population, three-quarters of a million people, were undocumented aliens, roughly twenty thousand of whose children were enrolled in Texas public schools. With recession adversely affecting employment, many of the state's taxpayers asked why they should bear the financial burdens of educating illegal aliens, as well as providing them with other benefits, such as food stamps and welfare payments.

The U.S. Supreme Court's 5-4 decision on *Plyler v. Doe* was delivered by Associate Justice William Joseph Brennan, Jr., a justice whom many observers considered a liberal but whose overall record was moderate. The *Plyler* majority ruling upheld a previous decision by the U.S. Fifth Circuit Court that had ruled for the defendants. Chief Justice Warren Burger vigorously dissented from the majority opinion, along with justices Byron White, William Rehnquist, and Sandra Day O'Connor.

On behalf of the Court's majority, Brennan declared that the 1975 Texas statute rationally served no substantial state interest and violated the equal protection clause of the Fourteenth Amendment. Ratified along with the Thirteenth and Fifteen Amendments during the post-Civil War Reconstruction Era, the Fourteenth Amendment guaranteed "that no State shall . . . deny to any person within its jurisdiction the equal protection of the laws." Although the overriding concern of Reconstruction politicians, judges, and states ratifying the Fourteenth Amendment was to afford protection to newly emancipated African Americans, the equal protection clause increasingly had been interpreted to mean what it stated: guaranteeing equal protection of the laws to any person—precisely the line of reasoning taken by Brennan.

Brennan and the Court majority likewise disagreed with the Texas argument that undocumented aliens did not fall "within its jurisdiction," thus excluding them and their children from Fourteenth Amendment guarantees. Such an exclusion, Brennan declared, condemned innocents to a lifetime of hardship and the stigma of illiteracy.

The *Plyler* decision was novel in two important respects. It was the first decision to extend Fourteenth Amendment guarantees to each person, irrespective of that person's citizenship or immigration status. Second, the Court majority introduced a new criterion for determining the applicability of Fourteenth Amendment protections: the doctrine of heightened or intermediate scrutiny. The Court avoided applying its previous standard of strict scrutiny. It recognized that education was not a fundamental right and that undocumented aliens were not, as it had previously phrased it, a "suspect class," in the sense that they, like African Americans, historically had been victims of racial discrimination. Heightened scrutiny was warranted, Brennan and the majority agreed, because of education's special importance to other social benefits and because children of undocumented aliens were not responsible for their status.

Chief Justice Burger and the three other dissenting, generally conservative, justices, who were staunch advocates of judicial restraint, strongly criticized Brennan and the majority for what the dissenters considered to be arguing political opinions instead of adhering to sound jurisprudence. The dissenters seriously questioned heightened scrutiny as a viable judicial standard and found that the Texas statute substantially furthered the state's legitimate interests.

The *Plyler* decision represented a significant departure from the decision rendered by Chief Justice Roger B. Taney in *Dred Scott v. Sandford* (1857), a decision that the Fourteenth Amendment was designed in part to nullify by political means. *Plyler's* heightened standard of scrutiny, however, continued through the mid-1990's to be controversial and confusing, both within the Supreme Court and among legal observers. The issue arising when the equal protection clause was applied to cases not involving racial discrimination had been raised in *Buck v. Bell* (1927), when Justice Oliver Wendell Holmes denounced such decision making as "the usual last resort of constitutional arguments."

In *Plyler*, Brennan and the majority saw no chance to apply the Court's already accepted classification of strict scrutiny to equal protection cases, because *Plyler's* defendants, the undocumented aliens, were not victims of institutionalized racial discrimination or of reverse discrimination. They were illegals as a consequence of their own conscious actions. Nevertheless, as legal scholars observed, in order to prevent hardship and stigmas from afflicting schoolchildren, who were not responsible for their parents' actions, the *Plyler* majority introduced an intermediate level of classification with their standard of heightened scrutiny. Such a standard raised questions about whether undocumented aliens and their families enjoyed rights to other government benefits, such as welfare assistance, medical care, and food stamps.

The difficulties confronted by Texas, by other Southwestern states, and by illegal aliens and their children were alleviated somewhat by a broad federal amnesty program launched in 1992.

Clifton K. Yearley

Bibliography
Aleinikoff, Thomas A., and David A. Martin. *Immigration: Process and Policy.* 2d ed. Saint Paul, Minn.: West, 1991. A careful review of modern U.S. immigration policies. Discusses the problems posed by illegal, undocumented aliens and the difficulties faced by government policymakers in coping with illegals.

Blasi, Vincent, ed. *The Burger Court.* New Haven, Conn.: Yale University Press, 1983. An authoritative yet readable analysis of the chief justiceship of Warren Burger, which did little to modify civil rights decisions of his predecessors. Also clarifies Brennan's attitudes and decisions.

Curtis, Michael Kent. *No State Shall Abridge.* Durham, N.C.: Duke University Press, 1986. A clear, scholarly exposition of the role played by the Fourteenth Amendment and the Bill of Rights in modern U.S. jurisprudence, including civil and criminal rights, racial and reverse discriminations, and interpretations of due process.

Hull, Elizabeth. *Without Justice for All.* Westport, Conn.: Greenwood Press, 1985. A precise study bearing on the problems raised in *Plyler*, the historical plight of resident and illegal aliens and their families, and the varying status of their constitutional rights.

Mirande, Alfredo. *Gringo Justice.* Notre Dame, Ind.: University of Notre Dame Press, 1990. A spirited, dismaying critique of U.S. judicial and political treatment of Hispanic immigrants by both the states and the federal government. Provides excellent context for understanding important aspects of the *Plyler* case.

Nelson, William. *The Fourteenth Amendment.* Cambridge, Mass.: Harvard University Press, 1988. An authoritative analysis of the evolution of the Fourteenth Amendment from a set of political principles to a vital part of twentieth century judicial decisionmaking. Good analyses of the Supreme Court's standards of scrutiny, including the intermediate or "heightened" scrutiny applied in *Plyler*.

Powell v. Alabama

U.S. SUPREME COURT
DECIDED NOVEMBER 7, 1932

- The Court ruled that the concept of due process requires states to provide effective counsel in capital cases when indigent defendants are unable to represent themselves.

In 1931, Ozie Powell and eight other black youths whose ages ranged from twelve to nineteen, known as the "Scottsboro boys," were tried and convicted before an all-white jury in Scottsboro, Alabama, charged with having raped two white women while traveling on a freight train. Although the Alabama constitution required the appointment of counsel for indigents accused of capital crimes, no lawyer was definitely appointed to represent the defendants until the day of their trial.

An atmosphere of racial hostility influenced the proceedings, and after a trial lasting one day, seven of the youths were sentenced to death, while the two youngest were transferred to the juvenile authorities. The trial attracted considerable attention, so that procommunist lawyers of the International Labor Defense volunteered to represent the young men on appeal. After the majority of the Alabama Supreme Court affirmed the convictions, the U.S. Supreme Court granted review.

The Court voted 7 to 2 to reverse the conviction and to remand the case to Alabama for a new trial. Writing for the majority, Justice George Sutherland did not speak of the Sixth Amendment, which had not yet been made applicable to the states, but rather he asked whether the defendants had been denied the right of counsel, contrary to the due process clause of the Fourteenth Amendment.

Sutherland noted that from the time of arraignment to the time of the trial, the defendants had not had "the aid of counsel in any real sense." The right to be heard implied the right to

Heywood Patterson (center), one of the Scottsboro defendants, in 1933. *(National Archives)*

be heard with the assistance of counsel, for even most educated and intelligent persons would not have the training or experience to represent themselves in a criminal trial. Sutherland was impressed with "the ignorance and illiteracy of the defendants" and with the "circumstances of public hostility." In this particular case, therefore, the failure of the trial court to make "an effective appointment of counsel" was a denial of due process within the meaning of the Fourteenth Amendment.

The Scottsboro boys case represented transitional steps in three important directions. First, the decision came very close to incorporating the right to counsel into the meaning of the Fourteenth Amendment, so that this portion of the Sixth Amendment would apply to the states. Second, it recognized that at least in capital cases, the state must provide counsel for indigents unable to defend themselves. Third, it included the provocative suggestion that the state had the obligation to provide "effective" assistance of counsel. These three issues would become increasingly important in subsequent cases.

Thomas T. Lewis

R.A.V. v. City of St. Paul

U.S. Supreme Court
Decided June 22, 1992

• This holding, invalidating an ordinance which made it a crime to burn a cross to harass African Americans, demonstrates how the Supreme Court affords a preferred status to First Amendment free speech, even reprehensible speech.

During the early morning hours of June 21, 1990, "R.A.V."—an unnamed seventeen-year-old, self-described as a white supremacist—and several other teenagers burned a makeshift wooden cross on the front lawn of the only African American family in their St. Paul, Minnesota, neighborhood. They were prosecuted for disorderly conduct in juvenile court under the city's "bias-motivated crime ordinance," which prohibited cross burning along with other symbolic displays that "one knows" or should know would arouse "anger, alarm or resentment in others on the basis of race, color, creed, religion, or gender."

The state trial court ruled that this ordinance was unconstitutionally overbroad because it indiscriminately prohibited protected First Amendment speech as well as unprotected activity. The Supreme Court of Minnesota reversed the lower court's decision and upheld the ordinance, which it interpreted to prohibit only unprotected "fighting words," face-to-face insults which are likely to cause the person to whom the words are addressed to attack the speaker physically.

The U.S. Supreme Court ruled unanimously in favor of R.A.V. and invalidated the ordinance, but the justices did not agree in their reasoning. Stating that they found the cross burning reprehensible, Justice Antonin Scalia, writing for the majority, nevertheless concluded that the ordinance was unconstitutional because it criminalized only specified "fighting words" based on the content of the hate message and, consequently, the government was choosing sides. He noted that the ordinance would prohibit a sign that attacked Catholics but would not prohibit a second sign that attacked those who displayed such an anti-Catholic bias.

Four justices concurred in the ruling of unconstitutionality, but Justice Byron White's opinion sharply criticized the majority opinion for going too far to protect racist speech. He reasoned that the ordinance was overbroad because it made it a crime to cause another person offense, hurt feelings, or resentment and because these harms could be caused by protected First Amendment speech. Justices Harry Blackmun and John Paul Stevens also wrote separate opinions complaining that hate speech did not deserve constitutional protection.

This holding calls into question numerous similar state laws designed to protect women and minorities from harassment and discrimination. Some of these individuals and groups may still invoke long-standing federal civil rights statutes, however, which carry severe criminal penalties of fines and imprisonment. In 1993, *R.A.V.*'s significance was called into question by the *Wisconsin v. Mitchell* decision upholding a state statute that increased a sentence for a crime of violence if the defendant targeted the victim because of the victim's race or other specified status.

Thomas E. Baker

Redd v. State of Georgia

Georgia Court of Appeals
April 6, 1910

• This Georgia court decision expanded the definition of public indecency, affirming the right of the state to regulate individual behaviors that society deems indecent.

The state of Georgia's 1895 penal code dictated that acts of public indecency were punishable as criminal misdemeanors. The plaintiffs in *Redd v. State of Georgia* had been convicted of public indecency for having deliberately displayed to a woman and her children a view of a bull and a cow copulating in an open field. The plaintiffs argued that their actions did not fall within the legal definition of public indecency, which, they asserted, "relates only to indecent exposure of the human person." Rejecting this interpretation, the court ruled that public indecency encompassed "all notorious public and indecent conduct, tending to debauch the public morals."

The court's interpretation was supported by an earlier decision in *McJunkins v. State*. Quoting from *McJunkins*, the court held that the term "public indecency" had no fixed legal meaning, that it was "vague and indefinite" and could not in itself imply a definite offense. The court's acceptance of this view, coupled with its refusal to limit acts of public indecency to those outlined in *McJunkins*—the inappropriate display of the human body or the production and distribution of obscene materials—allowed it to expand the legal definition of public indecency. The court ruled that the state's statute was "broad enough to cover all notorious public and indecent conduct, tending to debauch the public morals, even though it be unattended by an exposure of the human body."

Having expanded the legal definition of public indecency, the court went on to state that acts by themselves could not be considered indecent, unless "the time, the place, the circumstances, and the motives of the actors [are] considered." Accordingly, certain acts might be deemed decent in certain contexts and indecent in others. The court ruled that "a fair test to determine whether an act is notoriously indecent . . . is to consider whether the general run of the citizenry . . . would readily recognize it as such (all the attendant facts and circumstances and the motives of the actor being considered)."

Redd determined that individual behavior and the right to free expression were governed by contemporary social norms of decency. It supported assertions that individual behavior is open to public censure when its runs contrary to society's norms. Thus, the court classified the plaintiffs' behavior as indecent and open to censure because their deliberateness in displaying animal copulation to other people ran contrary to society's norms of decency at that time.

Thomas Aaron Wyrick

Reed v. Reed

U.S. Supreme Court
Decided November 22, 1971

- Finding for the first time that a state law violated the Fourteenth Amendment because it discriminated against women, the Court insisted that gender classifications must be rationally related to a legitimate state objective.

When Richard Reed, a minor, died without a will in Idaho, his separated parents, Cecil Reed and Sally Reed, filed separate petitions in probate court, each seeking appointment to administer the deceased's estate. In a joint hearing, the probate court followed the Idaho Code, which required a preference to the father because he was a male. In applying the statute, the probate judge could give no consideration to the relative capabilities of the two applicants to administer an estate.

Sally Reed appealed the judgment with the argument that a mandatory preference to males violated the equal protection clause of the Fourteenth Amendment. After losing the case in the Idaho Supreme Court, she appealed for a review by the U.S. Supreme Court. The Court had earlier indicated that the equal protection clause might forbid some kinds of classifications based on gender, but in contrast to categories of race, the Court had allowed states broad discretion to legislate different treatment for men and women, based on traditional sex roles that had been accepted as reasonable.

Departing from its previous leniency in the matter, the Court unanimously supported Sally Reed's position and ruled that the statute was incompatible with the state's obligation to provide "each person" with the "equal protection of the laws." The case, therefore, was remanded to the Idaho courts for new proceedings consistent with the Court's decision. In writing the official opinion, Chief Justice Warren Burger insisted that classifications of persons must not be arbitrary and must have "a fair and substantial relation to the object of the legislation." Burger conceded that there was some legitimacy for using a gender preference to reduce the workloads of the probate courts, but he found this rationale not sufficient to justify a mandatory preference without a hearing to determine the relative merits of the two petitioners. There was no rational basis to assume that men were always more qualified than women to administer wills.

The *Reed* decision was a landmark case that marked the Court's first use of the equal protection clause to strike down a statute on account of gender discrimination. Based on the history of the clause, Burger declined to consider whether gender is a "suspect" classification requiring strict judicial scrutiny, and his use of the "rational relationship test" would allow states much discretion in making gender distinctions. In later cases such as *Craig v. Boren* (1976), however, the Court would develop a more demanding test with a heightened level of scrutiny.

Thomas T. Lewis

Regents of the University of California v. Bakke

U.S. SUPREME COURT
RULING ISSUED JUNE 28, 1978

- The Bakke case established a compromise on the controversial issue of affirmative action in college admissions, deeming numerical quotas based on race to be impermissible but allowing race to be considered as one of several admission criteria.

During the 1950's and 1960's, the United States made substantial progress in civil rights, aided by Supreme Court decisions that found state-sponsored segregation of the races to be unconstitutional. With its decision in *Brown v. Board of Education* (1954), the Court signaled that the equal protection clause of the Fourteenth Amendment to the Constitution could not be reconciled with public policy that discriminated on the basis of race. The Civil Rights Act of 1964 enacted this idea into legislation. The 1960's also heralded the beginning of a new effort to correct the wrongs of racial discrimination through the adoption of affirmative action programs.

Supporters of affirmative action contended that the removal of legal barriers was inadequate to ensure equality of the races. For example, President Lyndon B. Johnson argued that the effects of years of discrimination could not be erased by the dismantling of legal segregation and that affirmative action to aid those who had been the victims of that discrimination was necessary. Agencies throughout the federal bureaucracy adopted regulations requiring or encouraging the use of affirmative action programs by recipients of federal funds. In response to a regulation of this type from the Department of Health, Education, and Welfare, many colleges and universities throughout the country altered their admissions policies in order to recruit minorities more actively.

The University of California at Davis Medical School (UCDMS) enrolled its first class in 1968. There were fifty students, three of whom were Asian and none of whom were African-American, Hispanic, or American Indian. Almost immediately, the school decided to create a special admissions program that would provide seats in each class for disadvantaged minorities. In 1970, eight seats were reserved for special admissions. In 1971, the total class size of the school was doubled to one hundred and the number of special admissions slots was doubled to sixteen. The admissions process became a two-track one, with applicants indicating whether they wanted to be considered as a disadvantaged minority. Persons found to qualify for special admissions competed against each other for the sixteen seats while all other applicants competed for the remaining seats. Applicants for special admissions did not have to meet the same requirements in terms of grade point averages and test scores as those competing in the general admissions process. Between 1968 and 1973, the year Allan Bakke first applied to Davis, the number of minority students enrolled in the medical school rose from three to thirty-one.

Allan Bakke was employed as an engineer with the National Aeronautics and Space Administration in California when he decided to apply to medical school in the fall of 1972. He had come to the decision that his true calling was in the practice of medicine. He applied to twelve medical schools that year and was rejected by all of them. Several of the schools cited Bakke's age, 33, as the cause of the rejection. Bakke had an admissions interview at UCDMS and received high marks in the ranking of candidates for admission but, because of his late application, missed by a few points the cut-off score for the few seats left at that time. Bakke visited the school after being rejected and talked with an admissions officer who encouraged him to apply again the next year and to consider challenging the special admissions program. Bakke believed that he would have been admitted to the school in 1973 if sixteen places had not been set aside.

Bakke applied for the 1974 class and was again rejected. This time it appeared that his views on the special admissions program, which he had discussed with an administrator during his interview, had kept him from gaining admission. Bakke decided to sue the medical school, arguing that the special admissions program violated his equal protection rights because the sixteen-seat quota was allocated purely on the basis of race. Bakke's case brought to the limelight a new equal protection question: Can members of the white majority be the victims of racial discrimination? Bakke contended that affirmative action programs like the one at the medical school created "reverse discrimination" and were no less a violation of the equal protection clause because the victim was a member of the majority race instead of the minority.

UCDMS argued that it had compelling reasons for creating the racial classification. It sought to remedy past societal discrimination that had kept minorities from becoming doctors. Additionally, it believed that upon completion of their medical training, minority doctors would be more likely to return to their communities and provide much-needed medical care. Finally, the school contended that ethnic diversity was an important asset to the educational environment and that the special admissions program helped ensure a more diverse student body.

The question of "reverse discrimination" had been before the courts only once before. In 1971, Marco DeFunis had challenged a similar special admissions program at the University of Washington Law School which he believed had kept him from being accepted at that school. The trial court agreed with DeFunis' claim and ordered the school to admit him. The law school complied but appealed the decision against its program. At the appeals level the court sided with the school and the case reached the U.S. Supreme Court in 1974, the same year Bakke began his suit.

The DeFunis case received considerable attention and clearly contributed to Bakke's decision to go ahead with his suit. In April of 1974 the Court decided to dismiss the DeFunis case as moot. DeFunis was about to graduate from the law school and the court held that no true legal controversy existed any longer. This decision opened the way for Bakke's case to be the flag bearer for the "reverse discrimination" argument.

The Superior Court of California agreed with Bakke's position. It found that the special admissions program constituted a racial quota in violation of the constitutions of the nation and the state and the Civil Rights Act of 1964. It said that UCDMS could not take race into account in its admissions decisions. It refused, however, to order Bakke's admission to the school, finding no evidence that Bakke would have been admitted had there been no affirmative action program. Both Bakke and the medical school appealed the decision. In 1976, the Supreme Court of California ruled in Bakke's favor, holding that the special admissions program was a violation of the equal protection clause of the Fourteenth Amendment and that Bakke must be admitted to the medical school. The medical school appealed this decision to the U.S. Supreme Court.

At the end of its 1977-1978 term, the Supreme Court announced its decision. Four justices, led by John Paul Stevens, believed the program to be a violation of Title VI of the Civil Rights Act of 1964, which forbids discrimination on the basis of race in any program receiving federal funds. These justices believed that the Court should go no further than this in ruling on the case. Four other justices, led by William Brennan, argued that affirmative action programs were acceptable because they remedied the effects upon minorities of centuries of discrimination.

These justices distinguished between invidious discrimination, which was forbidden by the Fourteenth Amendment, and what they saw as a benign discrimination, which was at the root of affirmative action programs. Some discrimination in favor of minorities was necessary if real equality instead of theoretical equality was the goal. Justice Harry Blackmun wrote, "In order to get beyond racism, we must first take account of race. . . . And in order to treat some persons equally, we must treat them differently."

Justice Lewis Powell wrote the decision that, because it allowed each of the other justices to join in at least part, became the ruling of the Court. Powell found that the UCDMS special admissions program was indeed unconstitutional. He argued that the equal protection clause prohibited policies based solely on racial factors unless there was some compelling state interest that could override the very high barrier to such classification. In examining the justifications offered by the medical school, he found only the academic interest in diversity convincing. He rejected the argument that past societal discrimination justified affirmative action.

Reverse discrimination required a showing that the agency practicing it (in this case, UCDMS) had in the past discriminated. Since the school had opened in 1968 and begun its special admissions program in 1970, no such history of discrimination existed. Powell also rejected the argument that the program was justified because it served the medical needs of disadvantaged minority communities. The medical school could provide no evidence that special admissions doctors were any more likely than others to return to these communities to practice medicine. Powell held that the program could not stand. In this part of his opinion, he was joined by the four justices in the Stevens coalition, creating a majority to strike down the special admissions program and compel Bakke's admission.

Powell did not rule out all affirmative action programs as violations of equal protection. In the medical school's third justification, diversity, he found some legitimacy because of the traditional freedom granted to academic institutions to set their educational goals. Powell said that the desire for diversity justified some consideration of race as a factor in admissions decisions. The flaw in the UCDMS program was that race appeared to be the only factor shaping decisions for the sixteen seats. In this part of his decision, Powell was joined by the four justices in the Brennan coalition, thus creating a majority for the position that race may be considered as one factor among others in admissions decisions.

The landmark Bakke case provided something for both opponents and supporters of affirmative action. While it accepted the idea of "reverse discrimination" made by Allan Bakke and vindicated his rights, it refused to reject the concept of affirmative action altogether. For college admissions officers, it provided a roadmap for how to go about pursuing affirmative action in admissions decisions without violating the equal protection clause. For policymakers in general, it warned against the use of numerical quotas for accomplishing affirmative action ends. The division on the Court heralded an extended battle in the courts over which kinds of affirmative action programs would be found to be constitutional and which would not.

In the years after *Bakke,* the courts struggled repeatedly, and contentiously, with questions regarding affirmative action in employment. *Bakke* raised more questions than it answered and brought to the forefront the breakdown of consensus on civil rights questions in the United States. When the issues of civil rights had been about the dismantling of legal barriers to equality, a broad consensus had existed about the justice of this course of action. It was generally agreed that the Constitution could not permit a legally segregated society.

After the landmark desegregation decisions of the 1950's and 1960's, the questions became more complicated and the moral imperatives less clear. What kind of equality did the Constitution require? Once the legal requirements of segregation were removed, was there any further affirmative obligation for society to remedy the wrongs of the past? To what extent could individuals not responsible for past discrimination be made to bear the burden for the past? These were questions much more difficult to navigate in the murky waters of constitutional interpretation.

For Allan Bakke, the impact was more clear cut. He enrolled in the University of California at Davis Medical School in the fall of 1978. In the spring of 1982, he graduated to a loud round of applause from the audience. For thousands of minority students around the country, the *Bakke* decision provided new opportunities in higher education. The Court majority permitting race to be considered as one factor ensured that special admissions programs would continue. What can never be calculated is whether more or fewer of these students were provided educational opportunities because of the decision.

Katy Jean Harriger

Bibliography

Dreyfuss, Joel, and Charles Lawrence III. *The Bakke Case: The Politics of Inequality*. New York: Harcourt Brace Jovanovich, 1979. Written by journalists in a readable narrative style that is sympathetic to arguments for affirmative action. Suggests that the focus of debate on qualifications obscured the underlying economic issues in affirmative action and signaled a fundamental change in race relations in the United States.

Eastland, Terry, and William J. Bennett. *Counting by Race: Equality from the Founding Fathers to Bakke and Weber*. New York: Basic Books, 1979. Presents an argument against pursuit of equality based on numerical quotas. Interesting historical discussion of different conceptions of equality in race relations in the United States.

Nieman, Donald G. *Promises to Keep: African-Americans and the Constitutional Order, 1776 to the Present*. New York: Oxford University Press, 1991. Readable historical essay with a good chapter at the end dealing with debate about affirmative action.

Schwartz, Bernard. *Behind Bakke: Affirmative Action and the Supreme Court*. New York: New York University Press, 1988. Provides behind the scenes insight into the decisionmaking process of the high court in this landmark case.

Sindler, Allan P. *Bakke, DeFunis, and Minority Admissions: The Quest for Equal Opportunity*. New York: Longman, 1978. Focuses on the issue of how to promote equal opportunity without engaging in reverse discrimination. Useful detailed study of underlying issues and court histories of Bakke and DeFunis cases.

Wilkinson, J. Harvie, III. *From Brown to Bakke: The Supreme Court and School Integration, 1954-1978*. New York: Oxford University Press, 1979. Chronicles role of Supreme Court in desegregation of education and argues that support for decisions breaks down as it moves from principle to imposing remedies of busing and affirmative action.

Reitman v. Mulkey

U.S. SUPREME COURT
DECIDED MAY 29, 1967

- California's adoption of Proposition 14, which repealed the state's fair housing laws, was struck down by the Supreme Court after the California Supreme Court interpreted the repeal as "authorizing" discrimination.

In 1959 and 1963, California established fair housing laws. These statutes banned racial discrimination in the sale or rental of private housing. In 1964, acting under the initiative process, the California electorate passed Proposition 14. This measure amended the state constitution so as to prohibit the state government from denying the right of any person to sell, lease, or refuse to sell or lease his or her property to another at his or her sole discretion. The fair housing laws were effectively repealed.

Mr. and Mrs. Lincoln Mulkey sued Neil Reitman in a state court, claiming that he had refused to rent them an apartment because of their race. They claimed that Proposition 14 was invalid because it violated the equal protection clause of the Fourteenth Amendment. If Proposition 14 was unconstitutional, the fair housing laws would still be in force. The Mulkeys won in the California Supreme Court, and Reitman appealed to the Supreme Court of the United States.

Justice Byron White's opinion for the five-justice majority admitted that mere repeal of an antidiscrimination statute would not be unconstitutional. In this case, however, the California Supreme Court had held that the intent of Proposition 14 was to encourage and authorize private racial discrimination. This encouragement amounted to "state action" that violated the equal protection clause of the Fourteenth Amendment.

The four dissenters in the case agreed on an opinion by Justice John M. Harlan. Harlan argued that California's mere repeal of its fair housing laws did not amount to encouraging and authorizing discrimination. If the repeal were to be seen that way, then a state could never rid itself of a statute whose purpose was to protect a constitutional right, whether of racial equality or some other. Harlan also suggested that opponents of antidiscrimination laws would later be able to argue that such laws not be passed because they would be unrepealable. Indeed, several ballot measures which have reversed or repealed civil rights laws protecting gays and lesbians have been struck down on the basis of *Reitman v. Mulkey*.

Reitman v. Mulkey has not had a major effect on American civil rights law. The Supreme Court has not been disposed to expand the "authorization" and "encouragement" strands of constitutional thought. The principle of "state action"—which is all that the Fourteenth Amendment equal protection rules can reach—has not been further broadened. Nevertheless, the precedent remains, with its suggestion that there is an affirmative federal constitutional duty on state government to prevent private racial discrimination.

Robert Jacobs

Reynolds v. Sims

U.S. SUPREME COURT
DECIDED JUNE 15, 1964

- For the first time taking action against state legislatures for ignoring constitutionally mandated requirements for redistricting, the Court specifically applied a "one person, one vote" solution to what it deemed to be inaccurate representation.

The 1960's witnessed a significant change in the apportionment of state legislative and congressional delegations. For the first time, the U.S. Supreme Court interfered with the apportionment practices of the states. The Court's action was an attempt to rectify what it deemed to be the malapportionment of a great majority of American state legislatures and of state delegations to the national House of Representatives

This situation had developed over the years because predominantly rural state legislatures continually ignored the population shifts that produced the tremendous growth of the country's cities in the twentieth century. In many cases, state legislatures, out of a fear that equitable redistricting would shift the rural-urban balance of power, deliberately ignored the provisions within their own state constitutions for periodic redistricting. The result was a constitutional abnormality that was distorting the democratic political process.

In a series of cases brought before the Court in the 1960's, the malapportionment problems were judicially corrected when the Court applied a "one person, one vote" principle. In 1964, a federal district court ordered the state of Alabama to reapportion but nullified two plans that did not apportion the legislative districts solely on the basis of population. The state appealed to the Supreme Court, which held that the equal protection clause of the Fourteenth Amendment requires that the seats in both houses be equally apportioned.

The existing apportionment of the Alabama state legislature

was struck down when the Court, in an 8-1 majority, applied the one person, one vote principle in the case. Writing for the majority, Chief Justice Earl Warren declared that restrictions on the right to vote "strike at the heart of representative government." The Court, he added, had "clearly established that the fundamental principle of representative government in this country is one of equal representation for equal numbers of people, without regard to race, sex, economic status, or place of residence within the state." The concept of one person, one vote was virtually a pure and intractable rule.

In his dissent, Justice John M. Harlan argued that the decision had the "effect of placing basic aspects of state political systems under the pervasive overlordship of the federal judiciary." This type of "judicial legislation" frightened not only Harlan but also a number of conservatives who did not want to see the Supreme Court become more active in producing equal voting rights.

The legacy of this case is clear: In *Reynolds* and several companion cases decided the same day, the Supreme Court determined that it had an obligation to interfere in the apportionment practices of the states in order to guarantee that no person was deprived of the right to vote. By guaranteeing those individual rights, the legislatures as well as the House of Representatives would more properly reflect the genuine complexion of American society.

Kevin F. Sims

Reynolds v. United States

U.S. SUPREME COURT
DECIDED MAY 5, 1879

• Upholding a congressional prohibition of polygamy in the territories, the Court established the principle that the First Amendment protects all religious beliefs but does not protect religiously motivated practices that harm the public interest.

George Reynolds, a member of the Mormon church and a resident of the territory of Utah, was tried in a federal territorial court for committing the crime of bigamy, in violation of an 1862 statute. At his trial, Reynolds presented evidence that the accepted doctrine of his church was that every male member had the duty, circumstances permitting, to practice plural marriage and that failure to do so would be punished by "damnation in the life to come." He further argued that the First Amendment prohibited Congress from placing such limitations on the free exercise of religion. The trial judge refused to instruct the jury that the defendant should be exempted from the law for actions motivated by his religious beliefs, and the jury returned a guilty verdict. Reynolds appealed to the U.S. Supreme Court.

The Court unanimously ruled to uphold Reynolds' conviction. Writing the majority opinion, Chief Justice Morrison R. Waite recognized that Congress cannot pass a law that prohibits the free exercise of religion, but he made a distinction between religious beliefs and religious conduct. While beliefs or opinions were fully protected, Congress was free to punish "actions

In writing the majority opinion on *Reynolds*, Chief Justice Morrison R. Waite (center) made a careful distinction between religious beliefs and religious conduct. *(Harris and Ewing/Collection of the Supreme Court of the United States)*

which were in violation of social duties or subversive of good order."

An obvious example, Waite pointed out, was the possible practice of human sacrifice. Historically, polygamy had always been punished as a crime in the common law and statutes of Britain, and this tradition had been uniformly followed in every state of the United States. In addition, Waite quoted several respected jurists who argued that polygamy promoted despotic government and had other undesirable consequences. Congress, therefore, possessed legitimate authority to criminalize polygamy in the territories, and there was no obligation to make an exception for those who followed different religious beliefs.

The *Reynolds* decision was the Court's first major consideration of a law that restrained the religious freedom of a minority, and it would become an important precedent because of Waite's formulation of the belief-conduct distinction. Implicitly, the Court acknowledged that Congress could not prohibit a religious practice without a legitimate state interest, but the Court did not try to articulate guidelines for the level of state interest required. In its later decisions, the Court would consistently follow *Reynolds* in its belief-conduct distinction, but the decision would not prove helpful in providing standards to determine what kinds of religious conduct might be protected.

The immediate impact of *Reynolds* was limited because the free exercise clause did not then apply to state laws, but the Court would often refer to the case after the clause was made binding on the states in *Cantwell v. Connecticut* (1940).

Thomas T. Lewis

Rhodes v. Chapman

U.S. SUPREME COURT
DECIDED JUNE 15, 1981

• In this case, the Supreme Court ruled that the "double celling" of inmates at a maximum-security prison in Ohio did not violate constitutional safeguards against cruel and unusual punishment.

Rhodes v. Chapman evolved from a class-action suit brought by two inmates at the Southern Ohio Correctional Facility, a maximum-security prison in Lucasville. Cellmates Kelly Chapman and Richard Jaworski, citing a federal statute, maintained that incarcerating two inmates in the same cell violated the protection against cruel and unusual punishment guaranteed by the Eighth and Fourteenth Amendments. The U.S. District Court for the Southern District of Ohio, after an extensive investigation, concurred. Among other supporting reasons for its decision, the court argued that double celling of long-term prisoners aggravated the various problems associated with close confinement. It further noted that the Ohio facility housed a prison population 38 percent larger than its designed capacity and that it failed to provide each inmate with the recommended standard of 50 to 55 square feet of living space. It found, too, that the prison had made double celling a practice rather than a temporary solution to crowded conditions.

After the United States Court of Appeals for the Sixth Circuit upheld the lower court's judgment, the case went to the Supreme Court, which reversed the lower courts' decisions and ruled that double celling did not constitute cruel and unusual punishment. The Court stated that the district court's findings were insupportable and that the data on which it based its judgment were "insufficient to support its constitutional conclusion." The majority opinion, presented by Justice Lewis F. Powell, Jr., held that there was no real evidence that double celling at the Ohio prison facility inflicted undue pain or imposed any hardship that was out of proportion to the crimes warranting the inmates' imprisonment. A concurring opinion, however, cautioned that the Court's decision should not be interpreted as an abrogation of its responsibility to scrutinize prison conditions to ensure that humane but realistic standards are maintained.

The lone dissenter, Justice Thurgood Marshall, argued that prison overcrowding and the double celling of prisoners, unchecked, would eventually have a deleterious effect on the mental and physical health of prisoners, in total disregard of modern standards of human decency. Marshall also expressed concern that the Court's ruling might be construed as an admonition to district courts, enjoining them to adopt a laissez-faire position toward the administration of state prison systems.

For those individuals who believe that hardened felons have been mollycoddled and encouraged to seek legal redress for minor and even frivolous complaints, the *Rhodes* decision has landmark significance. It reflected the rising anger and fear of the nation regarding crime; by the early 1980's, the country was growing increasingly unsympathetic to the rights of prisoners.

John W. Fiero

Richmond v. J. A. Croson Co.

U.S. SUPREME COURT
DECIDED JANUARY 23, 1989

- *Richmond v. J. A. Croson Co.* made it much more difficult for cities and states to establish race-conscious affirmative action programs.

In 1983 the City Council of Richmond, Virginia, adopted a minority set-aside program for city contracting. Under the plan, 30 percent of all city construction subcontracts were to be granted to (or "set aside" for) minorityowned business enterprises. The J. A. Croson Company, a contracting firm which had been the low bidder on a city project, sued the city when its bid was rejected in favor of a larger bid submitted by a minority-owned firm. Croson's position was that the minority set-aside violated the equal protection clause of the Fourteenth Amendment by establishing a racial classification.

Richmond argued that the minority set-aside was valid as an attempt to remedy past discriminations. An earlier case, *Ful-*

lilove v. Klutznick (1980), had approved a similar set-aside program for federal government contracts. The city pointed out that only 0.67 percent of its prime construction contracts had gone to minority firms between 1978 and 1983.

By vote of 6 to 3 the Supreme Court decided for the Croson Company. The opinion of the Court was written by Justice Sandra Day O'Connor. Justice O'Connor argued that the earlier federal case was not relevant because the federal government has legislative authority to enforce the Fourteenth Amendment. State governments are limited by it. Race-conscious affirmative action programs are valid only where there is a showing of past discrimination by the state government itself. In the case of the Richmond statute, there was no such showing. It was undeniable that there had been discrimination against minority contractors, but that discrimination was by private firms, not by the city itself. While the city has the power to remedy private discriminations, she argued, it may not do so by setting up a quota system which is itself racially biased.

Justice Thurgood Marshall wrote the major dissenting opinion. He argued that the majority's view of the facts was too narrow. The extraordinary disparity between contracts let to minority and nonminority firms showed that there was systematic and pervasive discrimination which could only be remedied in practice by a set-aside or quota program of the kind passed in Richmond. He pointed out, as he had in earlier cases, the irony of a constitutional rule which forbids racial classifications for benign purposes, given the long history of constitutionally permitted racial classifications for discriminatory purposes. Justice Marshall insisted that the court should not scrutinize racial classifications strictly so long as the purpose of the classification is benign. Justices William Brennan, Jr., and Harry A. Blackmun joined Marshall in his dissent.

Richmond v. J. A. Croson Co. cast doubt on the future of race-conscious programs designed to remedy past discriminations. At the very least it means that racial quotas, however well-meant, are likely to be held unconstitutional.

Robert Jacobs

Robinson v. California

U.S. Supreme Court
Decided June 25, 1962

- *Robinson v. California* which held that it was cruel and unusual punishment to incarcerate drug addicts simply because of their addictions, was for some critics emblematic of the Warren Court's "softness" on crime.

Robinson was convicted under a California statute making it a crime to be a drug addict and was sentenced to ninety days in jail. The statute did not require the state to prove that the accused had either bought or purchased drugs or that he or she possessed them—the mere status of being a drug addict was enough to convict a defendant. Robinson appealed, and the Supreme Court overturned the conviction on grounds that incarceration for ninety days for what amounts to an illness constitutes cruel and unusual punishment.

Because of such rulings as *Mapp v. Ohio* (1961), which extended guarantees against unreasonable search and seizure to state defendants, the Court overseen by Chief Justice Earl Warren was criticized for "coddling" criminals. *Robinson* was doubly controversial because it is based on the assumption that drug addiction is an illness over which the addict has no control. Indeed, six years later the Court declined to follow its own precedent in *Powell v. Texas* (1968), in which it upheld the criminal conviction of a chronic alcoholic, declaring that the state of knowledge regarding alcoholism was inadequate to permit the enunciation of a new constitutional principle.

Still, *Robinson* is important for making the cruel and unusual punishment clause of the Eighth Amendment applicable at the state as well as the federal level. The case was a continuation of the "due process revolution," championed initially by Justice Hugo Black, that reached its high-water mark during Earl Warren's tenure as chief justice. By means of the due process clause of the Fourteenth Amendment, the guarantees of the Bill of Rights limiting federal action were "incorporated" into the Fourteenth Amendment, thus becoming applicable to state governments.

The Fourteenth Amendment, passed in the wake of the Civil War, makes all persons born in the United States citizens whose privileges and immunities cannot be restricted and whose rights of due process and equal protection cannot be denied. Some framers of the amendment indicated that the privileges and immunities extended therein included the guarantees of the Bill of Rights, but this point was left ambiguous. In *Palko v. Connecticut* (1937), the Court explicitly addressed the issue for the first time, stating that some of the rights embodied in the first ten amendments to the Constitution were so fundamental that the Fourteenth Amendment obligated states to observe them.

Writing in dissent in *Adamson v. California* (1947), Justice Black argued that the Fourteenth Amendment obligated states to honor all aspects of the Bill of Rights. The Court has never quite adopted this view, but by the time Earl Warren's leadership ended in 1969, most of the Bill of Rights had been applied to the states.

Lisa Paddock

Roe v. Wade

U.S. SUPREME COURT
DECIDED JANUARY 22, 1973

• Invalidating nearly all state laws prohibiting abortion within the first three months of pregnancy, this landmark decision led to one of the most emotionally charged and divisive public issues in American history.

By the early 1970's, abortion laws in the United States had become an issue of public controversy. Among the factors promoting this interest were concern for overpopulation, the vigorous women's rights movement, the overwhelming approval of physicians for liberalized abortion policies, and awareness that approximately one million illegal abortions occurred in the United States each year. Although by 1973, many states had revised and liberalized their abortion laws, arguments over these reforms were heated and bitter. On one side were those who argued that women should have unrestricted control over their bodies, and that this autonomy should include the freedom to terminate pregnancy medically. On the other side were those who maintained abortion was contrary to certain moral values and religious principles. The issue finally reached the U.S. Supreme Court in the case of *Roe v. Wade*, and was decided in January, 1973.

Norma McCorvey (Jane Roe) was an unmarried, impoverished pregnant woman who wanted to terminate her pregnancy by abortion in Texas, a state that prohibited abortion as a serious crime, except in cases where medical advice held that the life of the mother was otherwise endangered. The Texas statute was typical of state laws at the time. Roe first brought suit in the United States District Court for the Northern District of Texas, naming a district attorney, Henry Wade, as defendant. She received a judgment essentially in her favor when the Texas abortion statute was found unconstitutional.

Both parties then appealed the decision to the higher federal courts; ultimately, the case was argued before the Supreme Court. Roe's attorneys were seeking an order from the Supreme Court assuring that abortion laws could not be enforced in the future. By the time the case reached the higher courts, Roe was no longer pregnant. Her attorneys had anticipated this development and cast the issue as a class action on behalf of all women with unwanted pregnancies.

By a decision of 7 to 2, the Supreme Court affirmed the decision of the United States District Court and struck down the Texas law. The majority opinion was written by Justice Harry Blackmun. Concurring opinions were written by Chief Justice Warren Burger and by Justices William O. Douglas and Potter Stewart. The majority made the following significant points in its decision. Although there was no direct mention of abortion in the U.S. Constitution, the Court subjected the Texas statute to two tests. The first asked whether a fundamental right was violated. Blackmun's opinion identified this as the right to privacy, which was encompassed in the personal liberty protected by the due process clause of the Fourteenth Amendment.

In support of this position, the Court cited several earlier decisions that maintained that an individual's right to decide matters pertaining to one's personal privacy usually was superior to the state's interest in restricting that right. Earlier decisions, for example, had held that the states were prohibited from passing laws restricting a person's right to marry whomever he or she chose, regardless of race, to educate his or her children in private schools, or to have access to and use contraceptives. The court had carved out a zone of privacy that included matters relating to marriage, procreation, and child rearing. Blackmun also pointed out that legislation criminalizing abortion dated only from the late nineteenth century. Thus, such laws were a relatively recent phenomenon in the United States. Such history put the *Roe* decision into the mainstream of traditional common law, allowing abortion during the early stages of pregnancy.

Having determined that the Constitution afforded women the right to determine whether to continue or terminate a pregnancy, the Court then dealt with the question of whether a state could overrule the constitutional right of the individual by demonstrating a compelling reason or reasons that it should pass laws regulating abortions.

In the one critical area, the Court ruled in favor of women's right to choose. The state of Texas had argued that it had a compelling reason to regulate abortion to protect the life of the fetus. The Court held, however, that "the unborn are not included within the definition of 'person' as used in the Fourteenth Amendment." Historically, the Court stated, the United States had never treated the rights of persons after birth the same as those of the unborn. The Constitution, for example, only regards "persons born or naturalized" as citizens. There is no provision for an income tax deduction for the unborn. Property rights usually begin at birth, and the unborn have no right of inheritance. Thus, a fetus, by law, was not a person, and the state had no compelling reason to pass laws to protect it.

The court also rejected the argument that the state had a compelling reason to prohibit abortions to protect the health of the mother. Blackmun's opinion cited statistics that legal, medical abortions early in pregnancy posed less of a threat to a woman's health than did normal childbirth.

The Court went further than establishing the constitutionality of abortion and laid down guidelines regarding the performing of abortions. In issuing these principles, the Court felt that it was dealing with a matter affecting the life and health of the pregnant woman and the potential for life of the unborn. The Court also sought to provide guidelines for state legislators in the drafting of abortion statutes in order to help stem the tide of future abortion cases in the federal courts.

The majority opinion stated that a woman did not have an absolute right to an abortion. The state had a legitimate interest in protecting a woman's health and potential human life and in maintaining proper standards. Before the end of the first trimester of pregnancy, the state could do nothing to prevent an abortion that had been decided upon by a woman in consultation with a physician licensed by the state. "From and after the end of the first trimester, and until the point in time when the fetus becomes viable," that is, able to live independently of the mother, the state could regulate the abortion procedure only to preserve and protect the life of the mother. After the fetus became viable, however, the state could prohibit abortions altogether, except in cases where the life or health of the mother was endangered.

Minority opinions written by Justices Byron White and William Rehnquist presented the antiabortion position. White asserted that the Court's decision had sustained the position that the convenience of the prospective mother was superior to "the life or potential life that she carries. The Court," he continued, without constitutional sanction, "simply fashions and announces a new constitutional right for pregnant mothers" and in doing so, "invests that right with sufficient substance to override most existing state abortion statutes." White concluded by holding that the Court had interfered incorrectly with the legislative processes of the states. Abortion, he stated, was an issue that "should be left with the people and to the political processes the people have devised to govern their affairs."

Rehnquist held that there was no historical foundation for the Court's position that the right to abortion was to be found in the Fourteenth Amendment. History, he argued, established the fact that a majority of states had had abortion laws for at least a century, and that the legislators who had passed these laws represented the sentiments of the citizenry. There was, then, no historical support for Roe's argument of the universal acceptability of a woman's "right" to an abortion.

The Court left many issues relating to abortion undecided, because they had not been contested in this case. A victory, however, had been won by those who favored women's freedom of choice with regard to the continuation or termination of a pregnancy. Abortion on demand, which had been advocated by the more extreme advocates of the proabortion, "prochoice" movement, had been prohibited. This part of the ruling gave hope to the antiabortion, "right-to-life" group, which began a campaign to secure a constitutional amendment prohibiting abortion.

J. Stewart Alverson,
updated by Mary Welek Atwell

Bibliography

Garrow, David J. *Liberty and Sexuality: The Right to Privacy and the Making of Roe v. Wade.* New York: Macmillan, 1994. An exhaustive study of the people and legal issues involved in a series of court decisions related to privacy, that culminated in *Roe v. Wade.*

Goldstein, Leslie Friedman. *Contemporary Cases in Women's Rights.* Madison: University of Wisconsin Press, 1994. Contains a long section on court cases dealing with reproductive rights, in particular a meticulous discussion of the precedents and results of *Roe v. Wade.*

Mohr, James C. *Abortion in America: The Origins and Evolution of National Policy.* New York: Oxford, 1978. The most comprehensive history of the political and social forces that contributed to the development of anti-abortion legislation in the United States in the late nineteenth century.

Schneider, Carl E., and Maris A. Vinovskis, eds. *The Law and*

Politics of Abortion. Lexington, Mass.: Heath, 1980. Legal scholars address, often critically, the principles underlying *Roe v. Wade*, as well as its political aftermath.

Siegel, Reva B. "Abortion as a Sex Equality Right: Its Basis in Feminist Theory." In *Mothers in Law*, edited by Martha Albertson Fineman and Isabel Karpin. New York: Columbia University Press, 1995. Argues for treating abortion rights as issues of sex equality rather than as part of the right to privacy.

Solinger, Rickie. *Wake Up Little Susie: Single Pregnancy and Race Before Roe v. Wade*. New York: Routledge, 1992. Discusses the political meaning of policies toward unwed motherhood prior to *Roe v. Wade*.

Tribe, Laurence H. *Abortion: The Clash of Opposites*. New York: W. W. Norton, 1990. A noted constitutional scholar examines abortion from philosophical, scientific, political, and legal perspectives.

Rosenfeld v. Southern Pacific

U.S. COURT OF APPEALS FOR THE NINTH CIRCUIT
DECIDED JUNE 1, 1971

• This U.S. Court of Appeals Ninth Circuit opinion strictly interpreted the Civil Rights Act of 1964 with regard to the prohibition of discrimination in employment based on sex, thus striking down a California law permitting sex discrimination in employment.

In 1966, Leah Rosenfeld applied for the job of sole agent-telegrapher in Thermal, California. Her employer refused to consider her application, stating that the decision had been made that women would not be employed in such a position. Rosenfeld responded by filing a complaint with the Equal Employment Opportunity Commission (EEOC) claiming that the refusal to hire women as agent-telegraphers violated the Civil Rights Act of 1964.

Southern Pacific argued that it could not hire women for the sole agent-telegrapher position under a California law that prohibited the employment of women in jobs involving lifting more than a certain amount of weight. The job, as defined by Southern Pacific, required the lifting of objects weighing as much as fifty pounds and extraordinarily long workdays during the harvest season. The Court responded by striking down the California law, ruling that prospective employees should be considered regardless of sex and "on the basis of individual capacity."

Donald C. Simmons, Jr.

Rostker v. Goldberg

U.S. SUPREME COURT
DECIDED JUNE 25, 1981

• The Supreme Court held that Congress' decision to authorize the president to require registration of males but not females for possible military service did not constitute gender discrimination in violation of the due process clause of the Fifth Amendment.

The Military Selective Service Act authorizes the president to require male citizens and male resident aliens between the ages of eighteen and twenty-six to register for the draft. Registration was discontinued in 1975. In 1980, President Jimmy Carter recommended that Congress reactivate the registration process and that Congress amend the act to permit the registration and possible conscription of women. Congress considered the president's recommendations at length and decided to reactivate the registration process but declined to permit the registration of women. A three-judge federal district court ruled that the challenged gender-based distinction violated the due process clause of the Fifth Amendment. By a 6-3 vote, the U.S. Supreme Court reversed that decision on direct appeal.

Justice William H. Rehnquist, joined by Chief Justice Warren Burger and Justices Potter Stewart, Harry Blackmun, Lewis Powell, and John Paul Stevens, wrote the majority opinion. Rehnquist emphasized the Court's traditional deference to Congress in cases involving the national defense and military affairs. Registering women had been "extensively considered" by Congress, and its decision to register only males was not an "accidental by-product of a traditional way of thinking about females." Congress' purpose was to prepare a draft of "combat troops," and since women were ineligible for combat, Congress exempted them.

Rehnquist noted that the gender classification was "not invidious." He reasoned that Congress was not choosing arbitrarily to burden one of two similarly situated groups, "such as would be the case with an all-black or all-white, or an all-Catholic or all-Lutheran, or an all-Republican or all-Democratic registration." He found that men and women are not "similarly situated" for purposes of a draft or draft registration "because of the combat restrictions on women."

Justice Byron White, joined by Justice William Brennan, dissented, noting that not all positions in the military must be filled by combat-ready men and that women could be registered to fill noncombat positions "without sacrificing combat-readiness." Justice Thurgood Marshall, joined by Justice Brennan, also dissented on grounds that the government had failed to show that registering women would "seriously impede" its efforts to achieve "a concededly important governmental interest in maintaining an effective defense."

This decision continues to be important because female military personnel who are ineligible for combat find themselves disadvantaged when they compete with combat-eligible male personnel for positions and promotion. In the 1990's, combat restrictions on women were eased. Such developments speak directly to Rehnquist's premise that male-only draft registration is not discriminatory because only males are eligible for combat.

Joseph A. Melusky

Roth v. United States

U.S. SUPREME COURT
DECIDED JUNE 24, 1957

• Ruling that obscene material is not protected by the First Amendment, the Court defined obscenity narrowly and put strict limits on the kinds of obscenity that might be proscribed by law.

Samuel Roth conducted a business in New York in the publishing and sale of books, magazines, and photographs. A federal statute made it a crime to send "obscene, lewd, lascivious, or filthy" materials or advertisements through the U.S. mail, and Roth was found guilty in district court for violating four counts of the statute. Contemporary with Roth's conviction, David Alberts was convicted in California of advertising obscenity in violation of the state's penal code. When Roth and Alberts each petitioned the U.S. Supreme Court for review, the Court accepted both cases and consolidated them into one decision. The major issue was whether the federal and state statutes, as interpreted, were consistent with the First Amendment's freedom of speech and press.

Historically, both the federal government and the states had long criminalized most forms of pornography, and in numerous cases the Court had recognized such laws as a reasonable means to promote the state's legitimate interest in "decency."

Between 1842 and 1956 the U.S. Congress had enacted twenty antiobscenity laws, and at least six times the Supreme Court had approved prosecutions under these laws. Some American courts continued to follow *Regina v. Hicklin* (1868), which looked at the effects of isolated passages on the most susceptible persons in society. Roth and Alberts had been convicted under a less restrictive standard, endorsed by Judge Learned Hand and many liberals, that considered the work as a whole and its impact on the average adult. Still, given the precedents, few observers considered that the Supreme

Court would strike down antiobscenity statutes.

The Court ruled 6 to 3 to uphold Roth's federal conviction and 7 to 2 to uphold Alberts' state convictions. Writing for the majority, Justice William Brennan summarized the Anglo-American tradition of proscribing obscenity, and he concluded that obscenity enjoyed no constitutional protection because it had been historically recognized as "utterly without redeeming social importance." Making a distinction between sex and obscenity, Brennan rejected the *Hicklin* test as "unconstitutionally restrictive." He endorsed the alternative test of "whether to the average person, applying contemporary community standards,

The longest-serving (1939-1975) justice on the Supreme Court, William O. Douglas (1898-1980) was a consistent champion of free speech and was a strong dissenter in the *Roth* case. *(Library of Congress)*

the dominant theme of the material taken as a whole appeals to the prurient interest."

Two liberal members of the Court, Justices William O. Douglas and Hugo L. Black, dissented and argued that the First Amendment protected all forms of expression. One member of the Court, John M. Harlan, distinguished between federal and state prosecution of obscenity, allowing the states greater power in the area.

The *Roth* decision was a landmark case because the Court for the first time limited government's prerogative to criminalize obscene material, and because it insisted on a narrow definition of obscenity. While allowing the continuation of antiobscenity laws, *Roth* recognized that all ideas were protected unless they were "utterly without redeeming social importance." Equally important was the explicit rejection of the *Hicklin* test, so that subsequent prosecutions had to be based on the influence of a work in its entirety on an average person of the community. In post-*Roth* cases, the Court would continue to be divided over the definition and protection of obscenity, a controversy that culminated in the three-pronged compromise of *Miller v. California* (1973).

Thomas T. Lewis

Rowan v. U.S. Post Office Department

U.S. Supreme Court
May 4, 1970

- In a case originating in a mail-order company's complaint that its constitutional right to free speech was violated by a federal postal law empowering people to stop unsolicited mailings, the Supreme Court issued a ruling favoring protection of individual rights to privacy over free speech.

Section 4009 of the 1967 U.S. Postal Revenue and Federal Salary Act, Title III, empowers individuals to order companies engaged in mass mailings to stop sending them unsolicited advertisements for material that they regard as "erotically arousing or sexually provocative." The law also permits individuals to order their names deleted from all mailing lists in the mail-order companies' possession. *Rowan v. U.S. Post Office Department* originated in a case brought by the owner of a mail-order company who claimed that the 1967 law violated his First and Fifth Amendment rights of free speech and due process. He also asserted that the law's section 4009 was "unconstitutionally vague, without standards, and ambiguous."

In deciding *Rowan*, the Court examined the subsections of section 4009 that outline the procedures for ordering the cessation of mailings to individual households. One subsection states that mailers can be ordered by private individuals "to refrain from further mailings . . . to designated addressees." Another subsection assigns the postmaster general the duty of issuing requested cessation orders to specified mailers. A third subsection requires mailers to remove the names of complainants from their mailing lists and prohibits the sale, transfer, or exchange of lists bearing their names. Upon determination of a violation, the postmaster general can ask the attorney general to issue a compliance order against the mailer.

The Court decision affirmed the right of private individuals to direct the cessation of mailings and the deletion of their names from mailing lists used in the distribution of unsolicited advertisements. Explaining the Court's opinion, Chief Justice Warren Burger wrote: "Weighing the highly important right to communicate . . . against the very basic right to be free of sights, sounds, and tangible matter we do not want, it seems to us that a mailer's right to communicate must stop at the mailbox of an unreceptive addressee." Burger added that "a mailer's right to communicate is circumscribed only by an affirmative act of the addressee." In sum, the Court ruled that a mailer's right to communicate is not significantly infringed upon when balanced by a recipient's right to be free from unwanted communications.

The Court also held that the appellant's due process was not violated, and that section 4009 of the law was not unconstitutionally vague. Burger noted that "the only administrative action not preceded by a full hearing is the initial issuance of the prohibitory order. Since the sender risks no immediate sanction by failing to comply with that order . . . it cannot be said that this aspect of the procedure denies due process." Furthermore, Burger reasoned that because "appellants know precisely what they must do on receipt of a prohibitory order," the appellant's vagueness argument was ruled invalid.

Thomas Wyrick

Rummel v. Estelle

U.S. SUPREME COURT
DECIDED MARCH 18, 1980

- The Court found no cruel and unusual punishment in a state's mandatory life-imprisonment statute as applied to a man convicted of three fraudulent offenses involving only $229.11.

In 1973, William Rummel was convicted under the Texas recidivist statute, which required a mandatory life sentence after three felony convictions, even for nonviolent offenses. In 1964 Rummel had been convicted of his first felony, the fraudulent use of a credit card to obtain goods worth $80.00. Four years later he had been found guilty of passing a forged check for $28.36.

Finally, in 1973 Rummel was charged with a third felony of receiving $120.75 by false pretenses. Rummel might have avoided the life sentence if he had yielded to the state's pressure to accept a plea bargain without a jury trial, but he insisted on a trial. Rummel sought relief in federal court, with the argument that his life sentence was "cruel and unusual" because it was grossly excessive and disproportionate to the penalties for more serious crimes. The district court and court of appeals rejected the argument, and Rummel appealed to the U.S. Supreme Court.

The Court voted 5 to 4 to affirm the constitutionality of Rummel's punishment. Writing for the majority, Justice William H. Rehnquist maintained that the doctrine that the Eighth Amendment prohibited sentences disproportionate to the severity of the crime was relevant only in death-penalty cases, because this penalty was unique in its total irrevocability. Rehnquist found that the Texas statute had two legitimate goals: to deter repeat offenders and to isolate recidivists from society as long as necessary after they had demonstrated their incapacity to obey the law. The states generally had the authority to determine the length of isolation deemed necessary for such recidivists. Rehnquist also made much of the fact that the Texas statute allowed the possibility of parole.

In an important dissent, Justice Lewis F. Powell, Jr., argued that the doctrine of disproportionality also applied to penalties in noncapital cases. He pointed to precedents that could be interpreted as prohibiting grossly excessive penalties, especially *Weems v. United States* (1910) and *Robinson v. California* (1962). Powell observed that in Texas, even those convicted of murder or aggravated kidnapping were not subject to a mandatory life sentence. In addition, he maintained that the possibility of parole should not be considered in assessing whether the penalty was grossly disproportionate.

The *Rummel* decision would prove to be limited and uncertain in its application as a precedent. In 1983, when the Court encountered a life sentence without any chance of parole based on a recidivist statute in *Solem v. Helm*, Justice Powell would write the majority opinion while Rehnquist would write a dissent. While *Solem* did not directly overturn *Rummel*, the *Solem* majority did endorse the idea that a prison sentence might be unconstitutional if it was disproportionate to punishments for other crimes. Yet in upholding a life sentence for the possession of 650 grams of cocaine in *Harmelin v. Michigan* (1991), the Court would indicate its continued reluctance to apply the doctrine of disproportionality in noncapital cases.

Thomas T. Lewis

Runyon v. McCrary

U.S. Supreme Court
Decided June 25, 1976

- In this case, the Supreme Court broadened the meaning of Title 42, section 1981 of the 1866 Civil Rights Act to outlaw discrimination in all contracts.

Parents of African American children brought suit in federal court against private schools in Virginia that had denied their children admission. Disregarding the defendant schools' argument that a government-imposed obligation to admit black students to their unintegrated student bodies would violate constitutionally protected rights of free association and privacy, the district and appellate courts both ruled in the parents' favor, enjoining the schools from discriminating on the basis of race.

The parents had based their case on a section of the 1866 Civil Rights Act that was still in effect. In 1968, the Supreme Court had held in *Jones v. Alfred H. Mayer Co.* that section 1982 of the act prohibited racial discrimination among private parties in housing. In *Runyon*, the Court broadened this holding to imply that section 1981, the act's right-to-contract provision, outlawed all discriminatory contracts, whether involving public or private parties—including one between private schools and the parents of student applicants.

In the wake of *Runyon*, lower federal courts employed section 1981 to outlaw racial discrimination in a wide variety of areas, including banking, security deposit regulations, admissions to amusement parks, insurance, and mortuaries. The breadth of the Court's interpretation in *Runyon* of section 1981 also caused it to overlap with Title VII of the Civil Rights Act of 1964, governing employment contracts.

This overlap, together with ongoing concern about the extensiveness of the interpretation of section 1981, caused the Court to consider overruling *Runyon* in *Patterson v. McLean*

Credit Union (1989). Instead, *Patterson* severely restricted *Runyon* by declaring that section 1981 did not apply to postcontractual employer discrimination. *Patterson* went so far as to declare that although section 1981 protected the right to enter into employment contracts, it did not extend to future breaches of that contract or to the imposition of discriminatory working conditions. Congress in turn overruled this narrow reading of section 1981 in the Civil Rights Act of 1991, which includes explicit language permitting courts to prohibit employment discrimination that takes place after hiring.

The reason for the Court's about-face with regard to section 1981 can be found in its changing political composition. *Runyon* was decided midway through Chief Justice Warren Burger's tenure, when the Court was dominated by justices who occupied the middle of the political spectrum. In 1986, however, one of two dissenters in *Runyon*, the conservative Justice William H. Rehnquist, succeeded Burger. Rehnquist, who had always been outspoken in his criticism of what he regarded as the Court's excess of liberalism under Chief Justice Earl Warren, dissented in *Runyon* on grounds that the Warren-era *Jones* case had been improperly decided. By 1989, when the Court handed down its decision in *Patterson*, Rehnquist had been joined by enough fellow conservative thinkers to overrule *Runyon*'s interpretation of section 1981 by one vote.

Lisa Paddock

Rust v. Sullivan

U.S. SUPREME COURT
DECIDED MAY 23, 1991

• This case is one of a series of decisions dating back to *Maher v. Roe* (1977) authorizing the government to make access to, and information about, abortion dependent on a woman's ability to pay for it.

Section 1008 of the Public Health Service Act prohibits the use of federal funds in family planning programs "where abortion is a method of family planning." Prior to 1988, the regulations implementing this provision prohibited family planning programs which received federal funds from performing abortions. In 1988, new regulations also prohibited such programs from abortion counseling and from mentioning abortion when referring pregnant women to other services or facilities. The new regulations were commonly referred to as the "gag rules" because they forbade family planning health care programs to mention abortion and required them, if asked about abortion, to respond only that it was not considered an appropriate method of family planning.

Health care providers that offered family planning services and doctors filed suit, challenging the constitutionality of the gag rules. They raised three arguments. First, they claimed that the Department of Health and Human Services was acting beyond the scope of its authority. Second, they said, the rules violated the free speech rights of family planning programs under the First Amendment. Third, they argued that the rules violated the right to privacy (upheld in *Roe v. Wade*, 1973) of individuals using the services of family planning programs. The Supreme Court, by a 5-4 vote, rejected all three arguments and held that the rules were constitutional.

In an opinion written by William Rehnquist, the Court stated that the statutory language was broad in scope and ambiguous. In such cases the Court defers to the interpretation adopted by the agency charged with administering the statute as long as it reflects a plausible construction of the statute's plain language and does not otherwise conflict with Congress' expressed intent. Nothing in the language of the statute or its legislative history prohibited the Department of Health and Human Services from adopting a more restrictive view concerning abortion as a method of family planning. The gag rules were supported by a reasoned analysis demonstrating that the new restrictions assure federal funds are spent on only authorized purposes and avoid creating the appearance of governmental support for abortion-related activities.

Second, the Court held that the regulations do not violate the

First Amendment free speech rights of family planning programs, their staffs, or their patients. The government may make a value judgment favoring childbirth over abortion and implement that judgment via the allocation of public funds. Such a preference is not discriminating on the basis of viewpoint, but ensuring that government funds are being spent for a chosen activity rather than another which the government has chosen not to support. The gag rules do not force clinic personnel or patients to give up all abortion-related speech. Rather, they require that certain speech must occur outside the government-funded family planning program. When the government chooses to subsidize one activity, nothing in the First Amendment requires it also to subsidize the presentation of an alternative point of view or service.

Third, the Court found that the gag rules do not violate a woman's right to choose whether to terminate her pregnancy. The government has no constitutional duty to subsidize an activity merely because it is constitutionally protected, and it may validly allocate public funds for services relating to childbirth but not to abortion. This allocation, according to the Court, places no insurmountable obstacle in the path of a woman wishing to terminate her pregnancy, and it leaves her with the same choices as if the government had chosen not to fund any family planning programs.

The gag rules do not place impermissible restrictions on patient/doctor discussions concerning a woman's right to make an informed and voluntary choice on whether to carry her pregnancy to term, because this information remains available through private health care providers not receiving funds under the Public Health Service Act. The Court decided that the fact that most women participating in family planning programs funded by the act are too poor to obtain private health care services was irrelevant. Such financial constraints on a woman's ability to enjoy the full range of constitutionally protected choices, the Court said, are the product not of governmental restrictions but rather of her personal financial circumstances.

Johnny C. Burris

San Antonio Independent School District v. Rodriguez

U.S. SUPREME COURT
DECIDED MARCH 21, 1973

- The Supreme Court ruled that education was not a fundamental right and that a school finance system that resulted in lower expenditures in school districts inhabited by poor people did not violate the equal protection clause of the Fourteenth Amendment.

Texas, like many other states, finances its public schools with both state and local funding. In the 1970's, the state, through its Minimum Foundation School Program, guaranteed a minimum level of education, but individual school districts were permitted to increase the amount spent on education by taxing property within the district. The constitutionality of this method of school financing was challenged by Demetrio Rodriguez, a Mexican American with three children enrolled in the Edgewood School District. The value of property in that district was low, and, though the people of Edgewood taxed themselves at the maximum rate permitted by law, they were able to raise only $26 per child.

State funds brought the total expenditure per child up to $356. The Alamo Heights District, inhabited by much wealthier people, taxed itself at a lower rate than Edgewood, but, because of the higher value of the property, was able to raise $333 per child. State funds raised that to $594 per child. Rodriguez believed that such a school finance system discriminated against persons on the basis of wealth. A federal district court agreed and held it unconstitutional. The state of Texas appealed to the Supreme Court.

In a close decision, with the justices divided 5-4, the Supreme Court reversed the district court and upheld the Texas school finance system. The Court recognized the difficulty of measuring the quality of education received and relating it to the amount of money spent. Although Rodriguez had sought to convince the Court that education was a fundamental right because of the close connection between education and the ability to exercise the constitutional right of freedom of speech and the right to vote, the Court conceded only that education was important to the effective exercise of those rights but denied that the Constitution guaranteed their most effective exercise. The Court did not express approval of the challenged school finance system but rather considered that American federalism placed the matter within the states' domain.

State supreme courts did, indeed, respond to inequities in school financing. Several of them held that their states' school finance systems, similar to that of Texas, violated their own state constitutions. The California Supreme Court had rendered such a decision even before the U.S. Supreme Court's decision in the Rodriguez case. After the *Rodriguez* decision, other state supreme courts took action. A state may not deny its people federal constitutional rights, but it may certainly accord them greater rights than the federal Constitution. In 1989, the school finance system upheld in the Rodriguez case was held to be in violation of the Texas Constitution by the Texas Supreme Court.

Patricia A. Behlar

Santobello v. New York

U.S. SUPREME COURT
DECIDED DECEMBER 20, 1971

- In this case, which granted the petitioner the right to either a resentencing or a new trial, the Supreme Court confirmed the binding nature of plea-bargaining agreements made by prosecutors with defendants in criminal proceedings.

In 1969, in New York, Rudolph Santobello was arraigned on two criminal counts of violating state antigambling statutes. At first, Santobello entered a plea of not guilty, but later, after negotiations with his prosecutors, he changed his plea to guilty to a lesser-included charge, which carried a maximum penalty of one year in prison. Between the entering of the new guilty plea and the sentencing there was a delay of several months, and in the interim Santobello obtained a new defense attorney, who immediately attempted to have the guilty plea removed and certain evidence suppressed. Both motions were denied.

At Santobello's sentencing, a new prosecutor recommended the maximum penalty of one year in prison. The defense quickly objected, using the argument that the petitioner's plea-bargaining agreement had stipulated that the prosecution would make no recommendation regarding sentencing. The judge, rejecting the relevancy of what prosecutors claimed they would do, sentenced Santobello to the full one-year term on the grounds that he was a seasoned and habitual offender. Subsequently, the Appellate Division of the Supreme Court of the State of New York unanimously upheld the conviction.

The U.S. Supreme Court found that the prosecution had breached the plea-bargaining agreement and remanded the case to the state court to determine whether the circumstances required only resentencing before a different judge or whether the petitioner should be allowed to withdraw his guilty plea and be granted a new trial on the two counts as originally charged. The fact that the breach in the plea-bargaining agreement was inadvertent was deemed irrelevant, as was the sentencing judge's claim that he was not influenced by the prosecutor's recommendation. Chief Justice Warren E. Burger, in the Court ruling, argued that the plea-bargaining procedure in criminal justice "must be attended by safeguards to ensure the defendant what is reasonably due in the circumstances." Therefore, any agreement made in the plea-bargaining process, because it is part of the inducement used to encourage a plea of guilty, constitutes "a promise that must be fulfilled."

In its decision in *Santobello*, the Supreme Court both confirmed its formal recognition of plea bargaining, first granted in *Brady v. United States* (1970), and established its binding nature. Although in later decisions it would review and somewhat modify its position, as, for example, in *Mabry v. Johnson* (1984), it established an extremely important principle: that prosecutors and courts could not unilaterally renege on promises made in plea-bargaining agreements. The *Santobello* decision had the effect of encouraging wider use of the plea-bargaining process, an important aid in expediting justice.

John W. Fiero

Scales v. United States

U.S. SUPREME COURT

DECIDED JUNE 5, 1961

- In this case, the Supreme Court found that laws providing penalties for active membership in organizations advocating overthrow of the government do not necessarily violate the Constitution's guarantees of due process and freedom of speech.

Scales, a member of the Communist Party of the United States, was convicted under the membership clause of the Smith Act of 1940, making it a crime knowingly to belong to an organization whose aim is overthrow of the federal government by force or violence. The Smith Act was one of several antisubversive measures Congress passed after the outbreak of World War II. Although its first section addressed attempts to subvert the military, in fact the act was seldom invoked during World War II.

Afterward it became one of the government's primary methods of combating domestic communism during the Cold War.

In *Dennis v. United States* (1951), the Supreme Court upheld the convictions of eleven Communist Party leaders under the conspiracy provisions of the act, a decision that led to the indictment of 141 state party leaders throughout the country. *Scales v. United States* resulted from those indictments, as did the earlier *Yates v. United States* (1957).

In *Yates*, the Court by a vote of 6 to 1 reversed the convictions of fourteen party leaders involved. The opinion of the Court, written by Justice John M. Harlan and emphasizing the distinction between advocacy of a subversive ideology and advocacy of subversive action, found the conspiracy provisions of the Smith Act defective, thus rendering them worthless. No further prosecutions were undertaken under them.

Between the time the Supreme Court handed down its decision in *Dennis* and that in *Yates*, personnel changes on the Court as well as an easing of Cold War tensions resulted in a reorientation. *Yates* produced a backlash in Congress, however, and by the time the Court decided *Scales*, it had again changed its attitude. Justice Harlan, joined by Justice Felix Frankfurter, changed sides, with the result that Scales's conviction was upheld by a vote of 5 to 4.

In a companion case, *Noto v. United States*, decided the same day as *Scales*, the Court dismissed the conviction of a Communist Party member under the membership clause of the Smith Act. Justice Harlan's opinions in the two cases were careful to distinguish between mere membership in organizations such as the Communist Party and "not only knowing membership, but purposive membership, purposive that is as to the organization's criminal ends." Construed in this fashion, the Smith Act membership clause violated neither the due process clause of the Fifth Amendment nor the free speech guarantee embodied in the First Amendment.

In both *Yates* and *Scales*, the Court interpreted the Smith Act more narrowly than it had in *Dennis*, with the result that finally only twenty-nine of the individuals indicted under the act served time in jail for their convictions.

Lisa Paddock

Schall v. Martin

U.S. SUPREME COURT
DECIDED JUNE 4, 1984

- In agreeing with a New York State family court in this preventive detention case, the Supreme Court limited the application of the Fourteenth Amendment's due process clause.

Schall v. Martin was a preventive detention case involving juveniles. New York State had enacted a Family Court Act pertaining to juvenile delinquents and to juveniles arrested and remanded to the family court prior to trial. If the family court determined that pretrial release of juveniles might result in their disappearance or place them or the general public at risk, it was authorized to detain them. Detention occurred only after notice was given to parents and other authorities, a hearing was held, a statement of facts and reasons was presented, and the "probable cause" that release might be harmful was established.

Juvenile detainees Gregory Martin, Luis Rosario, and Kenneth Morgan (along with thirty-three other juveniles introduced into the case) faced serious charges. Martin had been arrested in 1977, charged with first-degree robbery, second-degree assault, and criminal possession of a gun after he and two others struck another youth on the head with a loaded gun and beat him in order to steal his jacket and sneakers. He was found guilty of these crimes by a family court judge and placed on two years' probation. Martin was fourteen. Rosario, also fourteen, was charged with robbery and second-degree assault for trying to rob two men by putting a gun to their heads and beating them. He previously had been detained for knifing a student. Morgan, fourteen, had four previous arrests and had been charged with attempted robbery, assault, and grand larceny for robbing and threatening to shoot a fourteen-year-old girl and her brother.

Martin and the others brought suit claiming that their detention deprived them of a writ of *habeas corpus* and violated the
due process clause of the Fourteenth Amendment. The federal
district appeals court agreed that their detention "served as
punishment without proof of guilt according to requisite constitutional standards." Gregory Schall, commissioner of the
New York City Department of Juvenile Justice, appealed to the
Supreme Court. The case reached the Supreme Court at a time
when polls showed that crime was a major fear of the American
public and when a relatively conservative Court was exercising
judicial restraint and limiting the expansion of civil liberties.

Reading the majority 7-2 decision, Justice William Rehnquist
acknowledged that the due process clause of the Fourteenth
Amendment indeed applied to the pretrial detention of juveniles. He agreed with Schall, however, that when, as in these
cases, there was "serious risk" involved to both the juveniles
and the public by their release, the New York law was compatible with the "fundamental fairness" demanded by the due
process clause.

Clifton K. Yearley

Schenck v. United States

U.S SUPREME COURT
DECIDED MARCH 3, 1919

- The Supreme Court promulgated the "clear and present danger" doctrine as a guideline in freedom of speech
cases.

The Schenck case involved the constitutionality of the Espionage Act. Passed by Congress on June 15, 1917, that wartime
measure provided severe penalties for individuals convicted of
such treasonable offenses as aiding the enemy, obstructing
recruiting, instigating disloyalty among American troops, or
mailing seditious material. The passage of the statute reopened

the old conflict between military necessity and the Bill of Rights.

Charles T. Schenck, the general secretary of the Socialist Party, strongly opposed American participation in World War I. He expressed his resistance to the "capitalist" war by distributing about fifteen thousand leaflets that urged noncompliance with the 1917 Selective Service Act. He was indicted under the Espionage Act for plotting to obstruct the draft and for using the mails to circulate his leaflets. After a federal court convicted him and sentenced him to prison, Schenck appealed to the U.S. Supreme Court on the grounds that he had been deprived of his freedom of speech and press guaranteed by the First Amendment to the Constitution.

The nation's highest court was thus confronted with the

Edward D. White (1845-1921), chief justice at the time of the *Schenck* decision, was appointed by President William Howard Taft, who succeeded him as chief justice in 1921. *(Albert Rosenthal/Collection of the Supreme Court of the United States)*

challenge of reconciling the Espionage Act with the First Amendment. After hearing arguments in 1919, the Court upheld the constitutionality of the 1917 law. Justice Oliver Wendell Holmes, Jr., speaking for a unanimous Court, maintained that the First Amendment guarantee of freedom of speech and press is not absolute. "The most stringent protection of Free speech," he said, "would not protect a man in falsely shouting fire in a theater and causing a panic." Freedom of expression is always under restraint, particularly in wartime.

In his decision, Holmes formulated the clear and present danger doctrine as a criterion for judging between permissible and illicit speech: "The question . . . is whether the words are used in such circumstances and are of such a nature as to create a clear and present danger that they will bring about the substantive evil that Congress has a right to prevent." Applying the test to Schenck's distribution of antidraft circulars during World War I, Holmes ruled that the defendant's activities did pose an immediate danger to the nation's war effort. Schenck's conviction was upheld.

The major legacy of the case to American justice has been the clear and present danger precept. The test subsequently became an influential yardstick in freedom of speech cases. A version of Holmes's criterion permits advocacy to be punished only if its objective is to incite lawless behavior and if such behavior is likely to occur. If the perceived danger is not imminent or its likelihood is minimal, the government may not restrict freedom of speech.

Ronald W. Long

Shapiro v. Thompson

U.S. SUPREME COURT
DECIDED APRIL 21, 1969

- Ruling that one-year residence requirements for receiving welfare benefits were unconstitutional, the Court defended a broad right to establish residence in the state of one's choice and to enjoy equal rights with other residents.

After living in Connecticut for two months, Vivian Thompson applied for public assistance under the Aid to Families with Dependent Children (AFDC) program. Thompson, pregnant and a mother of one child, was denied assistance because she did not meet the state's one-year residency requirement. She then sued the welfare commissioner, Bernard Shapiro, in federal district court. The district court ruled in her favor based on two principles: that the residency requirement had a "chilling effect on the right to travel" and that it denied Thompson's guarantee of equal protection under the Fourteenth Amendment. Connecticut appealed the ruling to the U.S. Supreme Court, which accepted review and consolidated the case with others dealing with the same requirement to receive welfare.

The Supreme Court decided by a 6-3 vote to strike down the durational residency requirements, with Justice William Brennan delivering the opinion of the majority. Brennan observed that the right to migrate from state to state, implied in several places in the Constitution, was well established in the precedents of the Court. Concerning the second issue, the equal protection clause of the Fourteenth Amendment, Brennan wrote that the residency requirement created two classes of needy residents, with the two classes receiving unequal benefits. Since this classification restricted "the fundamental right of interstate movement," it could only be justified by a "compelling state interest." Although a state had a valid interest in restricting its expenditures, it could not promote this interest "by invidious discrimination between classes of its citizens."

The dissenters in the case accepted the constitutional principle of a right to travel, but they believed that the impact of residency requirements were indirect and quite insubstantial. Justice John M. Harlan attacked the expansion of judicial power that occurred when courts arbitrarily decided that fundamental rights required a more rigorous standard of review.

Shapiro was an important step in the Warren Court's development of "strict scrutiny" doctrine, which required states to show a compelling state interest to justify laws limiting fundamental rights or laws based upon "suspect classifications" such as race. Since the right to interstate migration was recognized as fundamental, *Shapiro* made it difficult for states to justify durational residency requirements for most services. Later the Court would invalidate residency requirements for voting, indigent medical care, and other basic services but would allow them for less basic services, upholding requirements for seeking divorce and for exemption from paying out-of-state tuition at public universities. Contrary to some expectations, *Shapiro* did not mark the beginning of a new governmental obligation to provide the economic necessities of life.

Thomas T. Lewis

Shaw v. Reno

U.S. SUPREME COURT
RULING ISSUED JUNE 28, 1993

- By calling for close scrutiny of a predominantly black congressional district whose shape it considered "bizarre," the Supreme Court struck a blow against the practice of drawing district boundaries to create "majority-minority" electoral districts.

After the 1990 census, the state legislature of North Carolina began the task of "reapportionment," or redrawing its electoral districts. Although about 22 percent of the state's population was African American, no blacks had been elected to Congress for almost a century. To remedy this, and ostensibly to meet provisions of the Voting Rights Act, the legislature created two majority-nonwhite districts. In order to avoid disturbing incumbents' districts, the legislature drew one of the two districts largely along an interstate highway, snaking 160 miles through the north-central part of the state. The resulting district was 53 percent black.

Five voters filed suit against the reapportionment plan, objecting that the race-based district violated their right to participate in a nonracial electoral process. The case reached the Supreme Court, whose 5-4 majority instructed the lower courts to reconsider the constitutionality of such a district in light of its "bizarre" shape and its "uncomfortable resemblance to political apartheid." In essence, the majority expressed its concern about the practice of creating districts on the basis of race and of establishing contorted geographical boundaries. The coupling of the two practices presumably could result in districts that patently violated the Constitution's equal protection clause, unless a compelling state interest could be demonstrated.

When the *Shaw* case was subsequently returned to North Carolina, a federal panel upheld the reapportionment plan after finding that the state did indeed have a compelling interest in complying with the VRA. Nevertheless, the Supreme Court's *Shaw* decision has been the basis for other important decisions concerning racially defined districts. In 1994, for example, a majority-black district in Louisiana was rejected by a federal district court invoking *Shaw*. The court expressed particular concern that the district was intentionally created on the basis of the voters' race. More significant, in 1995 the U.S. Supreme Court extended *Shaw*'s admonitions about racial reapportionment to argue that voters' rights are violated whenever "race was the predominant factor motivating the legislature's decision to place a significant number of voters within or without a particular district," irrespective of shape.

Shaw served as a watershed in the contest between advocates of racial representation and those who champion a "colorblind" electoral system. It came at a time when various racial issues that had for years remained largely outside of sharp political debate—affirmative action, welfare reform, and so forth—had been thrust into the center stage of American political discourse. Although *Shaw* by no means resolved these debates, it helped to clarify the battle lines.

Steve D. Boilard

Shelley v. Kraemer

U.S. SUPREME COURT
DECIDED MAY 3, 1948

- Although the Supreme Court acknowledged the right of private individuals to make racially restrictive covenants, the Court ruled that state action to enforce such covenants was a violation of the Fourteenth Amendment.

After J. D. Shelley, an African American, purchased a house in a predominantly white neighborhood of St. Louis, Missouri, one of the neighbors, Louis Kraemer, sought and obtained an injunction preventing Shelley from taking possession of the property. Unknown to Shelley, the neighboring landowners had signed a contractual agreement barring owners from selling their property to members of "the Negro or Mongolian race."

Supported by the National Association for the Advancement of Colored People (NAACP), Shelley challenged the constitutionality of the contract in state court, but the Missouri Supreme Court upheld its legality. Appealing to the U.S. Supreme Court, Shelley's case was argued by the NAACP's leading counsel, Charles Houston and Thurgood Marshall. President Harry S Truman put the weight of the executive branch in favor of the NAACP's position.

This was not the first time that the issue of residential segregation had appeared before the Court. In *Buchanan v. Warley* (1917), the Court had struck down state statutes that limited the right of property owners to sell property to a person of another race, but in *Corrigan v. Buckley* (1926) the Court upheld the right of individuals to make "private" contracts to maintain segregation. *Corrigan* was based on the establishment principle that the first section of the Fourteenth Amendment inhibited the actions of state governments, not those of individuals.

The Court refused to declare restrictive contracts unconstitutional, but it held 6-0 that the Fourteenth Amendment's equal protection clause prohibited state courts from enforcing the contracts, meaning that the contracts were not enforceable. The decision, written by Chief Justice Fred Vinson, emphasized that one of the basic objectives of the Fourteenth Amendment was to prohibit the states from using race to discriminate "in the enjoyment of property rights." The decision did not directly overturn *Corrigan*, but it interpreted the precedent as involving only the validity of private contracts, not their legal enforcement. In a companion case five years later, *Barrows v. Jackson* (1953), Chief Justice Vinson dissented when the majority used

Chief Justice Frederick Vinson (1890-1953) wrote the majority decision in *Shelley v. Kraemer. (James Whitmore/Collection of the Supreme Court of the United States)*

the *Shelley* rationale to block enforcement of restrictive covenants through private damage suits against covenant violators. Eliminating the last direct method for legally barring African Americans from neighborhoods, *Shelley* was an important early victory in the struggle against state-supported segregation. Civil rights proponents hoped that a logical extension of the case would lead to an abolition of the distinction between private and state action in matters of equal protection, but in later decisions such as *Moose Lodge No. 107 v. Irvis* (1972), the majority of judges were not ready to rule against private conduct that was simply tolerated by the state.

Thomas T. Lewis

Sheppard v. Maxwell

U.S. Supreme Court
Decided June 6, 1966

- In *Sheppard v. Maxwell*, the Supreme Court for the first time provided guidelines for trial courts on how to balance the interests of the media in reporting information about a criminal trial and the rights of a criminal defendant.

Problems related to too much media publicity about a criminal trial extend back to the 1800's, but it was not until the 1960's that the Supreme Court discussed the effects of publicity in criminal trials. Between 1959 and 1966, the Court reversed five convictions on the grounds that the amount of publicity had affected the defendant's right to a fair trial. It was not until 1966, when it decided *Sheppard v. Maxwell*, that it actually provided practical suggestions to the trial courts on how to solve the issues related to prejudicial publicity.

Sheppard involved the murder conviction of Sam Sheppard, a well-known physician in Cleveland accused of murdering his wife. Even before the arrest of the defendant in this case, the media published countless stories about him, accentuating his alleged failure to cooperate with the investigation and strongly arguing for his arrest. After an article demanded to know why there had been no public inquest, a three-day inquest took place where Sheppard's questioning was covered by television and radio.

Another article also seemed to influence the decision to arrest Sheppard, since he was arrested hours after the headline "Why Isn't Sam Sheppard in Jail?" was run. Many articles and editorials implied his guilt and discussed allegedly incriminating evidence that was never introduced at trial. During the trial itself, the media filled the courtroom, and the constant movement of reporters made it difficult for some witnesses to be heard. A special table for media representatives was set in the courtroom, and twenty people were assigned to it.

The court also reserved four rows of seats behind the bar railing for television and radio reporters and for representatives of out-of-town newspapers and magazines. A radio station was allowed to broadcast from a room adjacent the room where the jury rested and deliberated. Because of his proximity to reporters in the courtroom, it was almost impossible for the defendant to speak privately with his attorney during the proceedings. Despite this situation, the trial judge did not take steps to limit the effects of the publicity or the behavior of the press during the trial. The Supreme Court reversed the murder conviction, holding that the publicity surrounding the trial had deprived the defendant of his right to a fair trial.

In criticizing the trial court for allowing a "carnival atmosphere in the courtroom" and for failing to control the flow of publicity, the Supreme Court ordered lower courts to take an affirmative role in protecting the rights of the defendants from undue interference by the press. The Court enumerated some ways in which courts could make sure the publicity did not affect the defendant's right to a fair trial. For example, courts could regulate the conduct of reporters in the courtroom, change venue, order a continuance of the trial, isolate witnesses, and control the release of information to the media by law enforcement personnel and counsel.

Alberto Bernabe-Riefkohl

Sherbert v. Verner

U.S. SUPREME COURT
DECIDED JUNE 17, 1963

- The Supreme Court allowed individuals to make First Amendment claims against governmental policies that indirectly burdened their free exercise of religion and required government to show that any such burdens were justified by a compelling state interest.

Adell Sherbert, a member of the Seventh-day Adventist church, worked in a textile mill in South Carolina, and in 1959 her employer informed her that henceforth she would be required to work on Saturdays. Since it was against her religious beliefs to work on the Sabbath, she refused the new conditions, and she was fired. Not able to find employment consistent with her beliefs, she filed for state unemployment benefits. South Carolina law did not allow benefits for applicants who refused to accept work without good cause, and the unemployment office rejected her religious scruples as a justification.

Sherbert and her lawyers filed suit against the unemployment office at state court, but the South Carolina Supreme Court ruled in favor of the state agency. The state court relied on the recent precedent of *Braunfeld v. Brown* (1961), in which the U.S. Supreme Court had allowed for Sunday closing laws (blue laws) even if such laws disadvantaged Jewish merchants whose religious convictions prevented them from working on Saturdays. The state court concluded that the burdens on Sherbert were essentially the same as the economic hardships accepted in *Braunfeld*.

The U.S. Supreme Court, however, voted 7-2 that South Carolina's policy was in violation of the religious exercise clause of the First Amendment, made applicable to the states by the Fourteenth Amendment. Writing for the majority, Justice William Brennan began with the premise that religious exercise was a fundamental right and that any governmental burden on this right must be justified by a compelling state interest. In addition, Brennan wrote that the state had the obligation to adopt the alternative which was the least restrictive on religious practice, a test that had previously been used in free speech cases. The state was violating the First Amendment when it presented Sherbert with the "cruel choice" of either forfeiting an economic benefit or abandoning one of the precepts of her religion.

The two dissenters, supported by many informed observers, argued that Brennan's opinion contradicted the reasoning in *Braunfeld*, but Brennan maintained that the two cases were quite different. In the earlier case, he wrote, the state had demonstrated a compelling interest to provide a uniform day of rest for all workers, while in Sherbert the state had no compelling reason to refuse to modify its requirements for unemployment benefits.

Sherbert required governments to make exceptions in enforcing laws to accommodate religious practices unless the normal application of the law could be defended according to the tests that it served a compelling state interest and was the least restrictive alternative. The result was a maximum of protection for unpopular religious practices. In *Employment Division, Department of Human Resources of Oregon v. Smith* (1990), however, the Court ruled that indirect burdens were acceptable when state policies had a secular basis and were equally applicable to all citizens.

Thomas T. Lewis

Skinner v. Railway Labor Executives' Association

U.S. SUPREME COURT
DECIDED MARCH 21, 1989

• In this case the Supreme Court ruled that drug and alcohol testing in the workplace was not a violation of the Fourth Amendment.

The Fourth Amendment to the U.S. Constitution protects not only against unreasonable search and seizure of persons and places but also against the issuance of warrants for search and seizure unless just cause is demonstrated.

The Federal Railroad Administration (FRA), in response to evidence that drug and alcohol abuse was becoming a problem in the nation's railways, established regulations to address the problem. These regulations required blood and urine samples from employees to test for drugs or alcohol after train accidents where deaths, injuries, or property damage occurred. Employees also had to submit to breath or urine tests if there was reasonable suspicion that they were under the influence of drugs or alcohol, even if no accident had occurred.

Railway labor organizations filed suit in the U.S. District Court for the Northern District of California. The court held the regulations to be constitutional. The railway organizations then appealed in the U.S. Court of Appeals for the Ninth Circuit. The appeals court reversed the lower trial court's decision, holding that such tests were search and seizure without warrant and constituted a violation of an employee's Fourth Amendment rights.

The U.S. Supreme Court, on *certiorari*, reversed the court of appeals ruling and upheld the original decision, finding that Fourth Amendment rights had not been violated. In addition, the Court noted that the FRA regulations were well known to, and understood by, the railway workers subject to them.

The Court found that the tests were not unconstitutional even when a warrant had not been issued. The justices cited the need to ensure the safety of the public using the railways. Because evidence of drug or alcohol use could disappear from a person's body within a brief period of time, timely testing was essential for accurate results. Obtaining a warrant would take too long. Furthermore, they said that the railway did not need to prove that there was particular reason to suspect drug or alcohol use before testing employees who had not been involved in accidents. The justices pointed out the need to discourage all employees from using drugs or alcohol during working hours or shortly before. In general, the Court held that the greater good of protecting the public outweighed the private rights of individuals responsible for ensuring travel safety.

The opinion was written by Justice Anthony Kennedy with Chief Justice William H. Rehnquist and Justices Byron R. White, Harry A. Blackmun, Sandra Day O'Connor, and Antonin Scalia concurring. Justice John Paul Stevens concurred in part and concurred in the judgment. Justices Thurgood Marshall and William J. Brennan dissented.

Elizabeth Algren Shaw

Smith v. Allwright

U.S. SUPREME COURT
DECIDED APRIL 3, 1944

- The Supreme Court's ruling in this case overturned the all-white primary in Texas and inspired further efforts to increase African American access to the ballot.

The Jim Crow system of racial segregation that characterized the Southern states in the early twentieth century was made possible by the virtual exclusion of African Americans from politics. One of the most effective tools for limiting black political influence was the all-white primary. Under this arrangement—adopted by eight Southern states—primary elections were held to be "private" affairs, outside the reach of the Fourteenth Amendment's prohibition against discriminatory state action and the Fifteenth Amendment's ban on racial discrimination in voting. The Democratic Party was so dominant in most Southern states that winning its primary was tantamount to election.

Texas witnessed the most significant legal challenges to the white primary. In 1927 the U.S. Supreme Court ruled (in *Nixon v. Herndon*) that blacks could not be barred from primaries by state law. The legislature repealed its laws on primary voting and opened the way for the state Democratic convention to ban blacks from participation in its primaries. The Supreme Court upheld this approach in *Grovey v. Townsend* (1935) as "private" action that was beyond the reach of the Constitution. In 1941, however, the Court enlarged the scope of federal jurisdiction by ruling (in *United States v. Classic*) that Congress could regulate primary elections that selected candidates for federal elections.

The National Association for the Advancement of Colored People (NAACP) saw an opportunity. Sponsoring a suit by Lonnie Smith, a Houston dentist who had unsuccessfully tried to vote in the Democratic primary, the NAACP argued that the all-white primary was, in fact, a racially discriminatory and unconstitutional election.

The Supreme Court, by an 8-1 majority, agreed. Reversing its previous decision in the *Grovey* case, the Court held that the primary was part of the state's electoral machinery; Smith had been unconstitutionally denied the vote on racial grounds.

The Court's decision marked the end of the white primary. It not only enlarged the scope of voting rights held to be subject to constitutional protection but also inspired two decades of efforts to end racial discrimination in voting that culminated in the Voting Rights Act of 1965.

William C. Lowe

Snepp v. United States

U.S. Supreme Court
Decided February 19, 1980

- This decision held that agreements requiring government employees to submit their writings for review prior to publication did not violate their First Amendment rights.

As a condition of employment, agents of the Central Intelligence Agency (CIA) are required to sign an agreement that they will not publish any information during or after employment without prepublication clearance by the agency. In 1977 former CIA employee Frank W. Snepp III published a book, *Decent Interval*, that described CIA activities in Vietnam, without first submitting his manuscript for prepublication review. The government then sued him for breach of contract, requesting that an injunction be imposed requiring him to submit all future publications for prepublication review. The government also sought to control all profits earned from the sale of Snepp's book. A federal district court in Virginia sided with the government in 1978. Two years later the U.S. Supreme Court upheld the district court ruling in *Snepp v. United States*.

Snepp argued that the prepublication agreement constituted an unconstitutional prior restraint upon his freedom of expression. The Supreme Court ruled, however, that such agreements are reasonable and appropriate to prevent unauthorized disclosure of CIA sources and methods, because the government has a "compelling interest" in protecting both national security secrets and the appearance of agency confidentiality.

This ruling reaffirmed a previous decision of the Fourth Circuit Court of Appeals in *United States v. Marchetti* (1972), which had enjoined publication of *The CIA and the Cult of Intelligence* (1974) by Victor Marchetti and John Marks, until the manuscript was purged of classified information. A federal appeals court subsequently ruled that both secrecy agreements and prepublication agreements did not violate the First Amendment in *McGehee v. Casey* (1983).

The CIA cases involved government efforts to impose censorship upon massive quantities of information regarding government activities because of potential danger to national security. The government and the courts have routinely viewed these cases as matters of contract law. To defenders of free speech, however, these attempts to censor writings critical of the government raise several concerns. First, questions of whether material might endanger national security is left entirely to government agencies; the courts have been reluctant to intercede in these determinations. Therefore, the authority to weigh the arguments for and against censorship has been delegated to the censor. Second, because the information is relevant to government policies and decisions, opponents of censorship fear that both the right of authors to criticize the government and the people's right to know may be jeopardized by agency decisions. Third, these regulations constitute prior restraints upon publication. With few exceptions, the courts have overturned prior restraints because they impose direct burdens upon authors and publishers and because they deter critics from engaging in expression that might be deemed seditious. However, the CIA prepublication and secrecy agreements constitute one area where prior restraints have been upheld by the courts.

Richard A. Parker

Solem v. Helm

U.S. SUPREME COURT
DECIDED JUNE 28, 1983

- In this case, the Supreme Court interpreted the Eighth Amendment's prohibition on cruel and unusual punishments to limit the ability of states to impose life sentences for multiple convictions on nonviolent felony charges.

In 1979, Jerry Helm was convicted of issuing a "no account" check for one hundred dollars. This was his seventh felony conviction in South Dakota. In 1964, 1966, and 1969, he had been convicted of third-degree burglary. He had been convicted of obtaining money under false pretenses in 1972, and in 1973 he was convicted of grand larceny. Moreover, his third drunk-driving conviction in 1975 counted as a felony offense.

All the offenses were nonviolent, none involved personal, physical victimization of another person, and alcohol was a contributing factor in each case. Although the maximum penalty for writing a "no account" check would have been five years in prison and a five-thousand-dollar fine, Helm was sentenced to life imprisonment without possibility of parole because anyone convicted of four felonies under South Dakota law may be given the maximum penalty for a class 1 felony— even if he or she has never committed any class 1 felonies. The purpose of the tough sentencing law was to put habitual offenders away forever so that they could not commit additional offenses.

On appeal, the South Dakota Supreme Court rejected Helm's claim that the sentence of life without parole for a nonviolent offense constituted cruel and unusual punishment in violation of the Eighth Amendment. The U.S. court of appeals disagreed and invalidated Helm's sentence. When the U.S. Supreme Court reviewed the case, a narrow five-member majority agreed with Helm's argument.

In a prior decision (*Rummel v. Estelle*, 1980), the U.S. Supreme Court had permitted Texas to impose a life sentence on a man who, over the course of a decade, was convicted of three separate theft offenses in which he stole less than $250. The Supreme Court regarded the *Helm* case as different because South Dakota, unlike Texas, did not permit people with life sentences to become eligible for parole. Thus the realistic impact of Helm's sentence was much harsher than that of life sentences imposed in other states where prisoners typically earn an eventual parole release if they exhibit good behavior. The Court decided that Helm's punishment was disproportionate to his crimes because sentences of life without parole are typically reserved for people convicted of first-degree murder, kidnapping, or treason—not for people who commit nonviolent offenses involving modest amounts of money.

The importance of *Solem v. Helm* is that the Supreme Court placed limitations on the ability of the states to impose severe sentences on people convicted of multiple nonviolent felonies. The case also reinforced the Court's view that the Eighth Amendment contains an implicit requirement that sentences cannot be disproportionate to the crimes committed.

Christopher E. Smith

Stanford v. Kentucky

U.S. SUPREME COURT
DECIDED JUNE 26, 1989

- In this case, the Supreme Court held that the Eighth Amendment's prohibition against "cruel and unusual punishment" did not prevent the execution of individuals who were juveniles at the time they committed the crimes for which they were executed.

The Supreme Court's decision addressed two cases, one involving a seventeen-year-old male convicted of first-degree murder for having robbed a gas station and then raped, sodomized, and shot a station attendant to death, and the other involving a sixteen-year-old sentenced to death for having robbed a convenience store, stabbed the attendant, and left her to die. Both criminal defendants had been tried as adults.

The Supreme Court held that the Eighth Amendment's "cruel and unusual punishment" clause did not bar states from executing individuals who were sixteen and seventeen years of age at the time they committed the applicable crimes. The Court noted that such executions were not the kinds of punishment considered cruel and unusual at the time the Bill of Rights was adopted. Furthermore, the Court concluded that the executions at issue in the case were not contrary to "evolving standards of decency that mark the progress of a maturing society."

Justice Sandra Day O'Connor concurred in this holding but wrote separately to emphasize her belief that the Court had a constitutional obligation to assure in each case that a particular defendant's blameworthiness was proportional to the sentence imposed. Justice Antonin Scalia, who wrote the majority opinion and the opinion of four justices on this point, argued that the Court had never invalidated a punishment solely because of an asserted disproportion between the punishment and the defendant's blameworthiness.

Justices William J. Brennan, Thurgood Marshall, Harry A. Blackmun, and John Paul Stevens dissented. These justices stated that the "cruel and unusual punishment" clause of the Eighth Amendment bars the execution of any person for a crime committed while the person was under the age eighteen. Justice Brennan, writing for the dissenters, asserted that such executions violated contemporary standards of decency. He pointed out that the laws of a majority of states would not have permitted the executions at issue in this case and that in the vast majority of cases involving juvenile offenders, juries did not impose the death penalty. The justice concluded by arguing that the imposition of the death penalty for juvenile crimes served the interests of neither retribution nor deterrence.

Capital punishment in these cases did not serve the interests of retribution since, according to Justice Brennan, the penalty was disproportionate to the defendants' blameworthiness. The punishment did not advance the interests of deterrence since juveniles were not likely to make the kind of cost-benefit analysis that would dissuade them from committing a crime for fear of receiving the death penalty.

Timothy L. Hall

Sturges v. Crowninshield

U.S. SUPREME COURT
DECIDED FEBRUARY 17, 1819

- In this case, the Supreme Court provided its first evaluation of the constitutionality of state bankruptcy statutes.

Sturges and Crowninshield were parties to two contracts involving promissory notes dated March 22, 1811. When the defendant in the case, the maker of the notes, could not repay them, he was sued in federal court. The court relieved him from repaying his debts on the basis of the New York bankruptcy statute, passed April 3, 1811. The plaintiff, who had lent money in good faith and prior to enactment of the New York law, appealed this decision, basing his case on two arguments: first, that individual states did not have the power to pass bankruptcy laws, which were the exclusive province of Congress, and second, that even if states were vested with such power under the Constitution, the New York law was invalid because, in permitting discharge of debts incurred before the statute was passed, it violated the contract clause (Article I, section 10) of the Constitution, which prohibits states from passing laws that impair the obligations of contracts. The judges of the circuit court were divided as to whether the ruling in favor of the defendant should be overturned, thus obliging the Supreme Court to decide the appeal.

The Supreme Court, by a vote of 6 to 0, voided the New York statute. Although Chief Justice John Marshall, writing for the Court, rejected the argument that the federal government had exclusive jurisdiction over insolvency laws, he did find the New York law an unconstitutional state interference with contracts.

Although Article I, section 8 of the Constitution empowers Congress to establish "uniform Laws on the subject of Bankruptcies throughout the United States," in 1819 there was no national bankruptcy law. In the absence of a comprehensive national scheme, Marshall declared, states were free to create their own systems of bankruptcy relief—so long as they did not discharge contracts involving debt. Since this is the very point of bankruptcy laws, *Sturges v. Crowninshield* left states in confusion until the Court again addressed the question in *Ogden v. Saunders* (1827), holding that states could pass insolvency laws so long as they did not permit discharge of debts that predated the laws.

Ogden, however, did not resolve the bankruptcy problem. Although various states, primarily northern ones, did attempt schemes for discharging insolvent debtors, they found they had difficulty meeting the needs of both debtors and creditors. Some states, fearful that bankruptcy laws would discourage lending altogether, did not even enter the field. Finally, in 1898, Congress put the controversy to rest by passing national bankruptcy legislation which preempted state insolvency laws. Flaws in the administration of the system were further addressed with the Bankruptcy Reform Act of 1978, which created a separate system of bankruptcy courts to enforce the new legislation.

Lisa Paddock

Swann v. Charlotte-Mecklenberg Board of Education

U.S. SUPREME COURT
DECIDED APRIL 20, 1971

- In this case, the U.S. Supreme Court determined that lower courts may properly order local school boards to use extensive school busing to desegregate urban schools.

The original catalyst for this case was the plan of the school board of Charlotte, Mecklenberg County, North Carolina, to close some African American schools, create attendance zones for most of the schools in the district, and allow a "freedom-of-choice" provision under which students could transfer to any school in the district, provided that they could furnish their own transportation and the school was not already filled to capacity.

The litigation began on January 19, 1965, when eleven African American families, including Vera and Darius Swann and their son James, were convinced by attorney Julius L. Chambers to sue the district for relief. The plaintiffs challenged the plan on the premise that the closing of the African American schools would place the burden of desegregation on the African American students, and that the other features would only perpetuate segregation.

In 1965, federal district court judge J. Braxton Craven rejected the plaintiff's challenge and approved the school board's plan. A year later, the Court of Appeals for the Fourth Circuit affirmed Craven's ruling. At this point, Chambers opted not to appeal to the Supreme Court, because he feared that the Court would only affirm the lower rulings under the precedents established at that time.

After the Supreme Court's ruling in *Green v. County School Board of New Kent County, Virginia* in 1968, however, Chambers decided to petition for further relief. In *Green*, the justices ruled that freedom-of-choice plans did not aid in the process of desegregation, and that other methods must be used to comply with *Brown v. Board of Education* (1954). On September 6, 1968, the *Swann* plaintiffs filed a motion for further relief in the federal district court in Charlotte. The motion came before Judge James B. McMillan. Both parties agreed that the school system fell short of achieving the unitary status required by *Green*. Two plans were submitted, one by the school board and the other by a court-appointed expert from Rhode Island College, Dr. John Finger.

Judge McMillan essentially accepted the Finger plan, which required more desegregation than the school board was willing to accept. The board plan would have closed seven schools and reassigned the students involved. Attendance zones were to be restructured to achieve greater racial balance, but the existing grade structures were left intact. Furthermore, the board plan would modify the free transfer plan into an optional majority-to-minority transfer system (students in a racial majority in one

The court of Warren Burger (1907-1995) around the time of its *Swann* decision. *(Harris and Ewing/Collection of the Supreme Court of the United States)*

school could transfer to another where they would be in the minority).

Under the board plan, African American students would be reassigned to nine of the ten high schools in the district, thereby producing in each an African American population of between 17 and 36 percent. The tenth high school would have an African American population of 2 percent. The junior high schools would be rezoned so that all but one would have from none to 38 percent African Americans. One junior high school would have an African American population of 90 percent. Attendance at the elementary schools, however, still would be based primarily on the neighborhood concept. More than half the African American children at this level would remain in schools that were between 86 and 100 percent black.

The Finger plan used the board zoning plan for high schools, with one modification. Three hundred additional African American students would be transported to the nearly all-white Independence High School. This plan dealt similarly with the junior high schools. Nine satellite zones would be created, and inner-city African American students would be assigned to nine outlying, predominantly white junior high schools.

As was typically the case, the biggest controversy concerned the elementary school students. Rather than simply relying on zoning, Finger proposed that pairing and grouping techniques be used as well, with the result that all elementary schools would have a black student proportion that would range from 9 to 38 percent. Pairing occurs when two schools, one predominantly white and one predominantly black, are combined by either sending half the students in one school to the other for all grades or by sending all the children to one school for certain grades and then to the other school for the remaining grade levels. Bus transportation would be used for the affected students.

After the district court's busing order, McMillan was hanged in effigy. Crowds demonstrated at the courthouse, in front of the judge's house, and at the *Charlotte Observer*, a newspaper that had supported busing. McMillan and his family received threatening phone calls, his law office was fire-bombed by an arsonist, his car was dynamited, and his home was vandalized.

The Charlotte-Mecklenberg Board of Education appealed McMillan's busing order to the Fourth Circuit Court of Appeals. The appellate court vacated McMillan's order respecting elementary schools, and affirmed his ruling only on the secondary school plans. This time, because of the *Green* case, Chambers appealed the decision to the Supreme Court.

By the time the Supreme Court ruled on *Swann* in 1971, Earl Warren had retired as chief justice, and President Richard Nixon (who had publicly condemned forced busing) had filled Earl Warren's seat with Warren Burger in 1969. *Swann v. Charlotte-Mecklenberg Board of Education* dealt with the constitutionality of several different techniques to achieve desegregation. In writing the unanimous decision, Burger admitted that the Court had not, as of that time, provided federal district courts with comprehensive guidelines for implementing its 1954 landmark case, *Brown v. Board of Education of Topeka, Kansas.* He declared:

> Understandably, in an area of evolving remedies, those courts had to improvise and experiment without detailed or specific guidelines. This Court . . . appropriately dealt with the large constitutional principles; other federal courts had to grapple with the flinty, intractable realities of day-to-day implementation of those constitutional commands. Their efforts, of necessity, embraced a process of "trial and error," and our effort to formulate guidelines must take into account their experience.

In accepting the Finger plan, the justices ruled that federal district courts could decree as tools of desegregation the following: reasonable bus transportation, reasonable grouping of noncontiguous zones, the reasonable movement toward the elimination of one-race schools, and the use of mathematical ratios of blacks and whites in the schools as a starting point toward racial desegregation. Thus, the nation's highest tribunal had ruled that school districts could transport students in an effort to implement different techniques for the purpose of desegregating their schools.

Brian L. Fife

Bibliography

Barrows, Frank. "School Busing: Charlotte, N.C." *The Atlantic* 230, no. 5 (1972). Assesses the school desegregation plan's impact on the citizens of Mecklenberg County during its implementation.

Fiss, Owen. "The Charlotte-Mecklenberg Case—Its Significance for Northern School Desegregation." *University of Chicago Law Review* 38 (1971). Argues that the *Swann* ruling was not relegated to Southern school systems, and that districts in the North would be affected as well.

Gaillard, Frye. *The Dream Long Deferred.* Chapel Hill: University of North Carolina Press, 1988. Gaillard, a reporter for the *Charlotte Observer*, documents the desegregation process in the Charlotte-Mecklenberg school district.

Goldstein, Robert D. "A *Swann* Song for Remedies: Equitable Relief in the Burger Court." *Harvard Civil Rights-Civil Liberties Law Review* 13 (1978). Surveys three principles that the Supreme Court has applied in its review of injunctions against state officers.

Schwartz, Bernard. *Swann's Way: The School Busing Case and the Supreme Court.* New York: Oxford University Press, 1986. In interviewing members of the Supreme Court and other principal personages, Schwartz provides an inside account of the Court's decision making in *Swann.*

Sweatt v. Painter

U.S. Supreme Court
Decided June 5, 1950

• This unanimous Supreme Court declared that the "separate but equal" standard established in *Plessy v. Ferguson* was unattainable in higher education.

Plessy v. Ferguson (1896) established the "separate but equal" doctrine that provided the legal justification for segregation.

Civil rights organizations, including the National Association for the Advancement of Colored People (NAACP), although opposed to "separate but equal," decided to use the courts in an attempt to make sure that the "equal" part of the "separate but equal" doctrine was being enforced. In a series of cases running from 1936 to the *Sweatt* decision in 1950, the NAACP attacked the lack of law schools and graduate programs for blacks throughout the South.

If no professional schools existed, clearly the "separate but equal" doctrine was not being met. When African Americans started seeking admission to professional schools throughout the South, many states established "overnight" law schools and professional schools in order to comply with *Plessy*. These schools were certainly separate, but were they equal? Herman Sweatt, a Houston, Texas, postal worker, applied to admission to the University of Texas Law School in 1946. He was denied admission on the grounds that Texas had just created a law school for blacks. To avoid integration, Texas had rented a few rooms in Houston and hired two black lawyers as its faculty.

Sweatt refused to attend the "black law school," saying that it was inferior and he would be deprived of the "equal protection of the law." A unanimous Supreme Court sided with Sweatt, whose case was argued by Thurgood Marshall of the NAACP. Even if the facilities at the two Texas schools were equal, the Court concluded that inequality might exist with respect to other factors "which make for greatness in a law school." Such factors include the reputation of the faculty and administration and the prestige of the alumni. "It is difficult to believe," said Chief Justice Fred M. Vinson, Jr., "that one who had a free choice between these law schools would consider the question close."

The Court ordered that Sweatt be admitted to the University of Texas Law School. The *Sweatt* case marked the first time the Supreme Court found a black professional school to be unequal in quality. Although the Court refused to reexamine *Plessy v. Ferguson*, the decision in *Sweatt* paved the way for the NAACP to launch a direct assault in overturning *Plessy* in *Brown v. Board of Education* only four years later.

Darryl Paulson

Tennessee v. Garner

U.S. SUPREME COURT
DECIDED MARCH 27, 1985

• This case significantly limited the power of police officers to use deadly force in effecting an arrest.

Most arrests do not entail problems, but occasionally the accused will resist arrest or flee. There are also occasions when law enforcement officers must make an instantaneous decision on the severity of any threat posed to the officers. The common law developed the rule that law enforcement officers could use all necessary and reasonable force, including deadly force, to arrest a suspected felon, regardless of whether the suspect committed an act of violence or posed a threat to the arresting officers.

The common-law rule became increasingly controversial during the 1960's and 1970's, but courts adhered to it. There were numerous objections of a constitutional, legal, and humanistic nature. The main objection was that, in essence, the rule allowed police officers to become judge, jury, and even executioner. Indeed, many jurisdictions which did not use capital punishment allowed officers to use deadly force through "fleeing felon" statutes modeled after the common law.

In *Tennessee v. Garner,* a fifteen-year-old boy, Edward Garner, broke a window and entered an unoccupied residence in suburban Memphis on the night of October 3, 1974. A neighbor called the police. Two police officers responded and intercepted the minor as he ran from the back of the house to a six-foot cyclone fence in the backyard. By shining a flashlight on the suspect, the officers could tell that the suspect was a youth and apparently unarmed. There was therefore no indication that the boy had committed a felony involving violence, nor did he pose an apparent threat to the officers' safety.

The suspect ignored the officers' directive to stop. Instead, he tried to escape. One officer took aim and fatally shot the suspect in the back as he climbed over the fence. The officer had acted in accordance with his training, the Tennessee fleeing felon statute, and police department policy. The deceased had ten dollars worth of money and jewelry in his possession stolen from the house.

The decedent's father brought suit against the officers, their superiors, and the city under the federal civil rights statute to recover damages for wrongful death caused by violation of the decedent's constitutional rights. The lawsuit was filed in federal court in a successful attempt to circumvent the common law. The Supreme Court overturned the common-law rule in a 6-3 decision. Justice Byron White delivered the majority opinion, which held that deadly force may be used to effectuate an arrest only in cases where it is necessary to prevent the escape of the suspect and the officer has probable cause to believe that the suspect poses a significant threat of death or serious physical injury to the officer or others.

The Court noted that most major police departments have forbidden the use of deadly force against nonviolent suspects. The practical effect of *Tennessee v. Garner* was that lawsuits involving wrongful death causes of action against state law enforcement officers will be brought in federal courts and will invoke federal constitutional law.

Denis Binder

Terry v. Ohio

U.S. SUPREME COURT
RULING ISSUED JUNE 10, 1968

- In this case, the Supreme Court ruled that, if an officer had reasonable suspicion that he was dealing with an armed individual, he could subject that person to a limited search of the outer clothing, a procedure sometimes known as "stop and frisk."

In October, 1963, veteran detective Martin McFadden observed suspicious activity by two men in a Cleveland business district. Suspecting a daylight robbery, McFadden approached John Terry and Richard Chilton and identified himself as a police officer. When his attempts to question the men on their activities were ignored, McFadden seized the two and patted down their outer clothing. Feeling a weapon on each, McFadden removed the guns and arrested the men for carrying concealed weapons. In a pretrial motion, Terry and Chilton contended that the guns were seized during an illegal search. The Court of Common Pleas overruled the motion and sentenced the men to three years. Chilton died before the case was appealed.

In June, 1968, the Supreme Court ruled 8 to 1 to uphold Terry's conviction. Writing for the majority, Chief Justice Earl Warren concluded that the issue at hand was "whether it is always unreasonable for a policeman to seize a person and subject him to a limited search for weapons unless there is probable cause for an arrest." In deciding this issue, the Court divided the case into the "seizure" and the "search." The decision defined a seizure as occurring any time a police officer restrains an individual's freedom to walk away.

Determining the constitutionality of the search required a balance between the Fourth Amendment's protection from unreasonable searches and seizures with the safety to the individuals involved. Warren concluded that a limited search was allowable if based on "specific reasonable inferences" drawn upon "the facts in the light of [the officer's] experience." In addition, the Court stipulated that "the issue is whether a reasonably prudent man in the circumstances would be warranted in the belief that his safety or that of others was in danger." Dissenting with the decision, Justice William O. Douglas looked to the legal differences between "probable cause" and "reasonable suspicion." Relying on the protection found in the Fourth Amendment, Douglas saw the search in question as an "infringement on personal liberty" because McFadden had no probable cause for arrest prior to the search.

Terry v. Ohio allowed a significant change in police procedures. It provided a police officer, once identified as such, with a legal right to perform a limited search of suspicious individuals by means of a protective pat-down. This provision helped to lower the number of injuries and deaths during initial confrontations between individuals and police officers. In addition, the police were authorized to seize any nonthreatening contraband, such as drugs or drug paraphernalia, found during a *Terry* search. Recognizing the potential for abuse in allowing "stop and frisk" actions by police, however, the Court was careful to outline the Fourth Amendment limitations that apply to stop and frisk searches. In *Sibron v. New York*, a companion case to *Terry*, the Court held that if the reason for the search is to find evidence rather than to check for weapons, then any evidence found is inadmissible.

Jennifer Davis

Texas v. Johnson

U.S. SUPREME COURT
DECIDED JUNE 21, 1989

• This decision affirmed that the First Amendment protects symbolic forms of expression, including the right to burn the U.S. flag as a political protest.

While the Republican National Convention was meeting in Dallas, Texas, in 1984, Gregory Lee Johnson participated in a political demonstration protesting policies of the Reagan administration and of certain Dallas-based corporations. In front of Dallas' city hall, Johnson doused an American flag with kerosene and set it on fire.

As the flag burned, protesters chanted, "America, the red, white, and blue, we spit on you." Several witnesses testified that they had been seriously offended, but no one was physically injured or threatened with injury. Following this demonstration, a witness collected the flag's remains and buried them in his back yard. Johnson was then charged with the desecration of a venerated object in violation of the Texas penal code. He was convicted, sentenced to a year in prison, and fined two thousand dollars. A district appeals court affirmed Johnson's conviction; however, Texas' Court of Criminal Appeals then reversed the lower court decisions. Finally, the U.S. Supreme Court affirmed the reversal, by a 5-4 vote.

Associate Justice William J. Brennan, Jr., joined by justices Thurgood Marshall, Harry Blackmun, Antonin Scalia, and Anthony Kennedy, wrote the majority opinion. Brennan noted that the First Amendment protects "expressive conduct" as well as written and spoken words. While a state can prevent "imminent lawless action," Johnson's symbolic expression of dissatisfaction with government policies did not lead to a disturbance of the peace and did not threaten the state's interest in maintaining order. Instead, Johnson's expression was

Shortly after becoming chief justice in 1986, William Rehnquist issued a strong dissent in the case of *Texas v. Johnson*, arguing that the national flag deserved special protection. *(Supreme Court Historical Society)*

restricted because of the content of his message.

"If there is a bedrock principle underlying the First Amendment," Brennan observed, "it is that the Government may not prohibit the expression of an idea simply because society finds the idea itself offensive or disagreeable." Toleration of Johnson's criticism reinforces the freedom that the flag represents. Brennan continued, "the way to preserve the flag's special role is not to punish those who feel differently about such matters. It is to persuade them that they are wrong. . . . We can imagine no more appropriate response to burning a flag than waving one's own, no better way to counter a flag burner's message than by saluting the flag that burns."

In a dissenting opinion joined by justices Byron White and Sandra Day O'Connor, Chief Justice William H. Rehnquist emphasized the unique role of the flag and the "profoundly offensive" nature of Johnson's conduct. In a separate dissent, Justice John P. Stevens argued that Johnson was prosecuted not for his criticism of government policies but for the method he chose to express his views.

Public outcries against this Court decision led to enactment of the federal Flag Protection Act. However, in *United States v. Eichman* (1990), the Supreme Court reaffirmed *Texas v. Johnson* by ruling that Congress was improperly trying to suppress expression because of its communicative impact.

Joseph A. Melusky

Thornburgh v. American College of Obstetricians and Gynecologists

U.S. SUPREME COURT
DECIDED JUNE 11, 1986

- The Court upheld a woman's right to abortion, striking down a number of provisions that would have limited that right and placed restrictions on physicians.

In June, 1982, Pennsylvania enacted the Abortion Control Act, which placed severe restrictions on access to abortion. Before signing an abortion consent form, a woman had to read, or hear read, material about abortion alternatives, stages of fetal development, and psychological and physical harm that abortion might cause. Physicians were required to file extensive information about the women on whom they performed abortions and provide criteria by which fetal viability was determined in each case. A second physician was required to attest fetal viability. Additionally, physicians were required to use the abortion method that best protected the viability of the fetus. Failure to comply was a third-degree felony.

Following passage, a case was filed with the U.S. Court of Appeals, Third Circuit, by the American College of Obstetricians and Gynecologists against the state of Pennsylvania, represented by Governor Richard Thornburgh. This court ruled against all the major restrictions, citing earlier Supreme Court decisions. Pennsylvania then filed an appeal with the Supreme Court. Opponents of abortion were hopeful that an increasingly conservative Court would use this case to overturn the major provisions of *Roe v. Wade* (1973).

The Supreme Court, by a 5-4 majority, upheld the findings of the appeals court. The consent requirements were deemed an attempt to persuade women to change their minds, not to provide necessary information for informed consent. The restrictions placed on physicians were ruled as impinging on the doctor-patient relationship and limiting physicians' professional judgment. Restricting the method of abortion was viewed as giving fetal rights priority over the health and well-being of the mother. The Court did reaffirm the states' right to intervene on behalf of the fetus, but only during the last trimester of pregnancy. It also invoked the concept of *stare decisis* (let past decisions stand) in affirming a woman's right to abortion. It argued that constant reinterpretation of the law undermines societal stability.

The dissenting minority questioned the fundamental right to abortion, arguing that no such right is found in the Constitution. It declared its belief that *Roe v. Wade* had gone too far in affirming a woman's right to privacy, arguing that fetal rights should be strengthened. These issues have continued to be part of the public debate surrounding abortion and have reappeared in other state laws and cases brought before the Supreme Court. The narrow majority decision in this case continues to generate hope among abortion opponents that continued challenges will eventually result in strict and severe limitations being placed on abortion.

Charles L. Kammer

Tilton v. Richardson

U.S. SUPREME COURT

DECIDED OCTOBER 12, 1971

- The Court held that it is constitutional for the federal government to provide grants to private sectarian colleges for the construction of academic buildings used solely for secular purposes.

The Higher Education Facilities Act of 1963 provided private colleges, both religious and secular, with federal grants and loans to construct academic buildings. The subsidized buildings were not to be used for religious instruction or worship for at least twenty years, but one section of the act allowed buildings to be used for any purpose after that period. The act was administered by the commissioner of education, and the commissioner required institutions receiving grants to provide assurances that the religious restrictions would be observed.

Eleanor Tilton and other taxpayers filed suit in a federal district court against the federal officials who administered the act, charging that grants to four church-related colleges in Connecticut were a violation of the establishment clause of the First Amendment. After the district court dismissed the complaint, the taxpayers appealed their suit to the U.S. Supreme Court.

The Court ruled 5 to 4 to uphold the provisions of the 1963 law that allowed religious colleges and universities to obtain federal funding for buildings used only for secular instruction, but the Court found that the part of the law ending the ban on religious practices after twenty years to be an unconstitutional contribution to a religious body. In defending the major portion of the law, Chief Justice Warren Burger wrote that the crucial question was not whether the law provided some benefit to a religious institution but whether the primary effect of the law was to advance religion.

In making a distinction between the 1963 law and cases in which the Court had ruled against state subsidies to primary and secondary schools, Burger argued that church-related colleges were not dealing with impressionable children, that the colleges under consideration did not have religious indoctrination as one of their substantial purposes, that buildings were themselves religiously neutral with little need for government surveillance, and that onetime grants required only minimal inspection. Cumulatively, Burger concluded that these factors lessened the potential for the grants to cause divisive religious fragmentation. He did acknowledge, however, that it might be unconstitutional for government to provide grants to a college which had religious indoctrination as one of its primary missions.

Since first dealing with the issue in *Everson v. Board of Education* (1947), the Court has had a difficult time interpreting the establishment clause in its relationship to governmental assistance to students attending religious schools. Sometimes the Court has supported the strict separationist view, which is suspicious of even indirect aid to religious education, while in other cases the Court has tended to promote accommodation and emphasize neutrality. The *Tilton* decision indicated that the Court was willing to allow an extreme accommodationist position when the case involved religious colleges and universities.

Thomas T. Lewis

Times Film Corp. v. City of Chicago

U.S. Supreme Court

Decided March 20, 1961

- This case upheld the principle of prior restraint on films, thereby continuing a pattern of treating film differently than other media.

The controversy surrounding this court case arose after the Times Film Corporation, a foreign-film importer and distributor, applied for a permit to show the Austrian film, *Don Juan* (1956), an adaptation of Wolfgang Amadeus Mozart's opera *Don Giovanni*. While the film contained no obscenities or sexual scenes, Chicago's municipal code required that films be submitted for censorship review along with applications before they could be publicly shown. The import company did not submit the film, claiming that the city's censorship statute was "null and void on constitutional grounds." They further stated that content of the film should not be subjected to censorship and if the city objected to the film, criminal process should not be brought against it until after *Don Juan* had been shown. The city denied them the permit because of the corporation's refusal to submit the film.

The film company filed suit in federal district court, asking that the film be permitted to be shown without prior censorship review, arguing that having a censor review films "amounted to a prior restraint on freedom of expression prohibited by the First and Fourteenth Amendments." The city argued that it could not protect the citizens of Chicago against "dangers of obscenity" if prior viewing and censorship were not permitted. The district court dismissed the case and an appeals court upheld the decision.

The Times Film Corporation's lawyers then petitioned the Supreme Court, which agreed to hear the case. The case was unusual in that most suits were filed because films submitted for review had been refused due to the content. The lawyers argued against permitting censorship prior to the film's viewing. In the Court's ensuing 5-4 decision, Justice Tom C. Clark said that the prior restraint in submitting a film did not violate the First Amendment. Chief Justice Earl Warren, one of the dissenting justices, warned that other forms of censorship on "newspapers, journals, books, magazines, television, radio or public speeches" might be invoked as a result of this decision. He also stated that the censor in offering judgment of the film's content does not have obligations to the public but to those who have hired him.

Marilyn Elizabeth Perry

Tinker v. Des Moines Independent Community School District

U.S. SUPREME COURT

DECIDED FEBRUARY 24, 1969

- In this case, the Supreme Court decided that students attending public junior high and high school have a constitutional right to express their opinions on important public policy issues as long as they do not materially disrupt the school's educational program while doing so.

In December, 1965, several students met at one of their homes and agreed to wear black armbands to their respective schools to demonstrate their opposition to the war in Vietnam. School authorities, upon learning of the students' plans, adopted a policy requiring the suspension of any student who wore an armband to school and refused to remove it. Five students wore black armbands to school and were suspended from class and sent home when they refused to obey the school's policy. Three of these students and their parents filed suit in federal district court on the grounds that the suspension of the students violated their First Amendment rights to freedom of speech. The district court dismissed their complaint, and the Court of Appeals for the Eighth Circuit affirmed that decision.

The Supreme Court by a vote of 7 to 2 reversed the decision of the lower court. In ringing terms, the Court declared that students and teachers do not "shed their constitutional rights to freedom of speech or expression at the schoolhouse gate." The Court was particularly concerned that the school authorities permitted students to wear other political symbols to class without sanction but had determined to discipline only those students who wore armbands to protest the Vietnam War. This kind of regulatory discrimination against a specific viewpoint of speech directly challenged the most basic of free speech principles: Government cannot prohibit the expression of one opinion while allowing other points of view to be openly debated.

Despite its endorsement of the free speech rights of students in *Tinker*, the Court was careful not to undermine the legitimate authority of school officials. The majority opinion of Justice Abe Fortas made it clear that while students had a constitutionally protected right to express their beliefs at school, their freedom of speech was not unlimited in its scope. Student expressive activities could be appropriately regulated to prevent any disturbance of the school's educational programs.

The First Amendment did not protect disruptive speech or expression that impinged on the rights of other students. In the case before it, however, there was no evidence that the passive wearing of armbands caused disruption or interfered with school activities. The Court rejected the argument that the speculative concerns of school officials, who feared that a protest against the Vietnam War might prove disorderly, constituted a sufficient basis for forbidding the students' speech. "In our system," Justice Fortas wrote, "undifferentiated fear or apprehension of disturbance is not enough to overcome the right to freedom of expression."

The primary holding in *Tinker* is that bedrock principles of freedom of speech apply to public school students. No case prior to *Tinker* had stated this rule as forcefully or as clearly. The Court's decision in *Tinker* did not purport to resolve all the conflicts that might arise between student speakers and school authorities. Subsequent decisions have demonstrated, for example, that when student speech is part of the school's educational program and bears the imprimatur of the school, officials have the discretion to regulate nondisruptive expression on the grounds that it does not further the school's educational goals.

Alan E. Brownstein

Tison v. Arizona

U.S. SUPREME COURT

DECIDED APRIL 21, 1987

• In this case, the Supreme Court created a flexible standard for applying the death penalty to felony-murder accomplices who demonstrate reckless disregard for human life even though they do not directly participate in killing a victim.

On July 30, 1978, brothers Donny, age twenty-one, Ricky, age twenty, and Raymond Tison, age nineteen, smuggled guns into the Arizona State Prison and helped in the escape of their father Gary, a convicted murderer, and another convicted murderer. The group changed cars and made their escape on a desert highway. When they had a flat tire, they flagged down a passing car containing young parents, a baby, and a teenage cousin and held the family at gunpoint. Gary Tison ordered his sons to load their possessions into the young family's car. As the brothers loaded the car and pushed their own disabled car into the desert, their father and the other prison escapee brutally murdered the entire family, including the baby, with shotgun blasts at close range. The escaping group traveled for several more days before encountering a police roadblock. During the ensuing shootout, Donny was killed, Gary escaped into the desert but soon died from exposure, and Ricky, Raymond, and the other convict were captured.

As accomplices to the killing of the young family, Ricky and Raymond Tison were charged with felony murder. When they were sentenced to death, they appealed their sentences based on a Supreme Court decision (*Enmund v. Florida*, 1982) which had declared that felony-murder accomplices cannot be sentenced to death if they do not directly participate in the actual killing. After the Arizona Supreme Court upheld the sentences, the Tisons took their case to the U.S. Supreme Court.

In a 5-4 decision, the U.S. Supreme Court created a flexible standard for imposing the death penalty. The Court declared that felony-murder accomplices could receive the death penalty if they demonstrated "reckless disregard for human life," even if they did not directly participate in the killing. The justices used this new standard to uphold the capital sentences imposed on the Tisons because they viewed the brothers' active involvement in supplying weapons to convicted murderers and kidnapping the young family as a demonstration of "reckless disregard."

In *Tison v. Arizona* the Supreme Court gave state prosecutors greater flexibility to seek the death penalty against accomplices who participate in crimes that result in homicides. This new flexibility came at the price of greater inconsistency in the application of capital punishment. Under the prior rule, it was relatively clear which offenders were eligible for the death penalty, based on their direct participation in a killing. By contrast, under the *Tison* rule, jurors and judges applying the vague "reckless indifference" standard have broad opportunities to impose capital punishment based on their negative feelings toward the accomplice or their revulsion at the crime without precise consideration of the defendant's actual participation.

Christopher E. Smith

United Steelworkers of America v. Weber

U.S. SUPREME COURT

DECIDED JUNE 27, 1979

• The Court ruled that an employer could establish voluntary programs of racial preference, including quotas, in order to eliminate manifest racial imbalance, even without evidence that the employer was guilty of discrimination.

Title VII of the Civil Rights Act of 1964 made it illegal "to discriminate against any individual because of his race, color, religion, sex, or national origin." Within a few years, federal agencies began to use "racial imbalance" as *prima facie* evidence of invidious discrimination, and they encouraged employers to use numerical goals, timetables, and sometimes quotas to promote minority participation in areas of employment where they had been traditionally underrepresented. The Kaiser Corporation's plant in Gramercy, Louisiana, found that while African Americans made up 39 percent of the local workforce, they occupied fewer than 2 percent of the craft positions in the plant. Fearing that this imbalance might jeopardize government contracts, the corporation and the labor union agreed to a "voluntary" affirmative action plan that included a special training program for craft positions. Admission to the training program was based on seniority, except that half the positions were reserved for African Americans even if they had less seniority.

Brian Weber, a white employee with five years of experience, was disappointed when he was not admitted into the program while two black employees with less seniority did gain admission. He sued both the company and the union with the argument that he was a victim of discrimination in violation of the 1964 Civil Rights Act. After Weber prevailed in both the district court and the court of appeals, the union petitioned the U.S. Supreme Court to review the judgments.

The Court voted 5 to 2 to reverse the lower courts' decision and to uphold the affirmative action program at the Gramercy plant. Writing for the majority, Justice William J. Brennan looked to the spirit rather than the literal wording of Title VII. Since the purpose of the law was to advance employment opportunities for members of racial minorities, he reasoned that the law did not prohibit preferences as a means of integrating minorities into the mainstream of American society. The program, moreover, did not "unnecessarily trammel" the interests of Weber; it was only a "temporary measure" to stop when a target was reached. Further, it had the limited goal of ending "a manifest racial imbalance." Finally, Brennan noted that if the Court had "misperceived" the intent of Congress, the decision could be corrected easily by legislative action.

In a strongly worded dissent, Justice William H. Rehnquist proclaimed that "no racial discrimination in employment is permissible under Title VII." Noting the explicit wording of the law, he also quoted extensively from the congressional debates to show that the framers of Title VII envisioned a law allowing no preference based on race or gender.

The *Weber* decision was one of the Court's most controversial cases to deal with the question of "reverse discrimination." Supporters of race-conscious remedies for past societal discrimination were delighted that the Court did not apply the strict scrutiny test to an affirmative action program that involved racial preference and quotas. In later cases the justices would continue to be divided over the issue of *Weber*; they would tend to alternate between approving and disapproving affirmative action programs.

Thomas T. Lewis

Village of Skokie v. National Socialist Party of America

ILLINOIS SUPREME COURT
RULING ISSUED JANUARY 27, 1978

- The *Skokie* decision upheld a broad interpretation of free speech, declaring that the promotion of even as odious an ideology as Nazism is protected by the First Amendment.

Frank Collin, a neo-Nazi leader of the National Socialist Party of America (NSPA), sought permission to hold an NSPA demonstration in Marquette Park, a white neighborhood of Chicago. The city, fearing a repeat of riots and racial assaults which had occurred during the previous three summers, used various legal devices to deny the Nazi Party a parade permit. Collin met or circumvented those requirements, until ultimately the city required a $250,000 bond to pay for any damages which might arise from the parade. The American Civil Liberties Union (ACLU) helped Collin challenge the city's requirement in federal court.

While the Marquette case was being litigated, Collin decided to move his demonstration to the village of Skokie, a largely Jewish suburb whose citizens include several thousand survivors of the Holocaust. Like Marquette Park, Skokie tried to stop Collin's group from demonstrating, securing from the Cook County Circuit Court an injunction against the NSPA. Skokie also quickly passed several ordinances which restricted the granting of parade permits through strict insurance bond requirements, a prohibition on the display of certain military uniforms, and a prohibition on the dissemination of material promoting or inciting racial or religious hatred. Thus there were two issues to be contested: the ordinances and the injunction.

In *Village of Skokie v. National Socialist Party of America*, the Illinois Supreme Court invalidated the injunction on First

Amendment grounds, finding that there were not adequate grounds for the prior restraint of the NSPA's symbolic speech. Invoking *Cohen v. California* (1971), the Court rejected Skokie's claim that the symbols of the NSPA, including the swastika, amounted to "fighting words" which were not protected speech. The issue of the ordinances was decided by the U.S. district court in *Collin v. Smith*, which also held in favor of the NSPA. That ruling was upheld upon appeal to the U.S. appeals court.

Despite Collin's legal successes, various Jewish and other groups from around the country threatened to block the planned Nazi march on Skokie. As Collin considered his options, the federal district court in Chicago, obviously heeding the *Skokie* decision, ruled in *Collin v. O'Malley* (1978) that Collin be granted the original parade permit for Marquette Park without the bond requirement. Collin moved the demonstration back to Marquette Park.

The *Skokie* decision (along with *Collin v. Smith* and *Collin v. O'Malley*) reflected a firm commitment to a broad interpretation of free speech. Although the U.S. Supreme Court in earlier years had noted that free speech is not a limitless right (as in the case of "fighting words" against specific individuals), in these cases the federal and state courts refused to find hateful speech directed against a general group (in this case, Jews) to be unprotected.

Steve D. Boilard

Wallace v. Jaffree

U.S. SUPREME COURT
DECIDED JUNE 4, 1985

• The Court ruled against a state law permitting a moment of silence for "meditation or voluntary prayer" in the public schools, based on the law's sectarian intent.

In 1978, the Alabama legislature authorized a one-minute period of silence to begin each school day in the public schools, and about half of the states in the 1970's passed similar laws. Many citizens, especially in the South, wanted public schools also to conduct oral prayer activities. In 1981, the Alabama legislature specified that the period of silence could be used "for meditation or voluntary prayer," and the next year the legislature ignored Supreme Court precedents and authorized teachers to lead willing students in a vocal prayer.

Ishmael Jaffree, an outspoken humanist of Mobile County, became angry when teachers of his minor children conducted prayer activities, with peer ridicule for those not participating. After local officials refused to stop the practice, Jaffree filed a complaint in federal court against various officials, including Governor George Wallace. The complaint challenged the constitutionality of the 1981 and 1982 laws. Although the district court ruled against Jaffree, based on the argument that the Supreme Court had been mistaken in 1947 when it made the establishment clause applicable to the states, the court of appeals reversed the judgment and found that the two laws were unconstitutional because they advanced and encouraged religious activities.

The U.S. Supreme Court unanimously affirmed the unconstitutionality of the 1982 law allowing vocal prayers, and the Court voted 6 to 3 to strike down the 1981 law allowing a moment of silence for meditation or prayer. Writing the majority opinion, Justice John Paul Stevens focused all of his attention on the 1981 law. Failing to find any secular motive behind the law, Stevens argued that the expression "meditation or voluntary prayer" indicated the legislature's desire to "endorse prayer as a favored practice," and he quoted the sponsor as introducing the bill as "an effort to return voluntary prayer to our public schools." Stevens found no problem with the simple moment of silence as enacted in the law of 1978.

In a long and vigorous dissent, Justice William H. Rehnquist reviewed the history of the establishment clause and rejected the idea that the clause required a "wall of separation between church and state." He concluded that the Framers intended only to prevent a national establishment of religion and to prohibit federal preference for one religion over another. Chief Justice Warren Burger's dissent emphasized that only two years earlier, in *Marsh v. Chambers* (1983), the Court had relied on history to allow oral prayers in legislative sessions. He wrote that to treat prayer as a step toward an established religion "borders on, if it does not trespass, the ridiculous." The dissenters did not reject the idea that the establishment clause applied to the states through the Fourteenth Amendment.

In the *Jaffree* decision, the Court went rather far in insisting on neutrality between religion and secularism in the public schools. The majority of the Court made it clear that a moment of silence was acceptable so long as schools did not encourage students to use the time for religious activity. In 1992 the Court would again deal with the issue of state-encouraged prayer in *Weisman v. Lee*, ruling that invocations and benedictions at public school graduation ceremonies violated the First Amendment.

Thomas T. Lewis

Wards Cove Packing Co. v. Atonio

U.S. Supreme Court

Ruling issued June 5, 1989

• This decision threatened to narrow the scope of the law against employment discrimination sharply.

Five salmon canneries, owned by Wards Cove Packing Company and Castle & Cooke, recruited seasonal labor for the peak of the fishing season at remote areas in Alaska. Unskilled cannery workers were recruited from Alaska Natives in the region and through the Seattle local of the International Longshoreman's and Warehouseman's Union; two-thirds of these employees were either Alaska Natives or Filipino Americans, including Frank Atonio and twenty-one other plaintiffs.

Higher-paid on-site noncannery support staff, including accountants, boat captains, chefs, electricians, engineers, managers, and physicians, were recruited from company offices in Oregon and Washington, largely by word of mouth; some 85 percent of these employees were white. For all employees, the companies provided race-segregated eating and sleeping facilities.

Plaintiff cannery workers, who believed that they were qualified to hold support staff positions but were never selected for these higher-paying jobs, filed suit in 1974 against the companies under Title VII of the Civil Rights Act of 1964. Their argument was based on statistics that showed ethnic differences in the two classes of workers, cannery versus noncannery. In addition to evidence of segregated company housing, they asserted disparate treatment and adverse impact arguments regarding criteria and procedures used to screen them out. Among these criteria, they claimed that there were preferences for relatives of existing employees (nepotism), rehire preferences, English language requirements, failure to promote from within, and a general lack of objective screening and selection criteria. The procedures to which they objected were separate hiring channels and word-of-mouth recruitment rather than open postings of job opportunities.

Justice Byron White delivered the opinion of a divided Court (the vote was 5-4). According to the majority, the comparison between ethnic groups in the two types of jobs was irrelevant because they were drawn from different labor market pools. The Court then went beyond the case to assert that a statistical difference between ethnic groups does not give *prima facie* evidence of discrimination under Title VII unless intent to discriminate is proved. To provide that proof, plaintiffs must show that specific criteria, even vague and subjective criteria, statistically account for the difference. Moreover, an employer may defend criteria that have been proved to account for the difference if they are "reasoned."

The decision had a deleterious impact on efforts to redress employment discrimination, as it reversed the broad language of *Griggs v. Duke Power Co.* (1971) by requiring proof of intent, by allowing the use of separate hiring channels, and by no longer insisting that employers must prove that biased hiring criteria are absolutely essential for job performance. Congress responded by passing the Civil Rights Act of 1991, which codified the original *Griggs* ruling into law.

Michael Haas

Washington v. Davis

U.S. Supreme Court

Decided June 7, 1976

- The Supreme Court held that evidence of the disparate impact of challenged employment practices is insufficient to prove discrimination.

African American members of the Washington, D.C., Metropolitan Police Department, as well as unsuccessful applicants to the department, sued the department, claiming that its hiring and promotion policies were racially discriminatory. In particular, they cited a written test that a disproportionately high number of blacks failed. The district court found for the police department, but the appellate court, relying on the Supreme Court precedent of *Griggs v. Duke Power Co.* (1971), reversed that decision, finding the disparate impact of the test to be evidence of employment discrimination. When *Washington v. Davis* came before the Supreme Court, however, Justice Byron White's opinion for the Court stated unequivocally that evidence of discriminatory purpose must be present for such tests to be found unconstitutional. The lower appellate court was reversed.

Griggs had been a landmark employment discrimination case which made disparate impact the test for employment discrimination under Title VII of the 1964 Civil Rights Act. In *Washington*, however, the plaintiffs were claiming that the police department's employment practices violated their right to equal protection under the due process clause of the Fifth Amendment. The standards for determining discrimination proscribed under Title VII were not, said the Court, the same as those applied to a claim of unconstitutional racial discrimination, which requires some evidence of intent to discriminate. Here, the Court found, the personnel test at issue was neutral on its face; in addition, it was rationally related to a legitimate purpose: improving employees' communications skills.

The Court indicated that intent to discriminate could be inferred from a totality of circumstances, including disparate impact, but it declined to spell out a more precise test for unconstitutional employment discrimination. In fact, the majority opinion confused the issue. As Justice John Paul Stevens indicates in his concurring opinion, disparate impact and discriminatory purpose are often indistinguishable. When disparate impact becomes proof of discriminatory purpose, the two standards are conflated. Furthermore, by augmenting the consequences of past discrimination, employment policies not intended to be discriminatory can produce results identical to those resulting from conspicuously discriminatory ones.

The test for what constitutes evidence of discriminatory intent was left indeterminate until the Supreme Court strengthened it in *Personnel Administrator of Massachusetts v. Feeney* (1979) to the advantage of employers. In *Feeney*, the Court held that even if discriminatory results of a prospective statute are foreseeable at the time it is passed by the legislature, it is only unconstitutional if these results constitute the reason for passage. The consequences for subsequent civil rights litigants pressing discrimination suits against state employers were profound.

Lisa Paddock

Webster v. Reproductive Health Services

U.S. SUPREME COURT
RULING ISSUED JULY 3, 1989

- In this case, the Supreme Court confirmed the basic principles of *Roe v. Wade* with regard to a woman's right to abortion but significantly expanded the ability of the states to regulate abortion, at least partially eroding the intent of *Roe v. Wade*.

In June of 1986, the state of Missouri passed into law a statute which amended existing state laws regarding abortion. The following month, several health care professionals brought a class-action suit challenging the constitutionality of five provisions of the new law. These were (1) the pronouncement by the state legislature that life begins at conception, (2) the connected pronouncement that unborn children have a legally protectable right to life, (3) mandatory viability tests prior to abortions after twenty or more weeks of pregnancy, (4) prohibition against public facilities and personnel performing abortions except to save the life of the mother, and (5) prohibition against public funds or personnel being used to counsel women to have an abortion except in life-threatening situations. *Amicus curiae* briefs were submitted by the federal government not only supporting the Missouri law but also arguing that *Roe v. Wade* (1973), which had established constitutionally protected abortion rights, should be overturned altogether.

The Court responded in a divided and complex way. Provisions (1) and (2) were taken to be abstract theoretical constructs without legal consequence, and thus to be beyond the interests of the court. By a narrow 5-4 vote, the Court upheld the Missouri law (reversing district and appeals court decisions). Four of the majority justices believed that this decision effectively overturned or at least fundamentally altered the impact of *Roe v. Wade*. The fifth, Sandra Day O'Connor, supported the right of Missouri to regulate abortion in the ways listed above but opined that such a decision did not fundamentally disturb *Roe v. Wade*. Thus *Roe v. Wade* was upheld, also by a 5-4 vote, with O'Connor providing the fifth vote for each majority.

The Court's decision preserved a basic right to abortion for the first two trimesters of pregnancy but also gave the states considerable leeway in regulating abortions. This had two cross-cutting effects. Other states passed laws similar to Missouri's and included new provisions such as parental notification for minors, which the Court approved as long as they included a process for permitting exceptions where appropriate.

On the other hand, abortion rights advocates now found it easier to organize "pro-choice" voters against "pro-life" candidates and, more specifically, against George Bush in the 1992 presidential election. Despite an attempt to moderate his views, Bush was beaten in 1992 partly by voters who feared that the next Bush Supreme Court appointee would further erode or overturn *Roe v. Wade*. New president Bill Clinton appointed two pro-choice justices within his first two years in office.

Ira Smolensky

Weeks v. Southern Bell

U.S. COURT OF APPEALS FOR THE FIFTH CIRCUIT
DECIDED MARCH 4, 1969

• This opinion by a federal appeals court strictly interpreted the Civil Rights Act of 1964 with regard to the prohibition of discrimination in employment based on sex, thus opening many jobs to women.

In 1966, Lorena W. Weeks, an employee of Southern Bell for nineteen years, applied for the job of switchman. Her employer refused to consider her application, stating that the decision had been made that women would not be employed as switchmen.

Weeks responded by filing a complaint with the Equal Employment Opportunity Commission (EEOC) stating that the refusal to hire women as switchmen violated the Civil Rights Act of 1964. An investigation by the EEOC indicated that Weeks might have a valid claim of discrimination based on sex.

Southern Bell argued that the job of switchman was an exception to the law because it required the lifting of heavy objects and emergency work. The Court responded that Southern Bell had not proven the position to be an exception to the law. While "men are stronger on average than women," the court stated, "it is not clear that any conclusions about relative lifting ability would follow." The Court ruled that many women are capable of performing the duties of a switchman.

Donald C. Simmons, Jr.

Weeks v. United States

U.S. Supreme Court
Decided February 24, 1914

• In order to enforce the privacy values of the Fourth Amendment, the Court ordered that illegally obtained evidence must be excluded from criminal trials in federal courts; this order is commonly called the "exclusionary rule".

After Fremont Weeks was arrested for illegally sending lottery tickets through the U.S. mail service, a federal marshal accompanied by a police officer, without a search warrant, broke into Weeks's private home and seized incriminating evidence. Although the defendant argued that the search and seizure contradicted the requirements of the Fourth Amendment, the resulting evidence was used to convict him in a federal district court. Weeks appealed his case to the Supreme Court.

Until the *Weeks* decision, American courts had followed the common-law practice of allowing federal prosecutors to use evidence unlawfully seized by law enforcement officers. Many constitutional scholars had argued that the traditional practice encouraged governmental violations of liberties guaranteed in the Constitution, and they insisted that it was inconsistent with the Fourth Amendment's purpose of treating people's houses as their castles.

Based on this point of view, the Supreme Court in *Boyd v. United States* (1886) criticized and implicitly rejected the common-law practice, but the Court stopped short of explicitly ruling the inadmissibility of evidence obtained illegally. The *Boyd* pronouncements on privacy values, without any means of enforcement, appeared to have no impact on the behavior of those who enforced the laws.

In *Weeks* an impatient Court unanimously required federal courts thereafter to apply the exclusionary rule in all criminal prosecutions. In the official opinion, Justice William Day declared that without the exclusionary rule, the Fourth Amendment was of "no value" and "might as well be stricken from the Constitution." The noble goal of punishing the guilty must not be used as an excuse to sacrifice the "fundamental rights" established by the Constitution. Day's opinion did not clearly articulate whether the application of the exclusionary rule was an individual right guaranteed by the Constitution or whether it was simply a judicial device developed to prevent unreasonable searches and seizures. Although these two views would continue to be debated by the Court, most justices have accepted Day's conclusion that the exclusionary rule is the only practical means of requiring government to conform to constitutional rules.

The immediate impact of the *Weeks* decision was limited, because it did not apply to state courts where most criminal prosecutions took place. When the Court ruled that the Fourth Amendment was binding on the states in *Wolf v. Colorado* (1949), the Court did not require states to follow the exclusionary rule, and until *Elkins v. United States* (1960), the so-called silver platter doctrine permitted federal prosecutors to make use of evidence illegally seized by agents of the states. Finally, in *Mapp v. Ohio* (1961), the Supreme Court required the application of the exclusionary rule in state courts. The exclusionary rule has always been controversial, for it sometimes makes it more difficult to prosecute criminals. Critics argue that there are alternative means of protecting the rights of the Fourth Amendment, but defenders reply that the alternatives do not provide effective protection.

Thomas T. Lewis

Wesberry v. Sanders

U.S. SUPREME COURT
RULING ISSUED FEBRUARY 17, 1964

• This decision required that congressional districts within a state be approximately equal in size.

The topic of representation in Congress and state legislatures—with the related issues of apportionment and districting—was long avoided by the federal courts. When in the 1946 case of *Colegrove v. Green* the Supreme Court was asked to consider the imbalance in size of congressional districts in Illinois (which had not been redistricted since 1901), it declined to enter "the political thicket" and said that such matters were the proper concern of legislative bodies. In 1929, Congress had stopped mandating that states redraw district lines after each census. The result was that by the 1960's there were substantial inequalities in the sizes of congressional (and state legislative) districts in many states, a situation that usually meant the decided overrepresentation of rural populations.

An important indication that change might be on the way came in the case of *Baker v. Carr* (1962). In this case the U.S. Supreme Court ruled that questions of apportionment and districting were within the jurisdiction of federal courts, effectively reversing the doctrine it had followed in the *Colegrove* case. The court took up the question directly when it agreed to hear *Wesberry v. Sanders*. This case had its origins in a class-action suit by voters in Fulton County, Georgia, who claimed that they were cheated of fair representation. They pointed out that their urban and suburban fifth district was approximately three times larger than the rural ninth district, though each was represented by one congressman. The Court upheld their challenge by a 7-2 majority. It based its decision on Article I, section 2 of the Constitution, which says that representatives should be chosen "by the People of the several States." The court interpreted this to mean that one person's vote should be equal to another's.

Wesberry was followed by other "reapportionment decisions." In *Reynolds v. Sims* (also 1964) the Court reached a similar conclusion with regard to state legislative districts (though grounding its decision here in the Fourteenth Amendment's equal protection clause).

By mandating equality in population among congressional districts, the Court brought a considerable shift in congressional representation and political power from rural areas to urban and—especially—suburban ones that would continue for the rest of the century. Other decisions had a similar effect at the state level, though the Court did tolerate greater differences in size among state legislative districts than among congressional districts. Once established, the doctrine of "one person, one vote" raised other questions, such as the extent to which racial and ethnic considerations should be factored into apportionment and districting.

William C. Lowe

West Coast Hotel Co. v. Parrish

U.S. SUPREME COURT
DECIDED MARCH 29, 1937

• In this case, the U.S. Supreme Court upheld a state minimum wage law and signaled the end of an era declaring many similar state laws unconstitutional on the basis of substantive due process.

The state of Washington enacted a minimum wage law for women in 1913. Elsie Parrish, a hotel chambermaid, sued her employer, the West Coast Hotel Company, for her minimum wage under the terms of the Washington law. She was seeking $14.50 for forty-eight hours of work. The Washington Supreme Court upheld the law, and the employer appealed to the U.S. Supreme Court. Chief Justice Charles Evans Hughes, writing for the narrow five-member majority, upheld the law under the U.S. Constitution's Fourteenth Amendment. The majority held that the protection of women workers was a legitimate end for the states to regulate. Further, a minimum wage for women provides for their subsistence and is a permissible means for the state to achieve the desired end.

This decision reversed several earlier cases which had declared similar state statutes unconstitutional under the Lochner doctrine. This doctrine was generally based on the Court's 1905 decision in *Lochner v. New York*, which struck down a New York maximum hours law as unconstitutional. The Lochner doctrine applied the Fourteenth Amendment due process clause to invalidate state legislation under the grounds of substantive due process. The Court had held state regulation of business activities to be an invasion of the fundamental freedom of individuals to enter into contracts of their own free choice. Such an argument was used many times to strike down state laws as unconstitutional that protected workers such as maximum hours laws.

The West Coast Hotel Company case is significant in that it was decided during the era of the "Court-packing plan" of President Franklin D. Roosevelt, during which the Court majority changed and reversed some of its earlier decisions. The *West Coast Hotel* decision vote by Justice Owen J. Roberts is cited as the "switch in time that saved nine" when he apparently changed his vote from his position in an earlier case. The Court then started to uphold many pieces of the Roosevelt administration's New Deal legislation and signaled the beginning of the modern era of judicial scrutiny of state and federal legislation.

Subsequently, the rationale of the Court has been criticized for relying too much on an argument that it is necessary to provide special protection to women in the workplace. In many early cases, during the period 1906-1937, courts had been willing to uphold legislation that characterized women as weaker and in need of more state protection. These laws have since generally given way to less sexually stereotypical laws that apply to all employees, not simply women.

Scott A. White

West Virginia State Board of Education v. Barnette

U.S. SUPREME COURT
DECIDED JUNE 14, 1943

- In an important recognition of freedom of conscience, the Supreme Court held in favor of Jehovah's Witnesses children who had refused to salute the flag and recite the Pledge of Allegiance at their public school.

On June 3, 1940, the Supreme Court decided *Minersville School District v. Gobitis* and upheld a state law requiring public school children to salute the flag and recite the Pledge of Allegiance. The Justices voted 8-1 to reject the argument by Jehovah's Witnesses children and their parents that they should be excused from the ceremony because of their religious beliefs.

Reaction to the ruling was highly critical among scholars and in the legal profession. Newspaper editorials disapproved of the outcome. Local school officials reacted enthusiastically, however, enacting similar provisions all across the country. The heightened sense of loyalty and patriotism during World War II contributed to public outrages against Jehovah's Witnesses, including physical attacks and torchings of their meeting halls.

The Board of Education of West Virginia resolved that the flag salute and the Pledge of Allegiance be a regular part of the school day and that refusal to participate be regarded as an act

The Court of Harlan F. Stone (center) in *Barnette* was notable in that several of its members openly admitted having made the wrong decision in the 1940 *Gobitis* case that *Barnette* reversed. *(Bachrach/Collection of the Supreme Court of the United States)*

of insubordination. Jehovah's Witnesses children were expelled in large numbers and threatened with being sent to reformatories; their parents were threatened with criminal prosecution for causing delinquency. In response, the parents brought suit in federal court. They explained that according to their religious belief the flag ceremony violated the Book of Exodus prohibition against bowing down before graven images.

The Supreme Court had changed by the time this case reached it. Justice James Byrnes had replaced Justice James McReynolds. Chief Justice Charles Evans Hughes had retired, and Justice Harlan Stone, who had dissented in *Gobitis*, was elevated to chief justice. Justice Robert H. Jackson was appointed to Stone's seat. Other justices simply changed their mind, perhaps affected by the almost universal condemnation of the decision and its aftermath of violence. Justices Hugo Black, William O. Douglas, and Frank Murphy took the unusual step of announcing in an intervening case that they now believed that *Gobitis* had been wrongly decided.

On Flag Day, Justice Jackson announced the 6-3 decision overruling *Gobitis*. His words are a stirring defense of the values of free speech and freedom of religion: "If there is any fixed star in our constitutional constellation, it is that no official, high or petty, can prescribe what shall be orthodox in politics, nationalism, religion, or other matters of opinion or force citizens to confess by word or act their faith therein." Justice Felix Frankfurter, who authored the *Gobitis* decision, wrote an eloquent dissent defending the principle of judicial self-restraint and urging deference to local elected leaders.

This landmark decision signaled the justices' new institutional willingness to intervene actively against majorities and state laws on behalf of minorities and civil liberties. It remains an important part of the First Amendment doctrine that protects free speech and free exercise of religion.

Thomas E. Baker

Wickard v. Filburn

U.S. Supreme Court
Decided November 9, 1942

- This case effectively eliminated the use of the interstate commerce clause of the Constitution as a restraint on federal authority.

Beginning in 1933, the federal government attempted to raise farm prices by measures intended to restrict output. After the Agricultural Adjustment Act of 1933 had been declared unconstitutional in 1936, Congress adopted the Agricultural Adjustment Act of 1938. The law authorized the secretary of agriculture to establish a national acreage allotment for wheat that would be translated into a permissible quota for each farmer. Farmers were given an opportunity to reject the national quota level in an annual referendum vote. Production in excess of the quota would incur a financial penalty.

Roscoe Filburn, an Ohio farmer, produced 239 bushels of wheat in excess of his allotment and was assessed a penalty of $117. He obtained an injunction from a federal district court against Secretary of Agriculture Claude Wickard. Filburn used much of his wheat output on his own farm, chiefly for feed and seed. He claimed that the government policy went beyond the boundaries of interstate commerce. He further argued that a speech by Wickard had misled farmers into supporting the quota in the referendum, and that the increase in penalties by a statutory amendment in May, 1941, was improper when applied to production already undertaken.

The Supreme Court rejected Filburn's claim and upheld federal authority. The contentions concerning Wickard's speech and the penalty increase, both of which had been accepted by the district court, were dismissed. As for the commerce clause, the Court noted its previous broad construction in *United States v. Darby Lumber Co.* (1941), upholding the federal minimum-wage law. They acknowledged that the 1938 law extended regulatory authority to production not entering commerce but being consumed on the farm. Such an extension was not improper: "[E]ven if appellee's activity be local and though it may not be regarded as commerce, it may still . . . be reached by Congress if it exerts a substantial economic effect on interstate commerce." Home-consumed production of wheat in the aggregate was a potentially important influence on the price of wheat. The propriety of such regulation was a political question, said the Court, rather than an issue of constitutionality.

Taking this decision and the *Darby* case in combination, the Supreme Court clearly served notice that it was not inclined to limit the scope of federal authority by reference to the commerce clause. Thus the doctrine of *United States v. E. C. Knight Co.* (1895), that "commerce succeeds to [that is, follows] manufacture, and is not a part of it," was put aside. It is probably not mere coincidence that the *Filburn* case came during World War II, which involved such extreme extensions of federal authority as the military draft and direct controls over wages and prices. The decisions in *Filburn* and *Darby* also removed obstacles to later extensions of federal authority into employment discrimination, health and safety, and environmental protection.

Paul B. Trescott

Wisconsin v. Mitchell

U.S. Supreme Court
Decided June 11, 1993

- This hate crime case was the first of its type to be heard by the U.S. Supreme Court; this landmark decision has opened the way for more extensive hate crime legislation, and it signals that such legislation will be upheld as constitutional by the court in most cases.

Following a showing of the 1988 film *Mississippi Burning*, several African American men and boys congregated at an apartment complex to talk about the film. After a discussion of a scene in the film in which a young African American boy is beaten by a white man, the accused, Todd Mitchell, asked those who joined him outside if they were ready to go after a white man.

Walking on the opposite side of the street and saying nothing, fourteen-year-old Gregory Riddick approached the complex. Mitchell selected three individuals from the group to go after Riddick. The victim was beaten, and his tennis shoes were stolen.

In a Kenosha, Wisconsin, trial court, Mitchell was convicted as a party to the crime of aggravated battery. By Wisconsin law, this crime carries a maximum prison sentence of two years. Mitchell's sentence was extended to four years, however, under a state statute commonly known as the "hate crimes" statute. This statute provides for sentence extensions if it can be determined that the victim was selected because of his or her race, religion, color, disability, sexual orientation, national origin, or ancestry.

Mitchell appealed his conviction and the extended sentence. His conviction was upheld by the court of appeals, but the Supreme Court of Wisconsin reversed the decision of the appellate court. Wisconsin's Supreme Court held that the "hate crimes" statute violated the defendant's First Amendment protection for freedom of speech because it was unconstitutionally overbroad and punished only what the state legislature found to be offensive. Moreover, the state Supreme Court believed that this statute would have a "chilling effect" on a citizen's freedom of speech; that is, a citizen would fear reprisal for actions which might follow the utterance of prejudiced or biased speech.

The U.S. Supreme Court reversed the state court's decision. Chief Justice William Rehnquist wrote the opinion in this unanimous decision. The Court held that Mitchell's First Amendment rights to free speech had not been violated. The Court pointed out that the statute was not aimed at speech but at conduct, which is not protected by the First Amendment. The Court also addressed the "chilling effect" of the statute, finding that such would not be the case and that the state Supreme Court's hypothesis was far too speculative to be entertained. This decision indicates that the Supreme Court appears ready to uphold legislation designed to enhance punishment for criminal acts based on bigotry and bias without making bigoted or biased speech itself a crime.

Donna Addkison Simmons

Wisconsin v. Yoder

U.S. SUPREME COURT

DECIDED MAY 15, 1972

- Balancing the state's interest in education against the freedom to exercise one's religion, the Supreme Court insisted that any governmental burden on this freedom must be justified by a compelling state interest.

Jonas Yoder and two other members of Amish churches were convicted and fined five dollars each for violating Wisconsin's compulsory school attendance law, which required children to attend school until the age of sixteen. Following their religious traditions, these Amish parents refused to send their children, ages fourteen and fifteen, to school beyond the eighth grade. The parents argued that the Wisconsin law violated their free exercise of religion, as protected by the First and Fourteenth Amendments. After the Wisconsin Supreme Court ruled in favor of the parents, the state of Wisconsin appealed to the U.S. Supreme Court.

The Court voted 6 to 1 (although Justice William Douglas' dissent was only in part) to uphold the position of the parents. Writing for the majority, Chief Justice Warren Burger began with the premise that the free exercise of religion was a fundamental right that could be overbalanced only by state interests of the "highest order." The Amish objected to formal education beyond the eighth grade because they believed that secondary education exposed children to "worldly" influences that tended to distance Amish youth from their religious community. According to traditions of almost three centuries, Burger stated, it was impossible to separate the Amish faith from a simple, nonsecular mode of life, and government institutions were prohibited from evaluating the desirability of particular religious beliefs.

Burger acknowledged that normally the state might enforce compulsory education laws because of the state's interest that children learn to become "self-sufficient participants in society." The Amish community, however, had a long-established system of informal vocational training that prepared children for life in an agrarian community. Burger indicated that nonreligious motivations would not justify exemption from school-attendance laws.

In a partial dissent, Justice Douglas argued that the issue was the religious freedom of the children rather than that of the parents. He insisted that exemption should not be granted until the children were asked if they wished a high-school education. The majority refused to consider this point, however, since only the parents were parties to litigation, and because of traditional rights of parents to control the religious education of their children.

Yoder was important as the Court's most advanced reaffirmation of the principles of *Sherbert v. Verner* (1963), requiring that states accommodate religious practices according to the dual criteria of the compelling state interest test and the least restrictive alternative test. In *Employment Division, Department of Human Resources of Oregon v. Smith* (1990), however, the Court adopted a more restrictive view of the right for legal exemption based on religious exercise.

Thomas T. Lewis

Witherspoon v. Illinois

U.S. SUPREME COURT

DECIDED JUNE 3, 1968

• In this groundbreaking decision, the Supreme Court decided that prospective jurors with reservations about the death penalty could not be excluded from service in a criminal proceeding.

The Sixth Amendment to the U.S. Constitution guarantees accused citizens the right to trial by an impartial jury of peers. This deceptively simple guarantee has come under fire in cases too numerous to mention. During the 1960's, many noteworthy cases advanced to the Supreme Court regarding the composition and unanimity of the jury in criminal cases. In 1968, the *Witherspoon* case compounded the jury-selection question with the issue of capital punishment.

Using an Illinois statute, the prosecution at William Witherspoon's murder trial in Cook County, Illinois, eliminated almost half of the potential jurors by challenging those who had reservations about their ability to impose a death sentence. This exclusion occurred without any determination of the level of reservation; that is, the potential jurors were excluded for any degree of uncertainty about imposition of a death sentence. The defendant, Witherspoon, appealed his case on the grounds that such a broad exclusion of jurors prevented him from being tried by an impartial jury as guaranteed in the Sixth Amendment. Witherspoon claimed that a jury absent of those opposed or at least uncertain about capital punishment would under no circumstances be impartial or representative of the community.

The Supreme Court agreed in a majority opinion written by Justice Potter Stewart. Witherspoon's death sentence was voided by the Court; however, his conviction was not overturned. The Court agreed with the defendant that a jury devoid of objectors to capital punishment was sure to be "woefully short" of the impartiality guaranteed by the Sixth Amendment and extended to the states under the Fourteenth Amendment. In the majority opinion, the Court stated that those prospective jurors who expressed a total disinclination toward ever imposing the death penalty could be excluded; however, persons who merely had reservations in the matter could not be excluded for their reservations alone.

The Court went on to state that juries must attempt to mirror the feelings of the community. In any given community there will be a certain number of people who are unsure of their feelings about capital punishment. This point of view should not be avoided in jury selection, the Court ruled, as inclusion of such undecided jurors will insure neutrality on the sentencing issue and will allow the jury more adequately to reflect the conscience of the community.

While ruling that a jury totally committed to the imposition of the death penalty cannot be selected deliberately, as this would deprive a defendant of life without due process, the Court did not issue a constitutional rule that would have required the reversal of every jury selected under the Illinois statute. The Court did not state that a jury composed of persons in favor of capital punishment would be predisposed to convict, only that such a jury would be predisposed in the sentencing element of a trial.

The *Witherspoon* decision was an early test of the Supreme Court's position on capital punishment as well as on jury composition and selection. The Court indicated its willingness to uphold criminal convictions while examining the sentencing procedures being used in the states. At no point in its opinion did the Court express disfavor for the death penalty; rather, the opinion targeted only the constitutional implications of the jury-selection process. In other words, the *Witherspoon* decision indicated that within constitutional bounds, communities would be left to choose whether or not to impose the death penalty.

Donna Addkison Simmons

Wolf v. Colorado

U.S. SUPREME COURT
DECIDED JUNE 27, 1949

- The decision of the U.S. Supreme Court in this search and seizure case emphasized the importance of the individual protections guaranteed by the Fourth Amendment against illegal searches and seizures but failed to mandate use of the exclusionary rule in state courts.

The U.S. Supreme Court has heard a number of cases related to the protection against unlawful searches and seizures guaranteed by the Fourth Amendment of the U.S. Constitution. Until early in the twentieth century, rules of common law allowed the admission of illegally obtained evidence in criminal trials throughout the country. A case decided by the U.S. Supreme Court in 1914, *Weeks v. United States,* changed the rules of evidence in federal criminal proceedings by instituting an "exclusionary rule" that required the barring of illegally obtained evidence in those trials.

The exclusionary rule in criminal trials prohibits the use of evidence which has been gained from an unconstitutional search and seizure. This rule was designed to give teeth to the Fourth Amendment in order to protect the integrity of trial courts from tainted evidence and to decrease police misconduct in the collection of evidence.

Wolf v. Colorado was the first case to argue that this exclusionary rule should also be mandatory for state criminal proceedings. Wolf was accused and convicted of performing illegal abortions. The evidence introduced at trial included his appointment book, which had been taken by a deputy sheriff without a warrant. After acquiring the appointment book, the deputy sheriff questioned patients whose names he saw in the book. By doing so, he obtained enough evidence to charge the doctor with performing illegal abortions. Wolf appealed his conviction on the basis that the evidence used to convict him was a product of an illegal search and seizure in violation of his Fourth Amendment liberties.

Writing for the majority, Justice Felix Frankfurter stated with undeniable enthusiasm that the Fourth Amendment protections are a vital and basic part of the concept of "ordered liberty." That is to say, the protections against illegal searches and seizures are fundamental to the American notion of freedom. The Court sustained Wolf's conviction, however, and stopped short of requiring use of the exclusionary rule in state courts. Rather, state courts were given the option of using or not using evidence which was obtained illegally.

Justice Hugo Black wrote a concurring opinion, and Justice William Douglas wrote the dissenting opinion, which was joined by Justices Frank Murphy and Wiley Rutledge. It is important to note that the dissenting justices only disagreed with the Court's finding inasmuch as the Court failed to exclude the evidence.

This decision stood throughout the 1950's; however, by the turn of the decade, the Court was beginning to fine tune this position. Several loopholes in the earlier *Weeks* decision were closed, and by 1961, the Court was ready to hold the states accountable for Fourth Amendment protections through the application of the Fourteenth Amendment. *Mapp v. Ohio* (1961) extended the application of the exclusionary rule to state criminal proceedings, effectively overturning the decision rendered in *Wolf.*

This controversial rule of evidence has been revisited on numerous occasions in both judicial and political arenas. Indeed, throughout the 1970's and 1980's, the Court itself continued to redefine the criteria for determining that evidence had been obtained illegally. Critics of the exclusionary rule tout the numbers of criminals released and unpunished, the apathy among police forces across the nation, and so on. Advocates of the exclusionary rule seek to remind policy makers and the public of dangers of unrestrained governmental interference and police powers. Both sides continue to argue their cases in the light of the ever-changing political landscape.

Donna Addkison Simmons

Yates v. United States

U.S. SUPREME COURT
DECIDED JUNE 17, 1957

• The U.S. Supreme Court's decision in this case advanced protections for both freedom of speech and freedom of assembly or political association; this case rendered ineffective the government's attempt to prosecute members of the Communist Party of America under the Smith Act.

Following the rise of communism around the globe, leaders in the United States moved to stamp out any signs of communist activity in the country. Fourteen middle-level Communist Party leaders were accused under the Smith Act (1940) of organizing and participating in a conspiracy to advocate the forceful overthrow of the United States government. In a stunning 6-1 decision, with two justices not participating, the Supreme Court reversed their convictions, acquitting five and remanding the remaining nine for new trials.

The Court maintained that the government had waited much too long to charge the defendants with organizing the Communist Party in the United States. Indeed, the Court stated that the three-year statute of limitations had expired. The Court also found that the trial judge had been mistaken in his directions to the jury in regard to what they must find in order to convince the defendants on the advocacy charges. Finally, the Court declared the evidence in several cases to be entirely insufficient. After this decision was rendered, the government dropped all nine of the remanded cases.

The question before the court was simple enough. When placed in balance, which is of greater consequence: the value of preserving free speech or the value of preserving a government's interest which might be adversely affected by such speech? This basic question continues to raise controversy and foster strong emotions even though the issue of communism itself has been removed.

In an earlier case, *Dennis v. United States* (1951), the Court upheld the Smith Act as constitutional, allowing for numerous conspiracy convictions from 1951 through 1957. The Yates decision did not directly overrule Dennis, but it clarified the distinction between advocating illegal acts and holding abstract doctrinal beliefs which, the Court said, had been ignored by trial courts. After *Yates*, the government was required to show very specific illegal acts by the accused in order to gain a conviction. Membership in a political organization was insignificant in and of itself. Strict standards of proof had to be met.

This decision marked a dramatic and important change in the Court's attitude toward the Smith Act and a move away from the *Dennis* decision. Only four years later, however, the Court upheld a section of the Smith Act which made it a crime to be a member of a group advocating the overthrow by force of the government. This case, *Scales v. United States* (1961), was neither a retreat from *Yates* nor a return to *Dennis*, because the Court insisted that evidentiary requirements similar to those found in *Yates* be met. That is, a person's "membership" has to meet certain criteria. It must be both knowing and active. Additionally, the person must show "specific intent" to bring about the forceful overthrow of the government. This case, in combination with *Yates*, made conviction under the Smith Act virtually impossible.

Donna Addkison Simmons

Zablocki v. Redhail

U.S. SUPREME COURT
RULING ISSUED ON JANUARY 18, 1978

- The Court ruled that a Wisconsin law prohibiting the marriage of residents failing to comply with court-ordered child-support payments and obligations unconstitutionally interfered with the right of personal choice in marriage and family life.

On September 27, 1974, Roger Redhail was denied an application for a marriage license by Thomas Zablocki, the clerk of Milwaukee County, on the grounds that Redhail had not complied with state family law. The Wisconsin Family Code made Redhail's ability to marry dependent on his payment of child support from a previous relationship and on assurances that minor children were not and would not become wards of the state.

Redhail, unmarried, unemployed, and poor, had not paid court-ordered child support, and his illegitimate daughter had received benefits under the Aid to Families with Dependent Children program since her birth. He challenged the law. On August 31, 1976, a federal district court said that the Wisconsin law violated the equal protection clause of the Fourteenth Amendment to the U.S. Constitution. The Supreme Court agreed and ruled that the state significantly interfered with the fundamental right to marry, the most important relation in family life and a liberty protected by the Fourteenth Amendment. Individuals, including "deadbeat dads," may make personal decisions relating to marriage without unjustified governmental interference.

Steve J. Mazurana and Dyan E. Mazurana

Appendices

The Constitution of the United States of America

We the People of the United States, in Order to form a more perfect Union, establish Justice, insure domestic Tranquility, provide for the common defence, promote the general Welfare, and secure the Blessings of Liberty to ourselves and our Posterity, do ordain and establish this Constitution for the United States of America.

ARTICLE I.

SECTION 1. All legislative Powers herein granted shall be vested in a Congress of the United States, which shall consist of a Senate and House of Representatives.

SECTION 2. The House of Representatives shall be composed of Members chosen every second Year by the People of the several States, and the Electors in each State shall have the Qualifications requisite for Electors of the most numerous Branch of the State Legislature.

No Person shall be a Representative who shall not have attained to the Age of twenty five Years, and been seven Years a Citizen of the United States, and who shall not, when elected, be an Inhabitant of that State in which he shall be chosen.

Representatives and direct Taxes shall be apportioned among the several States which may be included within this Union, according to their respective Numbers, which shall be determined by adding to the whole Number of free Persons, including those bound to Service for a Term of Years, and excluding Indians not taxed, three fifths of all other Persons. The actual Enumeration shall be made within three Years after the first Meeting of the Congress of the United States, and within every subsequent Term of ten Years, in such Manner as they shall by Law direct. The number of Representatives shall not exceed one for every thirty Thousand, but each State shall have at Least one Representative; and until such enumeration shall be made, the State of New Hampshire shall be entitled to chuse three, Massachusetts eight, Rhode-Island and Providence Plantations one, Connecticut five, New-York six, New Jersey four, Pennsylvania eight, Delaware one, Maryland six, Virginia ten, North Carolina five, South Carolina five, and Georgia three.

When vacancies happen in the Representation from any State, the

Executive Authority thereof shall issue Writs of Election to fill such Vacancies.

The House of Representatives shall chuse their Speaker and other Officers; and shall have the sole Power of Impeachment.

SECTION 3. The Senate of the United States shall be composed of two Senators from each State, chosen by the Legislature thereof, for six Years; and each Senator shall have one Vote.

Immediately after they shall be assembled in Consequence of the first Election, they shall be divided as equally as may be into three Classes. The Seats of the Senators of the first Class shall be vacated at the Expiration of the second Year, of the second Class at the Expiration of the fourth Year, and of the third Class at the Expiration of the sixth Year, so that one third may be chosen every second Year; and if Vacancies happen by Resignation, or otherwise, during the Recess of the Legislature of any State, the Executive thereof may make temporary Appointments until the next Meeting of the Legislature, which shall then fill such Vacancies.

No Person shall be a Senator who shall not have attained to the Age of thirty Years, and been nine Years a Citizen of the United States, and who shall not, when elected, be an Inhabitant of that State for which he shall be chosen.

The Vice President of the United States shall be President of the Senate, but shall have no Vote, unless they be equally divided.

The Senate shall chuse their other Officers, and also a President pro tempore, in the Absence of the Vice President, or when he shall exercise the Office of President of the United States.

The Senate shall have the sole Power to try all Impeachments. When sitting for that Purpose, they shall be on Oath or Affirmation. When the President of the United States is tried, the Chief Justice shall preside: And no Person shall be convicted without the Concurrence of two thirds of the Members present.

Judgment in Cases of Impeachment shall not extend further than to removal from Office, and disqualification to hold and enjoy any Office of honor, Trust or Profit under the United States: but the Party convicted shall nevertheless be liable and subject to Indictment, Trial, Judgment and Punishment, according to Law.

SECTION 4. The Times, Places and Manner of holding Elections for Senators and Representatives, shall be prescribed in each State by the Legislature thereof; but the Congress may at any time by Law make or alter such Regulations, except as to the Places of chusing Senators.

The Congress shall assemble at least once in every Year, and such Meeting shall be on the first Monday in December, unless they shall by Law appoint a different Day.

SECTION 5. Each House shall be the Judge of the Elections, Returns and Qualifications of its own Members, and a Majority of each shall constitute a Quorum to do Business; but a smaller Number may adjourn from day to day, and may be authorized to compel the Attendance of absent Members, in such Manner, and under such Penalties as each House may provide.

Each House may determine the Rules of its Proceedings, punish its Members for disorderly Behaviour, and, with the Concurrence of two thirds, expel a Member.

Each House shall keep a Journal of its Proceedings, and from time to time publish the same, excepting such Parts as may in their Judgment require Secrecy; and the Yeas and Nays of the Members of either House on any question shall, at the Desire of one fifth of those Present, be entered on the Journal.

Neither House, during the Session of Congress, shall, without the Consent of the other, adjourn for more than three days, nor to any other Place than that in which the two Houses shall be sitting.

SECTION 6. The Senators and Representatives shall receive a Compensation for their Services, to be ascertained by Law, and paid out of the Treasury of the United States. They shall in all Cases, except Treason, Felony and Breach of the Peace, be privileged from Arrest during their Attendance at the Session of their respective Houses, and in going to and returning from the same; and for any Speech or Debate in either House, they shall not be questioned in any other Place.

No Senator or Representative shall, during the Time for which he was elected, be appointed to any civil Office under the Authority of the United States, which shall have been created, or the Emoluments whereof shall have been encreased during such time; and no Person holding any Office under the United States, shall be a Member of either House during his Continuance in Office.

SECTION 7. All Bills for raising Revenue shall originate in the House of Representatives; but the Senate may propose or concur with Amendments as on other Bills.

Every Bill which shall have passed the House of Representatives and the Senate, shall, before it becomes a Law, be presented to the President of the United States; If he approve he shall sign it, but if not he shall return it, with his Objections to that House in which it shall have originated, who shall enter the Objections at large on their Journal, and proceed to reconsider it. If after such Reconsideration two thirds of that House shall agree to pass the Bill, it shall be sent, together with the Objections, to the other House, by which it shall likewise be reconsidered, and if approved by two thirds of that House, it shall become a Law. But in all such Cases the Votes of both Houses shall be determined by yeas and Nays, and the Names of the Persons voting for and against the Bill shall be entered on the Journal of each House respectively. If any Bill shall not be returned by the President within ten Days (Sundays excepted) after it shall have been presented to him, the Same shall be a Law, in like Manner as if he had signed it, unless the Congress by their Adjournment prevent its Return, in which Case it shall not be a Law.

Every Order, Resolution, or Vote to which the Concurrence of the Senate and House of Representatives may be necessary (except on a question of Adjournment) shall be presented to the President of the United States; and before the Same shall take Effect, shall be approved by him, or being disapproved by him, shall be repassed by two thirds of the Senate and House of Representatives, according to the Rules and Limitations prescribed in the Case of a Bill.

SECTION 8. The Congress shall have Power To lay and collect Taxes, Duties, Imposts and Excises, to pay the Debts and provide for the common Defence and general Welfare of the United States; but all Duties, Imposts and Excises shall be uniform throughout the United States;

To borrow Money on the credit of the United States;

To regulate Commerce with foreign Nations, and among the several States, and with the Indian Tribes;

To establish an uniform Rule of Naturalization, and uniform Laws on the subject of Bankruptcies throughout the United States;

To coin Money, regulate the Value thereof, and of foreign Coin, and fix the Standard of Weights and Measures;

To provide for the Punishment of counterfeiting the Securities and current Coin of the United States;

To establish Post Offices and post Roads;

To promote the Progress of Science and useful Arts, by securing for limited Times to Authors and Inventors the exclusive Right to their respective Writings and Discoveries;

To constitute Tribunals inferior to the supreme Court;

To define and punish Piracies and Felonies committed on the high Seas, and Offenses against the Law of Nations;

To declare War, grant Letters of Marque and Reprisal, and make Rules concerning Captures on Land and Water;

To raise and support Armies, but no Appropriation of Money to that Use shall be for a longer Term than two Years;

To provide and maintain a Navy;

To make Rules for the Government and Regulation of the land and naval Forces;

To provide for calling forth the Militia to execute the Laws of the Union, suppress Insurrections and repel Invasions;

To provide for organizing, arming, and disciplining, the Militia, and for governing such Part of them as may be employed in the Service of the United States, reserving to the States respectively, the Appointment of the Officers, and the Authority of training the Militia according to the discipline prescribed by Congress;

To exercise exclusive Legislation in all Cases whatsoever, over such District (not exceeding ten Miles square) as may, by Cession of particular States, and the Acceptance of Congress, become the Seat of the Government of the United States, and to exercise like Authority over all Places purchased by the Consent of the Legislature of the State in which the Same shall be, for the Erection of Forts, Magazines, Arsenals, dock-Yards and other needful Buildings;—And

To make all Laws which shall be necessary and proper for carrying into Execution the foregoing Powers, and all other Powers vested by this Constitution in the Government of the United States, or in any Department or Officer thereof.

SECTION 9. The Migration or Importation of such Persons as any of the States now existing shall think proper to admit, shall not be prohibited by the Congress prior to the Year one thousand eight hundred and eight, but a Tax or duty may be imposed on such Importation, not exceeding ten dollars for each Person.

The Privilege of the Writ of Habeas Corpus shall not be suspended, unless when in Cases of Rebellion or Invasion the public Safety may require it.

No Bill of Attainder or ex post facto Law shall be passed.

No Capitation, or other direct, Tax shall be laid, unless in Proportion to the Census or Enumeration herein before directed to be taken.

No Tax or Duty shall be laid on Articles exported from any State.

No Preference shall be given by any Regulation of Commerce or Revenue to the Ports of one State over those of another: nor shall Vessels bound to, or from, one State, be obliged to enter, clear, or pay Duties in another.

No Money shall be drawn from the Treasury, but in Consequence of Appropriations made by Law; and a regular Statement and Account of the Receipts and Expenditures of all public Money shall be published from time to time.

No Title of Nobility shall be granted by the United States: And no Person holding any Office of Profit or Trust under them, shall, without the Consent of the Congress, accept of any present, Emolument, Office, or Title, of any kind whatever, from any King, Prince, or foreign State.

SECTION 10. No State shall enter into any Treaty, Alliance, or Confederation; grant Letters of Marque and Reprisal; coin Money; emit Bills of Credit; make any Thing but gold and silver Coin a Tender in Payment of Debts; pass any Bill of Attainder, ex post facto Law, or Law impairing the Obligation of Contracts, or grant any Title of Nobility.

No State shall, without the Consent of the Congress, lay any Imposts or Duties on Imports or Exports, except what may be absolutely necessary for executing it's inspection Laws: and the net Produce of all Duties and Imposts, laid by any State on Imports or Exports, shall be for the Use of the Treasury of the United States; and all such Laws shall be subject to the Revision and Control of the Congress.

No State shall, without the Consent of Congress, lay any Duty of Tonnage, keep Troops, or Ships of War in time of Peace, enter into any Agreement or Compact with another State, or with a foreign Power, or engage in War, unless actually invaded, or in such imminent Danger as will not admit of delay.

ARTICLE II.

SECTION 1. The executive Power shall be vested in a President of the United States of America. He shall hold his Office during the Term of four Years, and, together with the Vice President, chosen for the same Term, be elected, as follows

Each State shall appoint, in such Manner as the Legislature thereof may direct, a Number of Electors, equal to the whole Number of Senators and Representatives to which the State may be entitled in the Congress: but no Senator or Representative, or Person holding an Office of Trust or Profit under the United States, shall be appointed an Elector.

The Electors shall meet in their respective States, and vote by Ballot for two Persons, of whom one at least shall not be an Inhabitant of the same State with themselves. And they shall make a List of all the Persons voted for, and of the Number of Votes for each; which List they shall sign and certify, and transmit sealed to the Seat of the Government of the United States, directed to the President of the Senate. The President of the Senate shall, in the Presence of the Senate and House of Representatives, open all the Certificates, and the Votes shall then be counted. The Person having the greatest Number of Votes shall be the President, if such Number be a Majority of the whole Number of Electors appointed; and if there be more than one who have such Majority, and have an equal Number of Votes, then the House of Representatives shall immediately chuse by Ballot one of them for President; and if no Person have a Majority, then from the five highest on the List the said House shall in like manner chuse the President. But in chusing the President, the Votes shall be taken by States, the Representation from each State having one Vote; A quorum for this Purpose shall consist of a Member or Members from two thirds of the States, and a Majority of all the States shall be necessary to a Choice. In every Case, after the Choice of the President, the Person having the greatest Number of Votes of the Electors shall be the Vice President. But if there should remain two or more who have equal Votes, the Senate shall chuse from them by Ballot the Vice President.

The Congress may determine the Time of chusing the Electors, and the Day on which they shall give their Votes; which Day shall be the same throughout the United States.

No Person except a natural born Citizen, or a Citizen of the United States, at the time of the Adoption of this Constitution, shall be eligible to the Office of the President; neither shall any person be eligible to that Office who shall not have attained to the Age of thirty five Years, and been fourteen Years a Resident within the United States.

In Case of the Removal of the President from Office, or of his Death, Resignation, or Inability to discharge the Powers and Duties of the said Office, the Same shall devolve on the Vice President, and the Congress may by Law provide for the Case of Removal, Death, Resignation or Inability, both of the President and Vice President, declaring what Officer shall then act as President, and such Officer shall act accordingly, until the Disability be removed, or a President shall be elected.

The President shall, at stated Times, receive for his Services, a Compensation, which shall neither be increased nor diminished during the Period for which he shall have been elected, and he shall not receive within that Period any other Emolument from the United States, or any of them.

Before he enter the Execution of his Office, he shall take the following Oath or Affirmation:—"I do solemnly swear (or affirm) that I will faithfully execute the Office of President of the United States, and will to the best of my Ability, preserve, protect and defend the Constitution of the United States."

SECTION 2. The President shall be Commander in Chief of the Army and Navy of the United States, and of the Militia of the several States, when called into the actual Service of the United States; he may require the Opinion, in writing, of the principal Officer in each of the executive Departments, upon any Subject relating to the Duties of their respective Offices, and he shall have Power to grant Reprieves and Pardons for Offenses against the United States, except in Cases of Impeachment.

He shall have Power, by and with the Advice and Consent of the Senate, to make Treaties, provided two thirds of the Senators present concur; and he shall nominate, and by and with the Advice and Consent of the Senate, shall appoint Ambassadors, other public Ministers and Consuls, Judges of the supreme Court, and all other Officers of the United States, whose Appointments are not herein otherwise provided for, and which shall be established by Law: but the Congress may by Law vest the Appointment of such inferior Officers, as they think proper, in the President alone, in the Courts of Law, or in the Heads of Departments.

The President shall have Power to fill up all Vacancies that may happen during the Recess of the Senate, by granting Commissions which shall expire at the End of their next Session.

SECTION 3. He shall from time to time give to the Congress Information of the State of the Union, and recommend to their Consideration such Measures as he shall judge necessary and expedient; he may, on extraordinary Occasions, convene both Houses, or either of them, and in Case of Disagreement between them, with Respect to the Time of Adjournment, he may adjourn them to such Time as he shall think proper; he shall receive Ambassadors and other public Ministers; he shall take Care that the Laws be faithfully executed, and shall Commission all the Officers of the United States.

SECTION 4. The President, Vice President and all civil Officers of the United States, shall be removed from Office on Impeachment for, and Conviction of, Treason, Bribery, or other high Crimes and Misdemeanors.

ARTICLE III.

SECTION 1. The judicial Power of the United States, shall be vested in one supreme Court, and in such inferior Courts as the Congress may from time to time ordain and establish. The Judges, both of the supreme and inferior Courts, shall hold their Offices during good Behaviour, and shall, at stated Times, receive for their Services, a Compensation, which shall not be diminished during their Continuance in Office.

SECTION 2. The judicial Power shall extend to all Cases, in Law and Equity, arising under this Constitution, the Laws of the United States, and Treaties made, or which shall be made, under their Authority;—to all Cases affecting Ambassadors, other public Ministers and Consuls;—to all Cases of admiralty and maritime Jurisdiction;—to Controversies to which the United States shall be a Party;—to Controversies between two or more States; between a State and Citizens of another State; between Citizens of different States,—between Citizens of the same State claiming Lands under Grants of different States, and between a State, or the Citizens thereof, and foreign States, Citizens or Subjects.

In all Cases affecting Ambassadors, other public Ministers and Consuls, and those in which a State shall be Party, the supreme Court shall have original Jurisdiction. In all the other Cases before mentioned, the supreme Court shall have appellate Jurisdiction, both as to Law and Fact, with such Exceptions, and under such Regulations as the Congress shall make.

The Trial of all Crimes, except in Cases of Impeachment, shall be by Jury; and such Trial shall be held in the State where the said Crimes shall have been committed; but when not committed within any State, the Trial shall be at such Place or Places as the Congress may by Law have directed.

SECTION 3. Treason against the United States, shall consist only in levying War against them, or in adhering to their Enemies, giving them Aid and Comfort. No Person shall be convicted of Treason unless on the Testimony of two Witnesses to the same overt Act, or on Confession in open Court.

The Congress shall have Power to declare the Punishment of Treason, but no Attainder of Treason shall work Corruption of Blood, or Forfeiture except during the Life of the Person attainted.

ARTICLE IV.

SECTION 1. Full Faith and Credit shall be given in each State to the public Acts, Records, and judicial Proceedings of every other State; And the Congress may by general Laws prescribe the Manner in which such Acts, Records and Proceedings shall be proved, and the Effect thereof.

SECTION 2. The Citizens of each State shall be entitled to all Privileges and Immunities of Citizens in the several States.

A Person charged in any State with Treason, Felony, or other Crime, who shall flee from Justice, and be found in another State, shall on Demand of the executive Authority of the State from which he fled, be delivered up, to be removed to the State having Jurisdiction of the Crime.

No person held to Service or Labour in one State, under the Laws thereof, escaping into another, shall, in Consequence of any Law or Regulation therein, be discharged from such Service or Labour, but shall be delivered up on Claim of the Party to whom such Service or Labour may be due.

SECTION 3. New States may be admitted by the Congress into this Union; but no new State shall be formed or erected within the Jurisdiction of any other State; nor any State be formed by the Junction of two or more States, or Parts of States, without the Consent of the Legislatures of the States concerned as well as of the Congress.

The Congress shall have Power to dispose of and make all needful Rules and Regulations respecting the Territory or other Property belonging to the United States; and nothing in this Constitution shall be so construed as to Prejudice any Claims of the United States, or of any particular State.

SECTION 4. The United States shall guarantee to every State in this Union a Republican Form of Government, and shall protect each of them against Invasion; and on Application of the Legislature, or of the Executive (when the Legislature cannot be convened) against domestic Violence.

ARTICLE V.

The Congress, whenever two thirds of both Houses shall deem it necessary, shall propose Amendments to this Constitution, or, on the Application of the Legislatures of two thirds of the several States, shall call a Convention for proposing Amendments, which, in either Case, shall be valid to all Intents and Purposes, as Part of this Constitution, when ratified by the Legislatures of three fourths of the several States, or by Conventions in three fourths thereof, as the one or the other Mode of Ratification may be proposed by the Congress; Provided that no Amendment which may be made prior to the Year One thousand eight hundred and eight shall in any Manner affect the first and fourth Clauses in the Ninth Section of the first Article; and that no State, without its Consent, shall be deprived of it's equal Suffrage in the Senate.

ARTICLE VI.

All Debts contracted and Engagements entered into, before the Adoption of this Constitution, shall be as valid against the United States under this Constitution, as under the Confederation.

This Constitution, and the Laws of the United States which shall be made in Pursuance thereof; and all Treaties made, or which shall be made, under the Authority of the United States, shall be the supreme Law of the Land; and the Judges in every State shall be bound thereby, any Thing in the Constitution or Laws of any State to the Contrary notwithstanding.

The Senators and Representatives before mentioned, and the Members of the several State Legislatures, and all executive and judicial Officers, both of the United States and of the several States, shall be bound by Oath or Affirmation, to support this Constitution; but no religious Test shall ever be required as a Qualification to any Office or public Trust under the United States.

ARTICLE VII.

The Ratification of the Conventions of nine States, shall be sufficient for the Establishment of this Constitution between the States so ratifying the Same.

Done in Convention by the Unanimous Consent of the States present the Seventeenth Day of September in the Year of our Lord one thousand seven hundred and Eighty seven and of the Independence of the United States of America the Twelfth. In Witness whereof We have hereunto subscribed our Names,

G^{o}: Washington—Presid^{t} and deputy from Virginia

New Hampshire	John Langdon Nicholas Gilman		
		Delaware	Geo: Read Gunning Bedord jun John Dickinson Richard Bassett Jaco: Broom
Massachusetts	Nathaniel Gorham Rufus King		
Connecticut	Wm Sam^1 Johnson Roger Sherman	Maryland	James McHenry Dan of St Thos. Jenifer Dan^1 Carroll
New York	John Langdon		
		Virginia	John Blair— James Madison Jr.
New Jersey	Wil: Livingston David Brearley Wm Paterson Jona: Dayton		
		North Carolina	W^m. Blount Richd Dobbs Spaight. Hu Williamson
New Jersey	B Franklin Thomas Mifflin Robt Morris Geo. Clymer Thos. FitzSimons Jared Ingersoll James Wilson Gouv Morris	South Carolina	J. Rutledge Charles Cotesworth Pinckney Charles Pickney Pierce Butler
		Georgia	William Few Abr Baldwin

Attest William Jackson Secretary

Amendments to the U.S. Constitution

AMENDMENT I.

Congress shall make no law respecting an establishment of religion, or prohibiting the free exercise thereof; or abridging the freedom of speech, or of the press, or the right of the people peaceably to assemble, and to petition the Government for a redress of grievances.

[ratified December, 1791]

AMENDMENT II.

A well regulated Militia, being necessary to the security of a free State, the right of the people to keep and bear Arms, shall not be infringed.

[ratified December, 1791]

AMENDMENT III.

No Soldier shall, in time of peace be quartered in any house, without the consent of the Owner, nor in time of war, but in a manner to be prescribed by law.

[ratified December, 1791]

AMENDMENT IV.

The right of the people to be secure in their persons, houses, papers, and effects, against unreasonable searches and seizures, shall not be violated, and no Warrants shall issue, but upon probable cause, supported by Oath or affirmation, and particularly describing the place to be searched, and the persons or things to be seized.

[ratified December, 1791]

AMENDMENT V.

No person shall be held to answer for a capital, or otherwise infamous crime, unless on a presentment or indictment of a Grand Jury, except in cases arising in the land or naval forces, or in the Militia, when in actual service in time of War or public danger; nor shall any person be subject for the same offence to be twice put in jeopardy of life or limb, nor shall be compelled in any criminal case to be a witness against himself, nor be deprived of life, liberty, or property, without due process of law; nor shall private property be taken for public use without just compensation.

[ratified December, 1791]

AMENDMENT VI.

In all criminal prosecutions, the accused shall enjoy the right to a speedy and public trial, by an impartial jury of the State and district wherein the crime shall have been committed; which district shall have been previously ascertained by law, and to be informed of the nature and cause of the accusation; to be confronted with the witnesses against him; to have compulsory process for obtaining witnesses in his favor, and to have the assistance of counsel for his defence.

[ratified December, 1791]

AMENDMENT VII.

In Suits at common law, where the value in controversy shall exceed twenty dollars, the right of trial by jury shall be preserved, and no fact tried by a jury shall be otherwise re-examined in any Court of the United States, than according to the rules of the common law.

[ratified December, 1791]

AMENDMENT VIII.

Excessive bail shall not be required, nor excessive fines imposed, nor cruel and unusual punishments inflicted.

[ratified December, 1791]

AMENDMENT IX.

The enumeration in the Constitution, of certain rights, shall not be construed to deny or disparage others retained by the people.

[ratified December, 1791]

AMENDMENT X.

The powers not delegated to the United States by the Constitution, nor prohibited by it to the States, are reserved to the States respectively, or to the people.

[ratified December, 1791]

AMENDMENT XI.

The Judicial power of the United States shall not be construed to extend to any suit in law or equity, commenced or prosecuted against one of the United States by Citizens of another State, or by Citizens or Subjects of any Foreign State.

[ratified February, 1795]

AMENDMENT XII.

The Electors shall meet in their respective states, and vote by ballot for President and Vice President, one of whom, at least, shall not be an inhabitant of the same state with themselves; they shall name in their ballots the person voted for as President, and in distinct ballots the person voted for as Vice-President, and they shall make distinct lists of all persons voted for as President, and of all persons voted for as Vice-President, and of the number of votes for each, which lists they shall sign and certify, and transmit sealed to the seat of the government of the United States, directed to the President of the Senate;—The President of the Senate shall, in the presence of the Senate and House of Representatives, open all the certificates and the votes shall then be counted;—The person having the greatest number of votes for President, shall be the President, if such number be a majority of the whole number of Electors appointed; and if no person have such majority, then from the persons having the highest numbers not exceeding three on the list of those voted for as President, the House of Representatives shall choose immediately, by ballot, the President. But in choosing the President, the votes shall be taken by states, the representation from each state having one vote; a quorum for this purpose shall consist of a member or members from two-thirds of the states, and a majority of all the states shall be necessary to a choice. And if the House of Representatives shall not choose a President whenever the right of choice shall devolve upon them, before the fourth day of March next following, then the Vice-President shall act as President, as in the case of the death or other constitutional disability of the President.—The person having the greatest number of votes as Vice-President, shall be the Vice-President, if such number be a majority of the whole number of Electors appointed, and if no person have a majority, then from the two highest numbers on the list, the Senate shall choose the Vice-President; a quorum for the purpose shall consist of two-thirds of the whole number of Senators, and a majority of the whole number shall be necessary to a choice. But no person constitutionally ineligible to the office of President shall be eligible to that of Vice-President of the United States.

[ratified June, 1804]

AMENDMENT XIII.

SECTION 1. Neither slavery nor involuntary servitude, except as a punishment for crime whereof the party shall have been duly convicted, shall exist within the United States, or any place subject to their jurisdiction.

SECTION 2. Congress shall have power to enforce this article by appropriate legislation.

[ratified December, 1865]

AMENDMENT XIV.

SECTION 1. All persons born or naturalized in the United States and subject to the jurisdiction thereof, are citizens of the United States and of the State wherein they reside. No State shall make or enforce any law which shall abridge the privileges or immunities of citizens of the United States; nor shall any State deprive any person of life, liberty, or property, without due process of law; nor deny to any person within its jurisdiction the equal protection of the laws.

SECTION 2. Representatives shall be apportioned among the several States according to their respective numbers, counting the whole number of persons in each State, excluding Indians not taxed. But when the right to vote at any election for the choice of electors for President and Vice President of the United States, Representatives in Congress, the Executive and Judicial officers of a State, or the members of the Legislature thereof, is denied to any of the male inhabitants of such State, being twenty-one years of age, and citizens of the United States, or in any way abridged, except for participation in rebellion, or other crime, the basis of representation therein shall be reduced in the proportion which the number of such male citizens shall bear to the whole number of male citizens twenty-one years of age in such State.

SECTION 3. No person shall be a Senator or Representative in Congress, or elector of President and Vice President, or hold any office, civil or military, under the United States, or under any State, who, having previously taken an oath, as a member of Congress, or as an officer of the United States, or as a member of any State legislature, or as an executive or judicial officer of any State, to support the Constitution of the United States, shall have engaged in insurrection or rebellion against the same, or given aid or comfort to the enemies thereof. But Congress may by a vote of two-thirds of each House, remove such disability.

SECTION 4. The validity of the public debt of the United States, authorized by law, including debts incurred for payment of pensions and bounties for services in suppressing insurrection or rebellion, shall not be questioned. But neither the United States nor any State shall assume or pay any debt or obligation incurred in aid of insurrection or rebellion against the United States, or any claim for the loss or emancipation of any slave; but all such debts, obligations and claims shall be held illegal and void.

SECTION 5. The Congress shall have power to enforce, by appropriate legislation, the provisions of this article.

[ratified July, 1868]

AMENDMENT XV.

SECTION 1. The right of citizens of the United States to vote shall not be denied or abridged by the United States or by any State on account of race, color, or previous condition of servitude.

SECTION 2. The Congress shall have power to enforce this article by appropriate legislation.

[ratified February, 1870]

AMENDMENT XVI.

The Congress shall have power to lay and collect taxes on incomes, from whatever source derived, without apportionment among the several States, and without regard to any census or enumeration.

[ratified February, 1913]

AMENDMENT XVII.

The Senate of the United States shall be composed of two Senators from each State, elected by the people thereof, for six years; and each Senator shall have one vote. The electors in each State shall have the qualifications requisite for electors of the most numerous branch of the State legislatures.

When vacancies happen in the representation of any State in the Senate, the executive authority of such State shall issue writs of election to fill such vacancies: *Provided*, That the legislature of any State may empower the executive thereof to make temporary appointments until the people fill the vacancies by election as the legislature may direct.

This amendment shall not be so construed as to affect the election or term of any Senator chosen before it becomes valid as part of the Constitution.

[ratified April, 1913]

AMENDMENT XVIII.

SECTION 1. After one year from the ratification of this article the manufacture, sale, or transportation of intoxicating liquors within, the importation thereof into, or the exportation thereof from the United States and all territory subject to the jurisdiction thereof for beverage purposes is hereby prohibited.

SECTION 2. The Congress and the several States shall have concurrent power to enforce this article by appropriate legislation.

SECTION 3. This article shall be inoperative unless it shall have been ratified as an amendment to the Constitution by the legislatures of the several States, as provided in the Constitution, within seven years

from the date of the submission hereof to the States by the Congress.
[ratified January, 1919, repealed December, 1933]

AMENDMENT XIX.

The right of citizens of the United States to vote shall not be denied or abridged by the United States or by any State on account of sex.

Congress shall have power to enforce this article by appropriate legislation.
[ratified August, 1920]

AMENDMENT XX.

SECTION 1. The terms of the President and Vice President shall end at noon on the 20th day of January, and the terms of Senators and Representatives at noon on the 3d day of January, of the years in which such terms would have ended if this article had not been ratified; and the terms of their successors shall then begin.

SECTION 2. The Congress shall assemble at least once in every year, and such meeting shall begin at noon on the 3d day of January, unless they shall by law appoint a different day.

SECTION 3. If, at the time fixed for the beginning of the term of the President, the President elect shall have died, the Vice President elect shall become President. If a President shall not have been chosen before the time fixed for the beginning of his term, or if the President elect shall have failed to qualify, then the Vice President elect shall act as President until a President shall have qualified; and the Congress may by law provide for the case wherein neither a President elect nor a Vice President elect shall have qualified, declaring who shall then act as President, or the manner in which one who is to act shall be selected, and such person shall act accordingly until a President or Vice President shall have qualified.

SECTION 4. The Congress may by law provide for the case of the death of any of the persons from whom the House of Representatives may choose a President whenever the right of choice shall have devolved upon them, and for the case of the death of any of the persons from whom the Senate may choose a Vice President whenever the right of choice shall have devolved upon them.

SECTION 5. Sections 1 and 2 shall take effect on the 15th day of October following the ratification of this article.

SECTION 6. This article shall be inoperative unless it shall have been ratified as an amendment to the Constitution by the legislatures of three-fourths of the several States within seven years from the date of its submission.
[ratified January, 1933]

AMENDMENT XXI.

SECTION 1. The eighteenth article of amendment to the Constitution of the United States is hereby repealed.

SECTION 2. The transportation or importation into any State, Territory, or possession of the United States for delivery or use therein of intoxicating liquors, in violation of the laws thereof, is hereby prohibited.

SECTION 3. This article shall be inoperative unless it shall have been ratified as an amendment to the Constitution by conventions in the several States, as provided in the Constitution, within seven years from the date of the submission hereof to the States by the Congress.

[ratified December, 1933]

AMENDMENT XXII.

SECTION 1. No person shall be elected to the office of the President more than twice, and no person who has held the office of President, or acted as President, for more than two years of a term to which some other person was elected President shall be elected to the office of the President more than once. But this Article shall not apply to any person holding the office of President when this Article was proposed by the Congress, and shall not prevent any person who may be holding the office of President, or acting as President, during the term within which this Article becomes operative from holding the office of President or acting as President during the remainder of such term.

SECTION 2. This article shall be inoperative unless it shall have been ratified as an amendment to the Constitution by the legislatures of three-fourths of the several States within seven years from the date of its submission to the States by the Congress.

[ratified February, 1951]

AMENDMENT XXIII.

SECTION 1. The District constituting the seat of Government of the United States shall appoint in such manner as the Congress may direct:

A number of electors of President and Vice President equal to the whole number of Senators and Representatives in Congress to which the District would be entitled if it were a State, but in no event more than the least populous State; they shall be in addition to those appointed by the States, but they shall be considered, for the purposes of the election of President and Vice President, to be electors appointed by a State; and they shall meet in the District and perform such duties as provided by the twelfth article of amendment.

SECTION 2. The Congress shall have power to enforce this article by appropriate legislation.

[ratified March, 1961]

AMENDMENT XXIV.

SECTION 1. The right of citizens of the United States to vote in any primary or other election for President or Vice President, for electors for President or Vice President, or for Senator or Representative in Congress, shall not be denied or abridged by the United States or any State by reason of failure to pay any poll tax or other tax.

SECTION 2. The Congress shall have power to enforce this article by appropriate legislation.

[ratified January, 1964]

AMENDMENT XXV.

SECTION 1. In case of the removal of the President from office or of his death or resignation, the Vice President shall become President.

SECTION 2. Whenever there is a vacancy in the office of the Vice President, the President shall nominate a Vice President who shall take office upon confirmation by a majority vote of both Houses of Congress.

SECTION 3. Whenever the President transmits to the President pro tempore of the Senate and the Speaker of the House of Representatives his written declaration that he is unable to discharge the powers and duties of his office, and until he transmits to them a written declaration to the contrary, such powers and duties shall be discharged by the Vice President as Acting President.

SECTION 4. Whenever the Vice President and a majority of either the principal officers of the executive departments or of such other body as Congress may by law provide, transmit to the President pro tempore of the Senate and the Speaker of the House of Representatives their written declaration that the President is unable to discharge the powers and duties of his office, the Vice President shall immediately assume the powers and duties of the office as Acting President.

Thereafter, when the President transmits to the President pro tempore of the Senate and the Speaker of the House of Representatives his written declaration that no inability exists, he shall resume the powers and duties of his office unless the Vice President and a majority of either the principal officers of the executive department or of such other body as Congress may by law provide, transmit within four days to the President pro tempore of the Senate and the Speaker of the House of Representatives their written declaration that the President is unable to discharge the powers and duties of his office. Thereupon

Congress shall decide the issue, assembling within forty-eight hours for that purpose if not in session. If the Congress, within twenty-one days after receipt of the latter written declaration, or, if Congress is not in session, within twenty-one days after Congress is required to assemble, determines by two-thirds vote of both Houses that the President is unable to discharge the powers and duties of his office, the Vice President shall continue to discharge the same as Acting President; otherwise, the President shall resume the powers and duties of his office.

[ratified February, 1967]

AMENDMENT XXVI.

SECTION 1. The right of citizens of the United States, who are eighteen years of age or older, to vote shall not be denied or abridged by the United States or by any State on account of age.

SECTION 2. The Congress shall have power to enforce this article by appropriate legislation.

[ratified July, 1971]

AMENDMENT XXVII.

No law, varying the compensation for the services of the Senators and Representatives, shall take effect, until an election of Representatives shall have intervened.

[ratified May 7, 1992]

Supreme Court Justices

Alphabetical listing of Supreme Court justices. Birth and death dates are given in parentheses below name. Name in boldface indicates service as chief justice of the United States. Asterisk (*) after date in *Tenure* column indicates justice died while in office.

Name	Tenure	Appointed by	Highlights
Henry Baldwin (1780-1844)	1830-1844*	Jackson	First justice consistently to write separate opinions expressing his views. Significant opinion: *Holmes v. Jennison*, 39 U.S. 540 (1840). Other publication: *A General View of the Origin and Nature of the Constitution and Government of the United States* (1937).
Philip Pendleton Barbour (1783-1841)	1836-1841*	Jackson	Significant opinion: *New York v. Miln*, 36 U.S. 102 (1837).
Hugo Lafayette Black (1886-1971)	1937-1971	Franklin D. Roosevelt	Author of incorporation doctrine, which held that the major provisions of the Bill of Rights were imposed on the states through the due process clause of the Fourteenth Amendment. Significant opinions: *Adamson v. California*, 332 U.S. 46 (1947) (dissenting opinion); *Barenblatt v. United States*, 360 U.S. 109 (1959) (dissenting opinion); *Gideon v. Wainwright*, 372 U.S. 335 (1963); *Pointer v. Texas*, 380 U.S. 400 (1965); *Illinois v. Allen*, 397 U.S. 337 (1970); *New York Times Co. v. United States*, 403 U.S. 713 (1971) (concurring opinion).
Harry Andrew Blackmun (1908-1999)	1970-1994	Nixon	Defender of a general constitutional right of privacy. Significant opinions: *Roe v. Wade*, 410 U.S. 113 (1973); *Andresen v. Maryland*, 427 U.S. 463 (1976); *New York v. Burger*, 482 U.S. 691 (1987); *California v. Acevedo*, 500 U.S. 565 (1991).

Name	Tenure	Appointed by	Highlights
John Blair, Jr. (1732-1800)	1790-1796	Washington	Significant opinion: *Chisholm v. Georgia*, 2 U.S. 419 (1793).
Samuel Blatchford (1820-1893)	1882-1893*	Arthur	Wrote one of the earliest opinions interpreting the scope of the privilege against self-incrimination. Energetic supporter of substantive due process doctrine. Significant opinions: *Chicago, Milwaukee, and St. Paul Railway. Co. v. Minnesota*, 134 U.S. 418 (1890); *O'Neil v. Vermont*, 144 U.S. 323 (1892); *Councilman v. Hitchcock*, 142 U.S. 547 (1892).
Joseph P. Bradley (1813-1892)	1870-1892*	Grant	Author of *Boyd v. United States*, 116 U.S. 616 (1886), the first case offering a significant interpretation of the Fourth and Fifth Amendments. Significant opinions: *Legal Tender Cases*, 79 U.S. 603 (1871) (concurring opinion); *Civil Rights Cases*, 109 U.S. 3 (1885); *Munn v. Illinois*, 118 U.S. 557 (1886).
Louis Dembitz Brandeis (1856-1941)	1916-1939	Wilson	As a lawyer was a social reformer known as the "people's attorney." As a justice, argued states should be free to experiment with social and economic regulation and was a consistent defender of individual rights. Significant opinions: *Olmstead v. United States, 277 U.S. 438 (1928) (dissenting opinion); Whitney v. California*, 274 U.S. 357 (1927) (concurring opinion); *New State Ice Co. v. Liebmann*, 285 U.S. 262 (1932) (dissenting opinion).

Name	Tenure	Appointed by	Highlights
William Joseph Brennan, Jr. (1906-1997)	1956-1990	Eisenhower	Author of many important Warren Court-era opinions on individual rights; opposed death penalty. Significant opinions: *Baker v. Carr*, 369 U.S. 186 (1962); *Wong Sun v. United States*, 371 U.S. 471 (1963); *New York Times Co. v. Sullivan*, 376 U.S. 254 (1964); *United States v. Wade*, 388 U.S. 218 (1967); *Warden v. Hayden*, 387 U.S. 294 (1967); *Coleman v. Alabama*, 399 U.S. 1 (1970); *Gregg v. Georgia*, 428 U.S. 153 (1976) (dissenting opinion); *Craig v. Boren*, 429 U.S. 190 (1976); *Dunaway v. New York*, 442 U.S. 200 (1979); *Pennsylvania v. Muniz*, 496 U.S. 582 (1990).
David Josiah Brewer (1837-1910)	1890-1910*	Harrison	Believed many forms of governmental economic and social regulation were unconstitutional under substantive due process doctrine. Significant opinions: *Reagan v. Farmers' Loan & Trust Co.*, 154 U.S. 362 (1894); *In re Debs*, 158 U.S. 564 (1895); *Muller v. Oregon*, 208 U.S. 412 (1908).
Steven Gerald Breyer (1938-)	1994-	Clinton	
Henry Billings Brown (1836-1913)	1891-1906	Harrison	Author of "separate but equal" doctrine concerning racial classifications. Significant opinions: *Pollock v. Farmers' Loan & Trust Co.*, 158 U.S. 601 (1895) (dissenting opinion); *Plessy v. Ferguson*, 163 U.S. 537 (1896); *Holden v. Hardy*, 169 U.S. 366 (1898).

Name	Tenure	Appointed by	Highlights
Warren Earl Burger (1907-1995)	1969-1986	Nixon	Critical of Warren-era expansion of constitutional rights available to criminal defendants, but unsuccessful in reversing those decisions. Revived separation of powers as an important constitutional doctrine. Significant opinions: *Harris v. New York*, 401 U.S. 222 (1971); *South Dakota v. Opperman*, 428 U.S. 364 (1976); *United States v. Chadwick*, 433 U.S. 1 (1977); *Richmond Newspapers, Inc. v. Virginia*, 448 U.S. 555 (1980) (plurality opinion); *INS v. Chadha*, 462 U.S. 919 (1983); *Nix v. Williams*, 467 U.S. 431 (1984); *United States v. Sharpe*, 470 U.S. 675 (1985).
Harold Hitz Burton (1888-1964)	1945-1958	Truman	Generally, opposed expansion of rights for criminal defendants in state courts. Significant opinions: *Haley v. Ohio*, 332 U.S. 596 (1948) (dissenting opinion); *Henderson v. United States*, 339 U.S. 816 (1950); *Louisiana v. Resweber*, 329 U.S. 459 (1947) (dissenting opinion).
Pierce Butler (1866-1939)	1923-1939*	Harding	Opposed most New Deal regulatory measures. Significant opinions: *Olmstead v. United States*, 277 U.S. 438 (1928) (dissenting opinion); *United States v. Schwimmer*, 279 U.S. 644 (1929).
James Francis Byrnes (1879-1972)	1941-1942	Franklin D. Roosevelt	Last justice who became a lawyer without attending law school. Resigned from the Court to assist the president in the war effort. Served as secretary of state in the Truman administration.
John Archibald Campbell (1811-1889)	1853-1861	Pierce	Resigned soon after Alabama's secession from the Union and became assistant secretary of war for the Confederacy. Significant opinion: *Scott v. Sandford*, 60 U.S. 393 (1857) (concurring opinion).

Name	Tenure	Appointed by	Highlights
John Catron (1786-1865)	1837-1865*	Jackson	Significant opinions: *License Cases*, 46 U.S. 504 (1847); *Scott v. Sandford*, 60 U.S. 393 (1857) (concurring opinion).
Benjamin Nathan Cardozo (1870-1938)	1932-1938*	Hoover	Distinguished career on the New York Court of Appeals and the United States Supreme Court. One of the great jurists in American history. Significant opinions: *Palko v. Connecticut*, 302 U.S. 319 (1937); *Baldwin v. Seelig*, 294 U.S. 511 (1935); *Stewart Machine Co. v. Davis*, 301 U.S. 548 (1937). Other writings: *The Nature of the Judicial Process* (1921); *The Growth of the Law* (1924); *The Paradoxes of Legal Science* (1928).
Salmon Portland Chase (1808-1873)	1864-1873*	Lincoln	Ardent abolitionist. Presided over impeachment trial of President Andrew Johnson. Significant opinions: *Ex parte Milligan*, 71 U.S. 2 (1866) (concurring opinion); *Ex parte McCardle*, 74 U.S. 506 (1869); *United States v. Klein*, 80 U.S. 128 (1871).
Samuel Chase (1741-1811)	1796-1811*	Washington	Signer of the Declaration of Independence, ardent Federalist, and only justice ever impeached, although not convicted by the Senate. Significant opinions: *Ware v. Hylton*, 3 U.S. 199 (1796); *Calder v. Bull* 3 U.S. 386 (1798).
Tom Campbell Clark (1890-1977)	1949-1967	Truman	Author of *Mapp v. Ohio* opinion, which imposed the exclusionary rule on states. Retired from the Court when his son, Ramsey Clark, became attorney general. Significant opinions: *Jenks v. United States*, 353 U.S. 657 (1957) (dissenting opinion); *Mapp v. Ohio*, 367 U.S. 643 (1961); *School District of Abington v. Schempp*, 374 U.S. 203 (1963); *Sheppard v. Maxwell*, 384 U.S. 333 (1966).

Name	Tenure	Appointed by	Highlights
John Hessin Clarke (1857-1945)	1916-1922	Wilson	Resigned from the Court to advocate United States entry into the League of Nations. Significant opinions: *Abrams v. United States*, 250 U.S. 616 (1919); *Hammer v. Dagenhart*, 247 U.S. 251 (1918) (dissenting opinion).
Nathan Clifford (1803-1881)	1858-1881*	Buchanan	
Benjamin Robbins Curtis (1809-1874)	1851-1857	Fillmore	Defense counsel for President Johnson during his impeachment trial. Significant opinions: *Cooley v. Board of Wardens of the Port of Philadelphia*, 53 U.S. 299 (1851); *Scott v. Sandford*, 60 U.S. 393 (1857) (dissenting opinion).
William Cushing (1732-1810)	1790-1810*	Washington	In more than twenty years of service, wrote only nineteen opinions. Significant opinion: *Ware v. Hylton*, 2 U.S. 282 (1796).
William Cushing (1732-1810)	1796	Washington	Chief justice for one week before he decided to decline the office and remain as an associate justice.
Peter Vivian Daniel (1784-1860)	1842-1860*	Van Buren	Consistent advocate of states' rights. Significant opinions: *Cooley v. Board of Wardens of the Port of Philadelphia*, 53 U.S. 299 (1851) (concurring opinion); *Scott v. Sandford*, 60 U.S. 393 (1857) (concurring opinion).
David Davis (1815-1886)	1862-1877	Lincoln	Resigned from the Court to take a seat in the United States Senate. Significant opinion: *Ex parte Milligan*, 71 U.S. 2 (1866).
William Rufus Day (1849-1923)	1903-1922	Theodore Roosevelt	Author of the exclusionary rule remedy for Fourth Amendment violations in federal courts. Significant opinions: *Weeks v. United States*, 232 U.S. 383 (1914); *Hammer v. Dagenhart*, 247 U.S. 251 (1918).

Name	Tenure	Appointed by	Highlights
William Orville Douglas (1898-1980)	1939-1975	Franklin D. Roosevelt	An iconoclast and one of the most outspoken justices. Defender of a broad scope for First Amendment and other individual rights. Significant opinions: *Terminiello v. Chicago*, 337 U.S. 1 (1949); *Griswold v. Connecticut*, 381 U.S. 479 (1965); *Argersinger v. Hamlin*, 407 U.S. 25 (1972). Other writings: *Go East, Young Man* (1974); *The Court Years, 1939-1975* (1980); and more than thirty other books.
Gabriel Duvall (1752-1844)	1811-1835	Madison	One of the first members of the Court to hold strong antislavery views.
Oliver Ellsworth (1745-1807)	1796-1800	Washington	As a senator, the main author of the Judiciary Act of 1789, which established the federal court system.
Stephen Johnson Field (1816-1899)	1863-1897	Lincoln	A zealous advocate of substantive due process doctrine as a means of protecting business from governmental regulation. Survived an assassination attempt by a political rival. Significant opinions: *Slaughterhouse Cases*, 83 U.S. 36 (1873) (dissenting opinion); *Munn v. Illinois*, 94 U.S. 113 (1877) (dissenting opinion). Other writing: *Personal Reminiscences of Early Days in California* (1893).
Abe Fortas (1910-1982)	1965-1969	Lyndon B. Johnson	As a lawyer, successfully argued in *Gideon v. Wainwright*, 372 U.S. 335 (1963), that the right to counsel be applied to the states. Longtime adviser and confidant of President Johnson. Nominated for chief justice in 1968, but withdrew. Resigned after disclosure of alleged financial impropriety involving a former client. Significant opinions: *In re Gault*, 381 U.S. 1 (1967); *Tinker v. Des Moines Independent Community School District*, 393 U.S. 503 (1969).

Name	Tenure	Appointed by	Highlights
Felix Frankfurter (1882-1965)	1939-1962	Franklin D. Roosevelt	Opposed imposition of many provisions of the Bill of Rights on the states through the due process clause of the Fourteenth Amendment. Fought with Justice Black over this issue for more than twenty years. Significant opinions: *Adamson v. California*, 332 U.S. 46 (1947) (concurring opinion); *Wolf v. Colorado*, 338 U.S. 25 (1949); *Rochin v. California*, 342 U.S. 165 (1952).
Melville Weston Fuller (1833-1910)	1888-1910*	Cleveland	Opposed an expansive reading of the Congress' power under the commerce clause. Significant opinions: *United States v. E. C. Knight Co.*, 156 U.S. 1 (1895); *Pollock v. Farmers' Loan & Trust Co.*, 158 U.S. 601 (1895); *Champion v. Ames*, 188 U.S. 321 (1903) (dissenting opinion).
Ruth Bader Ginsburg (1933-)	1993-	Clinton	Argued cases before the Court which established intermediate scrutiny under the equal protection clause of the Fourteenth Amendment for gender-based regulations.
Arthur Joseph Goldberg (1908-1990)	1962-1965	Kennedy	Resigned to become ambassador to the United Nations with expectation that he would be permitted to settle the Vietnam War. Significant opinions: *Escobedo v. Illinois*, 378 U.S. 478 (1964); *Aguilar v. Texas*, 378 U.S. 108 (1964); *Griswold v. Connecticut*, 381 U.S. 479 (1965) (concurring opinion).
Horace Gray (1828-1902)	1882-1902*	Arthur	Significant opinions: *Sparf v. Hansen*, 156 U.S. 51 (1895); *United States v. Wong Kim Ark*, 169 U.S. 649 (1898).
Robert Cooper Grier (1794-1870)	1846-1870	Polk	Significant opinions: *Moore v. Illinois* 55 U.S. 13 (1852); The *Prize Cases*

Name	Tenure	Appointed by	Highlights
John Marshall Harlan (1833-1911)	1877-1911*	Hayes	No other justice has written as many dissenting opinons which later became the law of the land. Significant opinions: *Plessy v. Ferguson*, 163 U.S. 537 (1896) (dissenting opinion); *Pollock v. Farmers' Loan & Trust Co.*, 158 U.S. 601 (1895) (dissenting opinion); *Lochner v. New York*, 198 U.S. 45 (1905) (dissenting opinion); *Berea College v. Kentucky*, 211 U.S. 45 (1908) (dissenting opinion).
John Marshall Harlan II (1899-1971)	1955-1971	Eisenhower	Author of the modern approach to the scope of the Fourth Amendment. Significant opinions: *Katz v. United States*, 389 U.S. 347 (1967) (concurring opinion); *Simmons v. United States*, 390 U.S. 377 (1968); *Spinelli v. United States*, 393 U.S. 410 (1969).
Oliver Wendell Holmes, Jr. (1841-1935)	1902-1932	Theodore Roosevelt	Most influential justice in the twentieth century; wrote with an elegant style unmatched in the history of the Court. Significant opinions: *Lochner v. New York*, 198 U.S. 45 (1905) (dissenting opinion); *Schneck v. United States*, 249 U.S. 47 (1919); *Abrams v. United States*, 250 U.S. 616 (1919) (dissenting opinion); *Pennsylvania Coal Co. v. Mohan*, 260 U.S. 393 (1922). Other writings: *Kent's Commentaries on American Law* (12th edition); *The Common Law* (1881).
Charles Evans Hughes (1862-1948)	1910-1916	Taft	Resigned to run (unsuccessfully) as the Republican nominee for president in 1916; later served as secretary of state in the Harding Administration.
Charles Evans Hughes (1862-1948)	1930-1941	Hoover	Successfully defended the Court against President Roosevelt's Court-packing plan. Significant opinions: *Brown v. Mississippi*, 297 U.S. 278 (1936); *Home Building & Loan Association v. Blaisdell*, 290 U.S. 398 (1934); *NLRB v. Jones and Laughlin Steel Corp.*, 301 U.S. 1 (1937).

Name	Tenure	Appointed by	Highlights
Ward Hunt (1810-1886)	1873-1882	Grant	
James Iredell (1751-1799)	1790-1799*	Washington	Significant opinion: *Chisholm v. Georgia*, 2 U.S. 419 (1793) (dissenting opinion).
Howell Edmunds Jackson (1832-1895)	1893-1895*	Harrison	
Robert Houghwout Jackson (1892-1954)	1941-1954*	Franklin D. Roosevelt	Took a leave from the Court to serve as chief prosecutor in the Nuremberg war crimes trial of Nazi leaders. Publicly feuded with Justice Black over this and other matters. Significant opinion: *West Virginia State Board of Education v. Barnette*, 319 U.S. 624 (1943). Other writings: *The Struggle for Judicial Supremacy* (1941); *The Supreme Court in the American System of Government* (1955).
John Jay (1745-1829)	1789-1795	Washington	In 1795, resigned to become governor of New York, and in 1800 declined nomination as chief justice. Only author of *The Federalist Papers* to serve on the Supreme Court. Significant opinion: *Chisholm v. Georgia*, 2 U.S. 419 (1793).
Thomas Johnson (1732-1819)	1791-1793	Washington	Wrote only one opinion.
William Johnson (1771-1834)	1804-1834*	Jefferson	Only member of the Court during this period who directly challenged Chief Justice Marshall's views on the Constitution. Significant opinions: *Gibbons v. Ogden*, 22 U.S. 1 (1824) (concurring opinion); *United States v. Hudson and Goodwin*, 11 U.S. 32 (1832).

Name	Tenure	Appointed by	Highlights
Anthony McLeod Kennedy (1936-)	1988-	Reagan	Expanded administrative search exception to warrant requirement to individuals. Significant opinions: *Skinner v. Railway Labor Executives' Association*, 489 U.S. 602 (1989); *Illinois v. Perkins*, 496 U.S. 292 (1990).
Joseph Rucker Lamar (1857-1916)	1911- 1916*	Taft	Significant opinion: *Gompers v. Bucks Stove and Range Company*, 221 U.S. 418 (1911).
Lucius Quintus Cincinnatus Lamar (1825-1893)	1888- 1893*	Cleveland	Significant opinions: *In re Neagle*, 135 U.S. 1 (1890) (dissenting opinion); *Field v. Clark*, 143 U.S. 649 (1892) (dissenting opinion).
Henry Brockholst Livingston (1757-1823)	1807- 1823*	Jefferson	
Horace Harmon Lurton (1844-1914)	1910- 1914*	Taft	
John Marshall (1755-1835)	1801- 1835*	John Adams	The "great chief justice" who established preeminent role of the Supreme Court in interpreting the Constitution. No other justice has ever so dominated the Supreme Court. His last constitutional law decision held the Bill of Rights did not apply to the states. Significant opinions: *Marbury v. Madison*, 5 U.S. 137 (1803); *McCulloch v. Maryland*, 17 U.S. 316 (1819); *Gibbons v. Ogden*, 22 U.S. 1 (1824); *Barron v. Baltimore*, 32 U.S. 243 (1833).

Name	Tenure	Appointed by	Highlights
Thurgood Marshall (1908-1993)	1967-1991	Lyndon B. Johnson	Lead lawyer for the NAACP, successfully argued *Brown v. Board of Education* and other cases before the Supreme Court. Viewed the Constitution as providing significant protection for the individual against unjust actions by the government. Adamantly opposed to the death penalty. Significant opinions: *United States v. Wilson*, 420 U.S. 332 (1975); *Gregg v. Georgia*, 428 U.S. 153 (1976) (dissenting opinion); *Donovan v. Dewey*, 452 U.S. 594 (1981); *Oliver v. United States*, 466 U.S. 170 (1984) (dissenting opinion); *Skinner v. Railway Labor Executives' Association*, 489 U.S. 602 (1989) (dissenting opinion); *Florida v. Bostick*, 501 U.S. 429 (1991) (dissenting opinion).
Stanley Thomas Matthews (1824-1889)	1881-1889*	Garfield	Closest Senate confirmation vote (24-23). Significant opinions: *Hurtado v. California*, 110 U.S. 516 (1884); *Yick Wo v. Hopkins*, 118 U.S. 356 (1886).
Joseph McKenna (1843-1926)	1898-1925	McKinley	In 1924, after old age rendered him incompetent but he remained on the Court, the other justices agreed to decide no case where his vote was the deciding one. Significant opinions: *Hoke v. United States*, 227 U.S. 308 (1913); *Hammer v. Dagenhart*, 247 U.S. 251 (1918) (dissenting opinion); *Gilbert v. Minnesota*, 254 U.S. 325 (1920).
John McKinley (1780-1852)	1838-1852*	Van Buren	
John McLean (1785-1861)	1830-1861*	Jackson	Adamant antislavery justice. Significant opinions: *Prigg v. Pennsylvania*, 41 U.S. 539 (1842) (dissenting opinion); *Ex parte Dorr*, 44 U.S. 103 (1844); *Scott v. Sandford*, 60 U.S. 393 (1857) (dissenting opinion).

Name	Tenure	Appointed by	Highlights
James Clark McReynolds (1862-1946)	1914-1941	Wilson	Arguably, the most reactionary and bigoted, and certainly the least congenial justice ever to serve on the Supreme Court. Opposed use of individual rights in criminal cases and New Deal regulatory measures. Significant opinions: *Berger v. United States*, 255 U.S. 22 (1921) (dissenting opinion); *Carroll v. United States*, 267 U.S. 132 (1925) (dissenting opinion); *Pierce v. Society of Sisters*, 268 U.S. 510 (1925); *Stromberg v. California*, 283 U.S. 359 (1931) (dissenting opinion); *Powell v. Alabama*, 287 U.S. 45 (1932) (dissenting opinion).
Samuel Freeman Miller (1816-1890)	1862-1890*	Lincoln	Opposed using the Fourteenth Amendment to block state regulations of business activity and favored the use of individual rights to check the power of the federal government. Significant opinions: *Slaughterhouse Cases*, 83 U.S. 36 (1873); *Kilbourn v. Thompson*, 103 U.S. 168 (1881); *United States v. Lee*, 106 U.S. 196 (1882).
Sherman Minton (1890-1965)	1949-1956	Truman	Consistently held for the government in criminal cases. Significant opinions: *United States v. Rabinowitz*, 339 U.S. 56 (1950); *United States ex rel. Knauff v. Shaughnessy*, 338 U.S. 537 (1950).
William Henry Moody (1853-1917)	1906-1910	Theodore Roosevelt	Believed states were free to confer or withhold individual rights from criminal defendants. Significant opinion: *Twining v. New Jersey*, 211 U.S. 78 (1908); *Londoner v. Denver*, 210 U.S. 373 (1908).
Alfred Moore (1755-1810)	1800-1804	John Adams	Wrote only one opinion.

Name	Tenure	Appointed by	Highlights
Frank Murphy (1890-1949)	1940-1949*	Franklin D. Roosevelt	Argued vigorously for the availability of individual rights as checks on governmental power and opposed the expansion of the scope of warrantless searches and seizures. Significant opinions: *Thornhill v. Alabama*, 310 U.S. 88 (1940); *In re Yamashita*, 327 U.S. 1 (1946) (dissenting opinion); *Harris v. United States*, 331 U.S. 145 (1947) (dissenting opinion); *Wolf v. Colorado*, 338 U.S. 25 (1949) (dissenting opinion).
Samuel Nelson (1792-1873)	1845-1872	Tyler	Significant opinions: *Scott v. Sandford*, 60 U.S. 393 (1857) (concurring opinion); *Prize Cases*, 67 U.S. 635 (1863) (dissenting opinion); *Ex parte Milligan*, 71 U.S. 2 (1866) (dissenting opinion).
Sandra Day O'Connor (1930-)	1981-	Reagan	First woman to serve on the Supreme Court. Significant opinions: *Strictland v. Washington*, 466 U.S. 668 (1984); *Oregon v. Elstad*, 470 U.S. 298 (1985); *Florida v. Bostick*, 501 U.S. 429 (1991).
William Paterson (1745-1806)	1793-1806*	Washington	Significant opinions: *Hylton v. United States*, 3 U.S. 171 (1796); *Stuart v. Laird*, 5 U.S. 299 (1803).
Rufus Wheeler Peckham (1838-1909)	1896-1909*	Cleveland	Author of best-known substantive due process case, *Lochner v. New York*, 198 U.S. 45 (1905). Believed states were not required to offer defendants all of the rights found in the Bill of Rights. Significant opinions: *Crain v. United States*, 162 U.S. 625 (1896); *White v. United States*, 164 U.S. 100 (1896); *Allegeyer v. Louisiana*, 165 U.S. 578 (1897); *Maxwell v. Dow*, 176 U.S. 581 (1900).

Name	Tenure	Appointed by	Highlights
Mahlon Pitney (1858-1924)	1912-1922	Taft	Rejected attempts to apply the Bill of Rights to state criminal justice systems and read the scope of those rights narrowly in federal criminal cases. Significant opinions: *Frank v. Mangum*, 237 U.S. 309 (1915); *Pierce v. United States*, 252 U.S. 239 (1920); *Berger v. United States*, 255 U.S. 22 (1921) (dissenting opinion).
Lewis Franklin Powell, Jr. (1907-1998)	1972-1987	Nixon	Author of modern "open fields" exception to the Fourth Amendment and of opinion cutting back access to federal *habeas corpus* for state prisoners. Significant opinions: *Barker v. Wingo*, 407 U.S. 514 (1972); *Doyle v. Ohio*, 426 U.S. 610 (1976); *Stone v. Powell*, 428 U.S. 465 (1976); *Solem v. Helm*, 463 U.S. 277 (1983); *Oliver v. United States*, 466 U.S. 170 (1984); *Batson v. Kentucky*, 476 U.S. 79 (1986).
Stanley Forman Reed (1884-1980)	1938-1957	Franklin D. Roosevelt	Significant opinions: *McNabb v. United States*, 318 U.S. 347 (1943) (dissenting opinion); *Adamson v. California*, 332 U.S. 46 (1947); *Winters v. New York*, 333 U.S. 507 (1948); *Gallegos v. Nebraska*, 342 U.S. 55 (1951); *Carlson v. Landon*, 342 U.S. 524 (1952); *Brown v. Allen*, 344 U.S. 443 (1953).
William Hubbs Rehnquist (1924-)	1972-1986	Nixon	Opposed to the Warren-era expansion of constitutional rights of defendants. Author of many opinions limiting the scope of these decisions and adamant critic of the exclusionary rule. Significant opinions: *Rakas v. Illinois*, 439 U.S. 128 (1978); *Illinois v. Gates*, 462 U.S. 213 (1983).

Name	Tenure	Appointed by	Highlights
William Hubbs Rehnquist (1924-)	1986-	Reagan	Led the Court in the creation of more exceptions to the warrant requirement of the Fourth Amendment and of limitations on the use of the exclusionary rule. Significant opinions *Colorado v. Connelly*, 479 U.S. 157 (1986); *United States v. Salerno*, 481 U.S. 739 (1987); *Arizona v. Youngblood*, 488 U.S. 51 (1988); *Michigan Department of State Police v. Sitz*, 496 U.S. 444 (1990).
Owen Josephus Roberts (1875-1955)	1930-1945	Hoover	Changed his vote and saved the Supreme Court from President Franklin D. Roosevelt's Court-packing plan, commonly known as a "switch in time that saved the nine." Consistent defender of individual rights in criminal cases. Significant opinions: *Grau v. United States*, 287 U.S. 124 (1932); *Herndon v. Lowry*, 301 U.S. 242 (1937); *Hague v. Committee for Industrial Organization*, 307 U.S. 496 (1939); *Cantwell v. Connecticut*, 310 U.S. 296 (1940); *Betts v. Brady, 316 U.S. 455 (1942).*
John Rutledge (1739-1800)	1790-1791	Washington	Wrote no opinions and attended no sessions of the Supreme Court. Resigned to become chief justice of the South Carolina Court of Common Pleas.
John Rutledge (1739-1800)	1795	Washington	Took oath and presided over one session where two cases were heard before he was not confirmed by the Senate.
Wiley Blount Rutledge, Jr. (1894-1949)	1943-1949*	Franklin D. Roosevelt	Significant opinions: *Thomas v. Collins*, 323 U.S. 518 (1944); *In re Yamashita*, 327 U.S. 1 (1946) (dissenting opinion).

Name	Tenure	Appointed by	Highlights
Edward Terry Sanford (1865-1930)	1923-1930*	Harding	Held that the First Amendment applied to the states through the due process clause of the Fourteenth Amendment. Significant opinions: *Gitlow v. New York*, 268 U.S. 652 (1925); *Fiske v. Kansas*, 274 U.S. 380 (1927).
Antonin Scalia (1936-)	1986-	Reagan	Significant opinions: *Illinois v. Rodriguez*, 497 U.S. 177 (1990); *California v. Hodari D.*, 449 U.S. 621 (1991); *United States v. Williams*, 504 U.S. 36 (1992).
George Shiras (1832-1924)	1892-1903	Harrison	Dissenting opinions offered modern view of the protections offered by the Fifth Amendment. Significant opinions: *Mattox v. United States*, 156 U.S. 237 (1895) (dissenting opinion); *Wong Wing v. United States*, 163 U.S. 228 (1896); *Brown v. Walker*, 161 U.S. 591 (1896) (dissenting opinion).
David Hackett Souter (1939-)	1990-	Bush	
Edwin M. Stanton (1814-1869)	1869*	Grant	Died four days after he was confirmed by the Senate.
John Paul Stevens (1920-)	1975-	Ford	Significant opinions: *Payton v. New York*, 445 U.S. 573 (1980); *United States v. Jacobsen*, 466 U.S. 109 (1984); *Maryland v. Garrison*, 480 U.S. 79 (1987).

Name	Tenure	Appointed by	Highlights
Potter Stewart (1915-1985)	1958-1981	Eisenhower	Leader in development of Supreme Court's approach to interpreting the scope of the Fourth Amendment in modern times. Famous for his quip concerning attempts to define obscenity: "[P]erhaps I could never succeed in intelligibly [defining obscenity]. But I know it when I see it; and the motion picture involved in this case is not that." *Jacobellis v. Ohio*, 378 U.S. 184, 197 (1964) (concurring opinion). Significant opinions: *Massiah v. United States*, 377 U.S. 201 (1964); *Stoner v. California*, 376 U.S. 483 (1964); *Katz v. United States*, 389 U.S. 347 (1967); *Chimel v. California*, 395 U.S. 752 (1969); *Gregg v. Georgia*, 428 U.S. 153 (1976) (plurality opinion); *Brewer v. Williams*, 430 U.S. 387 (1977); *Rhode Island v. Innis*, 446 U.S. 291 (1980).
Harlan Fiske Stone (1872-1946)	1925-1941	Coolidge	Author of footnote four in *United States v. Carolene Products Co.*, 304 U.S. 144 (1938), a key doctrinal innovation leading to modern equal protection analysis under the Fourteenth Amendment.
Harlan Fiske Stone (1872-1946)	1941-1946*	Franklin D. Roosevelt	Led the Supreme Court during the difficult years of World War II.
Joseph Story (1779-1845)	1812-1845*	Madison	Intellectual leader of the Supreme Court who also wrote many of the most significant early commentaries on American law. Significant opinions: *Martin v. Hunter's Lessee*, 14 U.S. 304 (1816); *Charles River Bridge v. Warren Bridge Co.*, 36 U.S. 420 (1837) (dissenting opinion); *United States v. Schooner Amistad*, 40 U.S. 518 (1841); *Swift v. Tyson*, 41 U.S. 1 (1842). Other writings: *Commentaries on the Constitution of the United States* (1833) (3 volumes); *Commentaries on Equity Jurisprudence* (1834); and numerous other books and articles.

Name	Tenure	Appointed by	Highlights
William Strong (1808-1895)	1870-1880	Grant	Author of opinions opening jury service to African Americans. Significant opinions: *Strauder v. West Virginia*, 100 U.S. 303 (1880); *Ex parte Virginia*, 100 U.S. 339 (1880); *Virginia v. Rives*, 100 U.S. 313 (1880).
George Sutherland (1862-1942)	1922-1938	Harding	Intellectual leader of the Supreme Court's opposition to New Deal regulatory measures; supported selective application of the Bill of Rights to state criminal justice systems. Significant opinions: *Powell v. Alabama*, 287 U.S. 45 (1932); *Berger v. United States*, 295 U.S. 78 (1935); *Carter v. Carter Coal Co.*, 298 U.S. 238 (1936).
Noah Haynes Swayne (1804-1884)	1862-1881	Lincoln	Most consistent supporter of President Lincoln's orders concerning prosecution of the Civil War. Significant opinion: *Slaughterhouse Cases*, 83 U.S. 36 (1873) (dissenting opinion).
William Howard Taft (1857-1930)	1921-1930	Harding	Only president ever to serve on the Court. As chief justice he actively sought to influence appointments to the Supreme Court. Author of property-based view of the scope of the Fourth Amendment. Significant opinions: *Myers v. United States*, 272 U.S. 52 (1926); *Olmstead v. United States*, 277 U.S. 438 (1928).
Roger Brooke Taney (1777-1864)	1836-1864*	Jackson	Pro-slavery and states' rights chief justice; author of the infamous *Scott v. Sandford* opinion. Resisted many of President Lincoln's orders concerning the prosecution of the Civil War. Significant opinions: *Charles River Bridge v. Warren Bridge Co.*, 36 U.S. 420 (1837); *License Cases*, 46 U.S. 504 (1847); *Scott v. Sandford*, 60 U.S. 393 (1857).

Name	Tenure	Appointed by	Highlights
Clarence Thomas (1948-)	1991-	Bush	Most controversial modern Supreme Court appointment; accused of sexual harrassment during confirmation process.
Smith Thompson (1768-1843)	1824-1843*	Monroe	Significant opinion: *Cherokee Nation v. Georgia*, 30 U.S. 1 (1831) (dissenting opinion).
Thomas Todd (1765-1826)	1807-1826*	Jefferson	Never disagreed with Chief Justice Marshall on any constitutional issue.
Robert Trimble (1777-1828)	1826-1828*	John Q. Adams	Significant opinions: *The Antelope Case*, 25 U.S. 546 (1827); *Ogden v. Saunders*, 25 U.S. 213 (1827).
Willis Van Devanter (1859-1941)	1911-1937	Taft	Significant opinion: *McGrain v. Daugherty*, 273 U.S. 135 (1927).
Frederick Moore Vinson (1890-1953)	1946-1953*	Truman	Significant opinions: *Harris v. United States*, 331 U.S. 145 (1947); *Shelley v. Kraemer, 334 U.S. 1 (1948); Stack v. Boyle*, 342 U.S. 1 (1951); *Dennis v. United States*, 341 U.S. 494 (1951).
Morrison Remick Waite (1816-1888)	1874-1888*	Grant	Significant opinions: *United States v. Cruikshank*, 92 U.S. 542 (1876); *Munn v. Illinois*, 94 U.S. 113 (1876).

Name	Tenure	Appointed by	Highlights
Earl Warren (1891-1974)	1953-1969	Eisenhower	Second only to Chief Justice Marshall in impact on the Supreme Court's role. Led expansion of constitutional rights for defendants in state courts and the transformation of the meaning of the equal protection clause of the Fourteenth Amendment. Significant opinions: *Brown v. Board of Education*, 347 U.S. 483 (1954); *Watkins v. United States*, 354 U.S. 178 (1957); *Spano v. New York, 360 U.S. 315 (1959); Reynolds v. Sims*, 377 U.S. 533 (1964); *Miranda v. Arizona*, 384 U.S. 436 (1966); *Terry v. Ohio*, 392 U.S. 1 (1968).
Bushrod Washington (1762-1829)	1789-1829*	John Adams	Almost always agreed with Chief Justice Marshall's views. Significant opinion: *Ogden v. Saunders*, 25 U.S. 213 (1827).
James Moore Wayne (1790-1867)	1835-1867*	Jackson	Significant opinion: *Louisville, Cincinnati and Charleston Railroad Co. v. Letson*, 43 U.S. 497 (1844).
Byron Raymond White (1917-)	1962-1993	Kennedy	Critical of the exclusionary rule and expansive view of the scope of protection offered by the Fourth Amendment. Significant opinions: *Miranda v. Arizona, 384 U.S. 436 (1966) (dissenting opinion); Camara v. Municipal Court of the City and County of San Francisco, 387 U.S. 523 (1967); Duncan v. Louisiana, 391 U.S. 145 (1968); Chambers v. Maroney, 399 U.S. 42 (1970); United States v. Matlock, 415 U.S. 164 (1974); Stone v. Powell*, 428 U.S. 465 (1976) (dissenting opinion); *United States v. Leon, 468 U.S. 897 (1984); New Jersey v. T.L.O., 469 U.S. 325 (1985); California v. Greenwood*, 486 U.S. 35 (1988).
Edward Douglas White (1845-1921)	1894-1910	Cleveland	Significant opinion: *Rasmussen v. United States*, 197 U.S. 506 (1905).

Name	Tenure	Appointed by	Highlights
Edward Douglas White (1845-1921)	1910-1921*	Taft	Significant opinion: *Standard Oil Co. v. United States*, 221 U.S. 1 (1911).
Charles Evans Whittaker (1901-1973)	1957-1962	Eisenhower	Supplied the critical vote in a series of 5-4 decisions in which the Supreme Court rejected individual rights claims in state criminal cases. Significant opinions: *Draper v. United States*, 358 U.S. 307 (1959).
James Wilson (1742-1798)	1789-1798*	Washington	While on the Court, was imprisoned for failure to pay his debts. Significant opinions: *Chisholm v. Georgia*, 2 U.S. 419 (1793).
Levi Woodbury (1789-1851)	1845-1851*	Polk	Rejected abolitionists' arguments for limiting the impact of the fugitive slave clause of the Constitution. Significant opinion: *Jones v. Van Zandt*, 46 U.S. 215 (1847).
William Burnham Woods (1824-1887)	1881-1887*	Hayes	Significant opinions: *United States v. Lee*, 106 U.S. 196 (1882) (dissenting opinion); *United States v. Harris*, 106 U.S. 629 (1883); *Presser v. Illinois*, 116 U.S. 252 (1886).

Bibliography

Law

Abadinsky, Howard. *Law and Justice.* Chicago: Nelson-Hall, 1988.

Arthur, John, and William H. Shaw, eds. *Readings in Philosophy of Law.* Englewood Cliffs, N.J.: Prentice-Hall, 1984.

Black, Henry. *Black's Law Dictionary.* 6th ed. St. Paul, Minn.: West, 1990.

Cantor, Norman F. *Imagining the Law: Common Law and the Foundations of the American Legal System.* New York: Harper-Collins, 1997.

Cappalli, Richard B. *The American Common Law Method.* Irvington, N.Y.: Transnational, 1997.

Davidow, Robert P., ed. *Natural Rights and Natural Law: The Legacy of George Mason.* Fairfax, Va.: George Mason University Press, 1986.

Dworkin, R. M., ed. *The Philosophy of Law.* Oxford, England: Oxford University Press, 1977.

Fast, Julius, and Timothy Fast. *The Legal Atlas of the United States.* New York: Facts on File, 1997.

Feinbergm, Joel, and Hyman Gross, eds. *Philosophy of Law.* 2d ed. Belmont, Calif.: Wadsworth Publishing, 1980.

Finnis, John. *Natural Law and Natural Rights.* Oxford, England: Clarendon Press, 1992.

Glendon, Mary Ann, Michael Wallace Gordon, and Christopher Osakwe. *Comparative Legal Traditions in a Nutshell.* St. Paul, Minn.: West, 1982.

Gould, William B. *A Primer on American Labor Law.* 3d ed. Cambridge, Mass.: MIT Press, 1993.

Hart, H. L. A. *The Concept of Law.* Oxford: Clarendon Press, 1961.

Matthews, Elizabeth W. *The Law Library Reference Shelf: Annotated Subject Guide.* 3d ed. Buffalo, N.Y.: W.S. Hein, 1996.

Sawer, Geoffrey. *Law in Society.* Oxford: Clarendon Press, 1965.

Shenefield, John H. *The Antitrust Laws: A Primer.* 2d ed. Washington, D.C.: AEI Press, 1996.

Walker, David M. *The Oxford Companion to Law*. Oxford: Clarendon Press, 1980.

Walker, Geoffrey De Q. *The Rule of Law*. Carlton, Victoria, Australia: Melbourne University Press, 1988.

West Publishing Company *West's Encyclopedia of American Law*. Saint Paul, Minn.: West Publishing, 1998.

The U.S. Constitution

Anastaplo, George. *The Constitution of 1787: A Commentary*. Baltimore: Johns Hopkins University Press, 1989.

Baker, Thomas E. *"The Most Wonderful Work": Our Constitution Interpreted*. St. Paul, Minn.: West, 1996.

Bizzoco, Dennis, ed. *The Exhaustive Concordance to the United States Constitution*. Chattanooga, Tenn.: Firm Foundation Press, 1994.

Bloom, Allan. *Confronting the Constitution*. Washington, D.C.: AEI Press, 1990.

Burger, Warren E. *It Is So Ordered: A Constitution Unfolds*. New York: William Morrow, 1995.

Dworkin, R. M. *Freedom's Law: The Moral Reading of the American Constitution*. Cambridge, Mass.: Harvard University Press, 1996.

Farber, Daniel A., and Suzanna Sherry. *A History of the American Constitution*. St. Paul, Minn.: West, 1990.

Friendly, Fred, and Martha Elliot. *The Constitution: That Delicate Balance*. New York: Random House, 1984.

Galloway, Russell, and Rose E. Bird. *A Student's Guide to Basic Constitutional Analysis*. New York: Matthew Bender/Irwin, 1996.

Hamilton, Alexander, James Madison, and John Jay. *The Federalist Papers*. New York: New American Library, 1961.

Kammen, Michael, ed. *The Origins of the American Constitution: A Documentary History*. New York: Penguin Books, 1986.

Kelly, Alfred H,. Winfred A. Harbison, and Herman Belz. *The American Constitution: Its Origin and Development*. 6th ed. New York: W. W. Norton, 1983.

Kluge, Dave. *The People's Guide to the United States Constitution*. New York: Carol, 1994.

Kramnick, Isaac, and Laurence R. Moore. *The Godless Constitution: The Case Against Religious Correctness.* New York: Norton, 1996.

Kyvig, David E. *Explicit and Authentic Acts: Amending the U.S. Constitution, 1776-1995.* Lawrence: University Press of Kansas, 1996.

Lamm, Barbara. *The American Constitution in Context.* Commack, N.Y.: Nova Science Publishers, 1996.

Levy, Leonard W., et al., eds. *Encyclopedia of the American Constitution.* 4 vols. New York: Macmillan, 1986.

Mansfield, Harvey C. *America's Constitutional Soul.* Baltimore: Johns Hopkins University Press, 1991.

Mitchell, Ralph. *CQ's Guide to the U.S. Constitution.* 2d ed. Washington, D.C.: Congressional Quarterly, 1994.

Padover, Saul K., and Jacob W. Landynski. *The Living U.S. Constitution: Historical Background, Landmark Supreme Court Decisions: With Introductions, Indexed Guide, Pen Portraits of the Signers.* 3d rev. ed. by Jacob W. Landynski. New York: Meridian, 1995.

Peltason, J. W. *Corwin and Peltason's Understanding the Constitution.* 13th ed. San Diego, Calif.: Harcourt Brace, 1994.

Rakove, Jack N. *Original Meanings: Politics and Ideas in the Making of the Constitution.* New York: Alfred A. Knopf, 1996.

Stevens, Richard G. *The American Constitution and Its Provenance.* Lanham, Md.: Rowman & Littlefield, 1997.

Vile, John R. *A Companion to the United States Constitution and Its Amendments.* 2d ed. Westport, Conn.: Praeger, 1997.

Wolfe, Christopher. *How to Read the Constitution: Originalism, Constitutional Interpretation, and Judicial Power.* Lanham, Md.: Rowman & Littlefield, 1996.

Constitutional Law

Abramson, Jeffrey. *We, the Jury: Justice and the Democratic Ideal.* New York: Basic Books, 1994.

Barron, Jerome A., and C. Thomas Dienes. *Constitutional Law in a Nutshell.* 3d ed. St. Paul, Minn.: West, 1995.

Braveman, Daan, William C. Banks, and Rodney A. Smolla. *Constitutional Law: Structure and Rights in Our Federal System.* 3d ed. New York: Matthew Bender, 1996.

Chandler, Ralph C. *The Constitutional Law Dictionary.* 2 vols. Santa Barbara, Calif.: ABC-Clio, 1985.

Chemerinsky, Erwin. *Constitutional Law: Principles and Policies.* New York: Aspen Law & Business, 1997.

Coleman, Jules L., and Anthony J. Sebok, eds. *Constitutional Law and Its Interpretation.* New York: Garland, 1994.

Cook, Joseph G. *Constitutional Rights of the Accused.* 2d ed. 3 vols. Rochester, N.Y.: Lawyers Cooperative, 1985-1986.

Fisher, Louis. *American Constitutional Law.* 2d ed. New York: McGraw-Hill, 1995.

Goldwin, Robert A., and William A. Schambra, eds. *How Does the Constitution Secure Rights?* Washington: American Enterprise Institute, 1985.

Grasso, Kenneth L., and Cecilia Rodriguez Castillo, eds. *Liberty Under Law: American Constitutionalism, Yesterday, Today, and Tomorrow.* Lanham, Md.: University Press of America, 1997.

Hyman, Harold M., and William M. Wiecek. *Equal Justice Under Law: Constitutional Development, 1835-1875.* New York: Harper and Row, 1982.

Lockard, Duane, and Walter F. Murphy. *Basic Cases in Constitutional Law.* 2d ed. Washington, D.C.: Congressional Quarterly Press, 1987.

McClellan, James. *Liberty, Order, and Justice: An Introduction to the Constitutional Principles of American Government.* Cumberland, Va.: James River Press, 1989.

Siegel, Larry J., ed. *American Justice: Research of the National Institute of Justice.* St. Paul, Minn.: West, 1990.

Stone, Geoffrey R., et al. *Constitutional Law.* 2d ed. Boston: Little, Brown, 1991.

Judicial Review

Choper, Jesse H. *Judicial Review and the National Political Process.* Chicago: University of Chicago Press, 1980.

Clinton, Robert Lowry. *Marbury v. Madison and Judicial Review.* Lawrence: University Press of Kansas, 1989.

Cox, Archibald. *The Court and the Constitution.* Boston: Houghton Mifflin, 1987.

Ely, John Hart. *Democracy and Distrust: A Theory of Judicial Review.* Cambridge, Mass.: Harvard University Press, 1980.

Garraty, John A., ed. *Quarrels That Have Shaped the Constitution*. Rev. ed. New York: Perennial Library, 1987.

Johnston, Richard E. *The Effect of Judicial Review on Federal-State Relations in Australia, Canada, and the United States*. Baton Rouge: Louisiana State University Press, 1969.

Kutler, Stanley I. *Judicial Power and Reconstruction Politics*. Chicago: University of Chicago Press, 1968.

The Incorporation Doctrine

Alderman, Ellen, and Caroline Kennedy. *In Our Defense: The Bill of Rights in Action*. New York: Avon Books, 1991.

Berger, Raoul. *The Fourteenth Amendment and the Bill of Rights*. Oklahoma City: University of Oklahoma Press, 1989.

Berger, Raoul. *Government by Judiciary: The Transformation of the Fourteenth Amendment*. Cambridge, Mass.: Harvard University Press, 1977.

Cortner, Richard. *The Supreme Court and the Second Bill of Rights: The Fourteenth Amendment and the Nationalization of Civil Liberties*. Madison: University of Wisconsin Press, 1981.

Curtis, Michael Kent. *No State Shall Abridge*. Durham, N.C.: Duke University Press, 1986.

Konvitz, Milton R., ed. *Bill of Rights Reader: Leading Constitutional Cases*. 5th rev. ed. Ithaca, N.Y.: Cornell University Press, 1973.

Nelson, William. *The Fourteenth Amendment*. Cambridge, Mass.: Harvard University Press, 1988.

The U.S. Judicial System

Abraham, Henry J. *The Judicial Process: An Introductory Analysis of the Courts of the United States, England, and France*. 6th Ed. New York: Oxford University Press, 1993.

Blank, Blanche D. *The Not So Grand Jury: The Story of the Federal Grand Jury System*. Lanham, Md.: University Press of America, 1993.

Bodenhamer, David. *Fair Trial: Rights of the Accused in American History*. New York: Oxford University Press, 1992.

Brenner, Susan W., and Gregory G. Lockhart. *Federal Grand Jury Practice*. St. Paul, Minn.: West, 1996.

Calvi, James V., and Susan E. Coleman. *American Law and Legal Systems*. 3d ed. Upper Saddle River, N.J.: Prentice Hall, 1997.

Clement, Mary. *The Juvenile Justice System: Law and Process*. Boston: Butterworth-Heinemann, 1997.

Farnsworth, E. Allan. *An Introduction to the Legal System of the United States*. 3d ed. Dobbs Ferry, N.Y.: Oceana, 1996.

Fine, Toni M. *American Legal Systems: A Resource and Reference Guide*. Cincinnati, Ohio: Anderson, 1997.

Lesser, Maximus A., and William S. Hein. *The Historical Development of the Jury System*. Buffalo, N.Y.: W. S. Hein, 1992.

Levy, Leonard. *Origins of the Fifth Amendment: The Right Against Self-Incrimination*. New York: Oxford University Press, 1968.

Williams, Mary E., ed. *The Jury System*. San Diego, Calif.: Greenhaven Press, 1997.

The Courts

Bator, Paul M., and Daniel J. Meltzer, eds. *Hart and Wechsler's The Federal Courts and the Federal System*. 3d ed. Westbury, N.Y.: Foundation Press, 1988.

Carp, Robert A., and Ronald Stidham. *The Federal Courts*. 2d ed. Washington, D.C.: Congressional Quarterly Press, 1991.

Fino, Susan P. *The Role of State Supreme Courts in the New Judicial Federalism*. New York: Greenwood, 1987.

Glick, Henry R. *State Court Systems*. Englewood Cliffs, N.J.: Prentice-Hall, 1973.

Horowitz, Donald L. *The Courts and Social Policy*. Washington, D.C.: Brookings Institution, 1977.

Institute of Judicial Administration. *A Guide to Court Systems*. 5th ed. New York: Author, 1971.

Marcus, Maeva. *Origins of the Federal Judiciary: Essays on the Judiciary Act of 1789*. New York: Oxford University Press, 1992.

Mayers, Lewis. *The American Legal System*. Littleton, Colo.: Rothman, 1981.

Meador, Daniel J. *American Courts*. St. Paul, Minn.: West, 1991.

Mezey, Susan Gluck. *In Pursuit of Equality: Women, Public Policy, and the Federal Courts*. New York: St. Martin's Press, 1992.

Posner, Richard A. *The Federal Courts: Crisis and Reform*. Cambridge, Mass.: Harvard University Press, 1985.

Pound, Roscoe. *Organization of Courts*. Westport, Conn.: Greenwood Press, 1979.

Surrency, Erwin C. *History of the Federal Courts*. New York: Oceana, 1987.

Tarr, G. Alan *State Supreme Courts in State and Nation*. New Haven, Conn.: Yale University Press, 1988.

Wheeler, Russell R., and Cynthia E. Harrison. *Creating the Federal Judicial System*. 2d ed. Washington, D.C.: Federal Judicial Center, 1994.

Wright, Charles A. *The Law of Federal Courts*. 5th ed. St. Paul, Minn.: West, 1994.

U.S. Supreme Court: Structure and Functions

Abraham, Henry J. *The Judiciary: The Supreme Court in the Governmental Process*. 7th ed. Boston: Allyn & Bacon, 1987.

Anzovin, Steven, and Janet Podell. *The U.S. Constitution and the Supreme Court*. New York: H. W. Wilson, 1988.

Baum, Lawrence. *The Supreme Court*. 5th ed. Washington, D.C.: Congressional Quarterly Press, 1995.

Biskupic, Joan, and Elder Witt. *Guide to the U.S. Supreme Court*. 3d ed. Washington, D.C.: Congressional Quarterly, 1997.

Biskupic, Joan, and Elder Witt. *The Supreme Court at Work*. 2d ed. Washington, D.C.: Congressional Quarterly Inc., 1997.

Congressional Quarterly's Guide to the U.S. Supreme Court. 2d ed. Washington, D.C.: Congressional Quarterly Press, 1990.

Cooper, Phillip J., and Howard Ball. *The United States Supreme Court: From the Inside Out*. Upper Saddle River, N.J.: Prentice Hall, 1996.

Epstein, Lee. *The Supreme Court Compendium: Data, Decisions, and Developments*. Washington, D.C.: Congressional Quarterly, 1994.

Franck, Matthew J. *Against the Imperial Judiciary: The Supreme Court vs. the Sovereignty of the People*. Lawrence: University Press of Kansas, 1996.

Greenberg, Ellen. *The Supreme Court Explained*. New York: W. W. Norton, 1997.

Hall, Kermit L., ed. *The Oxford Companion to the Supreme Court of the United States*. New York: Oxford University Press, 1992.

Hamilton, Jack A., ed. *The Supreme Court: Guardian or Ruler?* New York: Scholastic Book Services, 1968.

McCloskey, Robert G., and Sanford Levinson. *The American Supreme Court.* 2d ed. Chicago: University of Chicago Press, 1994.

McGurn, Barrett. *America's Court: The Supreme Court and the People.* Golden, Colo.: Fulcrum, 1997.

McKeever, Robert J. *The United States Supreme Court: A Political and Legal Analysis.* New York: Manchester University Press, 1997.

Paddock, Lisa, and Paul M. Barrett. *Facts About the Supreme Court of the United States.* New York: H. W. Wilson, 1996.

Schwartz, Bernard. *Decision: How the Supreme Court Decides Cases.* New York: Oxford University Press, 1996.

Wasby, Stephen L. *The Supreme Court in the Federal Judicial System.* 4th ed. Chicago: Nelson-Hall, 1993.

Witt, Elder, ed. *The Supreme Court A to Z: A Ready Reference Encyclopedia.* Washington, D.C.: Congressional Quarterly Press, 1993.

U.S. Supreme Court: History and Cases

Blasi, Vincent, ed. *The Burger Court.* New Haven, Conn.: Yale University Press, 1983.

Campbell, Douglas S. *The Supreme Court and the Mass Media: Selected Cases, Summaries, and Analyses.* New York: Praeger, 1990.

Davis, Abraham L., and Barbara L. Graham. *The Supreme Court, Race, and Civil Rights.* Thousand Oaks, Calif.: Sage Publications, 1995.

Devol, Kenneth S. *Mass Media and the Supreme Court: Legacy of the Warren Years.* 4th ed. New York: Hastings House, 1990.

Eastland, Terry, ed. *Benchmarks: Great Constitutional Controversies in the Supreme Court.* Grand Rapids, Mich.: W.B. Eerdmans, 1995.

Fehrenbacher, Don E. *The Dred Scott Case: Its Significance in American Law and Politics.* New York: Oxford University Press, 1978.

Friendly, Fred W. *Minnesota Rag: The Dramatic Story of the Landmark Supreme Court Case That Gave New Meaning to Freedom of the Press*. New York: Random House, 1981.

Irons, Peter. *The Courage of Their Convictions: Sixteen Americans Who Fought Their Way to the Supreme Court*. New York: Free Press, 1988.

James, Leonard F. *The Supreme Court in American Life*. Glenview, Ill.: Scott, Foresman, 1964.

Manfredi, Christopher P. *The Supreme Court and Juvenile Justice*. Lawrence, University Press of Kansas, 1998.

O'Brien, David M. *Storm Center: The Supreme Court in American Politics*. 4th ed. New York: W. W. Norton, 1996.

Rehnquist, William H. *The Supreme Court: How It Was, How It Is*. New York: William Morrow, 1987.

Smith, Christopher E. *The Rehnquist Court and Criminal Punishment*. New York: Garland, 1997.

Spann, Girardeau A. *Race Against the Court: The Supreme Court and Minorities in Contemporary America*. New York: New York University Press, 1993.

Tucker, David F. B. *The Rehnquist Court and Civil Rights*. Aldershot; Brookfield, USA: Dartmouth, 1995.

Watson, George, and John A. Stookey. *Shaping America: The Politics of Supreme Court Appointments*. New York: HarperCollins, 1995.

Wilkins, David E. *American Indian Sovereignty and the U.S. Supreme Court: The Masking of Justice*. Austin: University of Texas Press, 1997.

U.S. Supreme Court: Justices

Cushman, Clare. *The Supreme Court Justices: Illustrated Biographies, 1789-1995*. 2d ed. Washington, D.C.: Congressional Quarterly, 1995.

Lewis, Walker. *Without Fear or Favor: A Biography of Chief Justice Roger Brooke Taney*. Boston: Houghton Mifflin, 1965.

Mason, Alpheus Thomas. *William Howard Taft: Chief Justice*. New York: Simon and Schuster, 1965.

Schwartz, Bernard. *Super Chief: Earl Warren and His Supreme Court, a Judicial Biography*. New York: New York University Press, 1983.

Tushnet, Mark V. *Making Civil Rights Law: Thurgood Marshall and the Supreme Court, 1936-1961.* New York: Oxford University Press, 1994.

Tushnet, Mark V. *Making Constitutional Law: Thurgood Marshall and the Supreme Court, 1961-1991.* New York: Oxford University Press, 1997.

Urofsky, Melvin I., ed. *The Supreme Court Justices: A Biographical Dictionary.* New York: Garland, 1994.

Criminal Justice System

Abadinsky, Howard. *Crime and Justice: An Introduction.* Chicago: Nelson-Hall, 1987.

Austern, David. *The Crime Victim's Handbook.* New York: Viking Press, 1987.

Baker, Liva. *Miranda: The Crime, the Law, and the Politics.* New York: Atheneum, 1983.

Bidinotto, Robert J. *Criminal Justice? The Legal System Versus Individual Responsibility.* 2d ed. Irvington-on-Hudson, N.Y.: Foundation for Economic Education, 1996.

Champion, Dean J. *Criminal Justice in the United States.* Columbus, Ohio: Merrill, 1990.

Champion, Dean J. *Felony Probation: Problems and Prospects.* Westport, Conn.: Praeger, 1988.

Champion, Dean J. *Probation and Parole in the United States.* Columbus, Ohio: Merrill, 1990.

Chavez, Linda, and Gerald A. Reynolds. *Race and the Criminal Justice System: How Race Affects Jury Trials.* Washington, D.C.: Center for Equal Opportunity, 1996.

Cole, George F. *The American System of Criminal Justice.* 7th ed. Belmont, Calif.: Wadsworth, 1995.

Currie, Elliott. *Crime and Punishment in America.* New York: Henry Holt, 1998.

Friedman, Lawrence M. *Crime and Punishment in American History.* New York: Basic Books, 1993.

Israel, Jerold, and Wayne LaFave. *Criminal Procedure.* 3d ed. St. Paul, Minn.: West Publishing, 1980.

Kamisar, Yale. *Police Interrogation and Confessions: Essays in Law and Policy.* Ann Arbor: University of Michigan Press, 1980.

Katz, Burton S. *Justice Overruled: Unmasking the Criminal Justice System*. New York: Warner Books, 1997.

Kender, Suzanne E., ed. *Crime in America*. New York: H. W. Wilson, 1996.

Keve, Paul W. *Crime Control and Justice in America: Searching for Facts and Answers*. Chicago: American Library Association, 1995.

Roberson, Cliff, and Max Futrell. *An Introduction to Criminal Justice Research*. Springfield, Ill.: Charles C Thomas, 1988.

Samaha, Joel. *Criminal Justice*. 3d ed. St. Paul, Minn.: West, 1994.

Schmalleger, Frank, and Gordon M. Armstrong. *Crime and the Justice Systems in America: An Encyclopedia*. Westport, Conn.: Greenwood Press, 1997.

Walker, Samuel. *Popular Justice: A History of American Criminal Justice*. 2d ed. New York: Oxford University Press, 1998.

Whitebread, Charles, and Christopher Slobogin. *Criminal Procedure: An Analysis of Cases and Concepts*. 3d ed. Westbury, N.Y.: Foundation Press, 1993.

Capital Punishment

Bedau, Hugo A. *The Courts, The Constitution, and Capital Punishment*. Lexington, Mass.: Lexington Books, 1977.

Bedau, Hugo A. *The Death Penalty in America: Current Controversies*. New York: Oxford University Press, 1997.

Bedau, Hugo A., and Chester M. Pierce. *Capital Punishment in the United States*. New York: AMS Press, 1975.

Berger, Raoul. *Death Penalties: The Supreme Court's Obstacle Course*. Cambridge, Mass.: Harvard University Press, 1982.

Cornelius, William J. *Swift and Sure: Bringing Certainty and Finality to Criminal Punishment*. Irvington-on-Hudson, N.Y.: Bridge Street Books, Inc., 1997.

Hook, Donald D., and Lothar Kahn. *Death in the Balance: The Debate over Capital Punishment*. Lexington, Mass.: Lexington Books, 1989.

Johnson, Robert. *Condemned to Die: Life Under Sentence of Death*. Prospect Heights, Ill.: Waveland Press, 1989.

Latzer, Barry. *Death Penalty Cases: Leading U.S. Supreme Court Cases on Capital Punishment*. Boston: Butterworth Heinemann, 1997.

Megivern, James J. *The Death Penalty: A Historical and Theological Survey*. New York: Paulist Press, 1997.

Meltsner, Michael. *Cruel and Unusual: The Supreme Court and Capital Punishment*. New York: Random House, 1973.

Radelet, Michael L., ed. *Facing the Death Penalty: Essays on Cruel and Unusual Punishment*. Philadelphia: Temple University Press, 1989.

Randa, Laura E. *Society's Final Solution: A History and Discussion of the Death Penalty*. Lanham, Md.: University Press of America, 1997.

Vila, Bryan, and Cynthia Morris. *Capital Punishment in the United States: A Documentary History*. Westport, Conn.: Greenwood Press, 1997.

Zimring, Franklin E., and Gordon Hawkins. *Capital Punishment and the American Agenda*. Cambridge, England: Cambridge University Press, 1986.

The U.S. Bill of Rights

Alley, Robert S. *School Prayer: The Court, the Congress, and the First Amendment*. Buffalo, N.Y.: Prometheus Books, 1994.

Berns, Walter. *The First Amendment and the Future of American Democracy*. New York: Basic Books, 1970.

Friendly, Fred W. *The Good Guys, the Bad Guys, and the First Amendment: Free Speech vs. Fairness in Broadcasting*. New York: Random House, 1976.

Garry, Patrick M. *The American Vision of a Free Press: An Historical and Constitutional Revisionist View of the Press as a Marketplace of Ideas*. New York: Garland, 1990.

Garry, Patrick M. *Scrambling for Protection: The New Media and the First Amendment*. Pittsburgh, Pa.: University of Pittsburgh Press, 1994.

Halbrook, Stephen P. *A Right to Bear Arms: State and Federal Bills of Rights and Constitutional Guarantees*. New York: Greenwood Press, 1989.

Hemmer, Joseph J., Jr. *The Supreme Court and the First Amendment*. New York: Praeger, 1986.

Hentoff, Nat. *The First Freedom: The Tumultuous History of Free Speech in America*. New York: Delacorte Press, 1980.

Hickok, Eugene W., Jr., ed. *The Bill of Rights: Original Meaning and Current Understanding.* Charlottesville: University of Virginia Press, 1991.

Hohenberg, John. *Free Press/Free People: The Best Cause.* New York: Columbia University Press, 1971.

Ingelhart, Louis E. *Press and Speech Freedoms in America, 1619-1995: A Chronology.* Westport, Conn.: Greenwood Press, 1997.

Konvitz, Milton R. *First Amendment Freedoms: Selected Cases on Freedom of Religion, Speech, Press, Assembly.* Ithaca, N.Y.: Cornell University Press, 1963.

Labunski, Richard E. *The First Amendment Under Siege: The Politics of Broadcast Regulation.* Westport, Conn.: Greenwood Press, 1981.

Ladenson, Robert F. *A Philosophy of Free Expression and Its Constitutional Applications.* Lanham, Md.: Rowman & Littlefield, 1983.

Leahy, James E. *The First Amendment, 1791-1991: Two Hundred Years of Freedom.* Jefferson, N.C.: McFarland, 1991.

Lewis, Anthony. *Make No Law: The Sullivan Case and the First Amendment.* New York: Random House, 1991.

Malcolm, Joyce L. *To Keep and Bear Arms: The Origins of an Anglo-American Right.* Cambridge, Mass.: Harvard University Press, 1994.

Murphy, Paul L. *The Meaning of Freedom of Speech: First Amendment Freedoms from Wilson to FDR.* Westport, Conn.: Greenwood Press, 1972.

O'Brien, David M. *The Public's Right to Know: The Supreme Court and the First Amendment.* New York: Praeger, 1981.

Pember, Don R. *Privacy and the Press: The Law, the Mass Media, and the First Amendment.* Seattle: University of Washington Press, 1972.

Polenberg, Richard. *Fighting Faiths: The Abrams Case, the Supreme Court, and Free Speech.* New York: Viking Press, 1987.

Powe, Lucas A., Jr. *American Broadcasting and the First Amendment.* Berkeley: University of California Press, 1987.

Rogers, Donald J. *Press Versus Government: Constitutional Issues.* New York: Julian Messner, 1986.

Schwartz, Bernard. *The Great Rights of Mankind: A History of the American Bill of Rights*. New York: Oxford University Press, 1977.

Smith, Rodney K. *Public Prayer and the Constitution: A Case Study in Constitutional Interpretation*. Wilmington, Del.: Scholarly Resources, 1987.

Stevens, John D. *Shaping the First Amendment: The Development of Free Expression*. Beverly Hills, Calif.: Sage Publications, 1982.

Stone, Geoffrey R., Richard A. Epstein, and Cass R. Sunstein, eds. *The Bill of Rights in the Modern State*. Chicago: University of Chicago Press, 1992.

Van Alstyne, William W. *Interpretations of the First Amendment*. Durham, N.C.: Duke University Press, 1984.

Zerman, Melvyn B. *Taking on the Press: Constitutional Rights in Conflict*. New York: Thomas Y. Crowell, 1986.

Civil Liberties

Alderman, Ellen, and Caroline Kennedy. *The Right to Privacy*. New York: Alfred A. Knopf, 1995.

Barker, Lucius J., and Twiley W. Barker, Jr. *Civil Liberties and the Constitution*. 7th ed. Englewood Cliffs, N.J.: Prentice-Hall, 1994.

Belknap, Michal R. *Cold War Political Justice: The Smith Act, the Communist Party, and American Civil Liberties*. Westport, Conn.: Greenwood Press, 1977.

Bracken, Harry M. *Freedom of Speech: Words Are Not Deeds*. Westport, Conn.: Praeger, 1994.

Cohen, William, and David J. Danelski. *Constitutional Law: Civil Liberty and Individual Rights*. 3d ed. Westbury, N.Y.: Foundation Press, 1994.

Frankel, Marvin E. *Faith and Freedom: Religious Liberty in America*. New York: Hill & Wang, 1994.

Garvey, John H., and Frederick F. Schauer. *The First Amendment: A Reader*. 2d ed. St. Paul, Minn.: West, 1996.

Gates, Henry Louis, ed. *Speaking of Race, Speaking of Sex: Hate Speech, Civil Rights, and Civil Liberties*. New York: New York University Press, 1994.

Kirk, Russell, and Mitchell S. Muncy. *Rights and Duties: Reflections On Our Conservative Constitution*. Dallas, Tex.: Spence, 1997.

Koop, C. Everett. *The Right to Live, the Right to Die*. Wheaton, Ill.: Tyndale House, 1976.

Lynn, Barry W., and Marc D. Stern, Oliver S. Thomas. *The Right to Religious Liberty: The Basic ACLU Guide to Religious Rights*. 2d ed. Carbondale: Southern Illinois University Press, 1995.

Mendelson, Wallace. *The American Constitution and Civil Liberties*. Homewood, Ill.: Dorsey Press, 1981.

Smith, F. LaGard. *ACLU: The Devil's Advocate: The Seduction of Civil Liberties in America*. Colorado Springs, Colo.: Marcon, 1996.

Smith, Steven D. *Foreordained Failure: The Quest for a Constitutional Principle of Religious Freedom*. New York: Oxford University Press, 1995.

Urofsky, Melvin I., and Philip E. Urofsky, eds. *The Right to Die: A Two-Volume Anthology of Scholarly Articles*. New York: Garland, 1996.

Wallace, Mendelson. *The American Constitution and Civil Liberties*. Homewood, Ill.: Dorsey Press, 1981.

Yates, Michael. *Power on the Job: The Legal Rights of Working People*. Boston: South End Press, 1994.

Censorship

Amey, Lawrence, et al., eds. *Censorship*. 3 vols. Pasadena, Calif.: Salem Press, 1996.

Clor, Harry M., ed. *Censorship and Freedom of Expression: Essays on Obscenity and the Law*. Chicago: Rand McNally, 1971.

Cohen, Jeremy. *Congress Shall Make No Law: Oliver Wendell Holmes, the First Amendment, and Judicial Decision Making*. Ames: Iowa State University Press, 1989.

De Grazia, Edward. *Girls Lean Back Everywhere: The Law of Obscenity and the Assault on Genius*. New York: Random House, 1992.

De Grazia, Edward, and Roger K. Newman. *Banned Films: Movies, Censors, and the First Amendment*. New York: R. R. Bowker, 1982.

Ernst, Morris L., and Alexander Lindey. *The Censor Marches On: Recent Milestones in the Administration of the Obscenity Law in the United States.* 1940. Reprint. New York: Da Capo Press, 1971.

Foerstel, Herbert N. *Free Expression and Censorship in America: An Encyclopedia.* Westport, Conn.: Greenwood Press, 1997.

Friedman, Leon. *Obscenity: The Complete Oral Arguments Before the Supreme Court in the Major Obscenity Cases.* New York: Chelsea House, 1970.

Green, Jonathon. *The Encyclopedia of Censorship.* New York: Facts on File, 1990.

Hurwitz, Leon. *Historical Dictionary of Censorship in the United States.* Westport, Conn.: Greenwood Press, 1985.

Moretti, Daniel S. *Obscenity and Pornography: The Law Under the First Amendment.* London: Oceana, 1984.

Pally, Marcia. *Sense and Censorship: The Vanity of the Bonfires.* New York: Americans for Constitutional Freedom and the Freedom to Read Foundation, 1991.

Schauer, Frederick F. *The Law of Obscenity.* Washington: Bureau of National Affairs, 1976.

Sobel, Lester A., ed. *Pornography, Obscenity, and the Law.* New York: Facts on File, 1978.

Sunderland, Lane V. *Obscenity: The Court, the Congress, and the President's Commission.* Washington: American Enterprise Institute, 1975.

Abortion and Reproductive Rights

Dienes, C. Thomas. *Law, Politics, and Birth Control.* Urbana: University of Illinois Press, 1972.

Garrow, David J. *Liberty and Sexuality: The Right to Privacy and the Making of Roe v. Wade.* New York: Macmillan, 1994.

Goldstein, Leslie Friedman. *Contemporary Cases in Women's Rights.* Madison: University of Wisconsin Press, 1994.

Himes, Norman E. *Medical History of Contraception.* New York: Schocken Books, 1970.

Knight, James W., and Joan C. Callahan. *Preventing Birth: Contemporary Methods and Related Moral Controversies.* Salt Lake City: University of Utah Press, 1989.

Meyer, Cheryl L. *The Wandering Uterus: Politics and the Reproductive Rights of Women.* New York: New York University Press, 1997.

Mohr, James C. *Abortion in America: The Origins and Evolution of National Policy.* New York: Oxford, 1978.

Reed, James. *The Birth Control Movement and American Society: From Private Vice to Public Virtue.* Princeton, N.J.: Princeton University Press, 1983.

Reynolds, Moira D. *Women Advocates of Reproductive Rights: Eleven Who Led the Struggle in the United States and Great Britain.* Jefferson, N.C.: McFarland, 1994.

Schneider, Carl E., and Maris A. Vinovskis, eds. *The Law and Politics of Abortion.* Lexington, Mass.: Heath, 1980.

Solinger, Rickie. *Wake Up Little Susie: Single Pregnancy and Race Before Roe v. Wade.* New York: Routledge, 1992.

Stotland, Nada Logan. *Social Change and Women's Reproductive Health Care: A Guide for Physicians and Their Patients.* New York: Praeger, 1988.

Tone, Andrea. *Controlling Reproduction: An American History.* Wilmington, Del.: SR Books, 1997.

Tribe, Laurence H. *Abortion: The Clash of Opposites.* New York: W. W. Norton, 1990.

Civil Rights

Abraham, Henry J., and Barbara A. Perry. *Freedom and the Court: Civil Rights and Liberties in the United States.* 7th ed. New York: Oxford University Press, 1998.

Ashmore, Harry S. *Civil Rights and Wrongs: A Memoir of Race and Politics, 1944-1996.* Rev. ed. Columbia: University of South Carolina Press, 1997.

Belknap, Michal R. *Federal Law and Southern Order: Racial Violence and Constitutional Conflict in the Post-Brown South.* Rev. ed. Athens: University of Georgia Press, 1995.

Blumberg, Rhoda L. *Civil Rights: The 1960's Freedom Struggle.* Boston: Twayne, 1991.

Bradley, David, and Shelley Fisher Fishkin, eds. *The Encyclopedia of Civil Rights in America.* New York: M. E. Sharpe, 1997.

Braeman, John. *Before the Civil Rights Revolution: The Old Court and Individual Rights.* New York: Greenwood Press, 1988.

Branch, Taylor. *Parting the Waters: America in the King Years, 1954-63*. New York: Simon & Schuster, 1988.

Brooks, Roy L., Gilbert P. Carrasco and Gordon A. Martin. *Civil Rights Litigation: Cases and Perspectives*. Durham, N.C.: Carolina Academic Press, 1995.

Bullock, Charles S., III, and Charles M. Lamb. *Implementation of Civil Rights Policy*. Monterey, Calif.: Brooks-Cole, 1984.

Cashman, Sean D. *African-Americans and the Quest for Civil Rights, 1900-1990*. New York: New York University Press, 1991.

Friedman, Leon. *The Civil Rights Reader: Basic Documents of the Civil Rights Movement*. New York: Walker & Company, 1968.

Gaillard, Frye. *The Dream Long Deferred*. Chapel Hill: University of North Carolina Press, 1988.

Govan, Reginald C., and William L. Taylor, eds. *One Nation Indivisible: The Civil Rights Challenge for the 1990's*. Washington, D.C.: Citizens' Commission on Civil Rights, 1989.

Graham, Hugh D., ed. *Civil Rights in the United States*. University Park: Pennsylvania State University Press, 1994.

Greenberg, Jack. *Crusaders in the Courts: How a Dedicated Band of Lawyers Fought for the Civil Rights Revolution*. New York: Basic Books, 1994.

Lewis, Anthony. *Portrait of a Decade: The Second American Revolution*. New York: Random House, 1964.

Lewis, David L., and Charles W. Eagles. *The Civil Rights Movement in America: Essays*. Jackson: University Press of Mississippi, 1986.

Luker, Ralph. *Historical Dictionary of the Civil Rights Movement*. Lanham, Md.: Scarecrow Press, 1997.

Murray, Paul T. *The Civil Rights Movement: References and Resources*. New York: G. K. Hall, 1993.

Nieman, Donald G. *Promises to Keep: African-Americans and the Constitutional Order, 1776 to the Present*. New York: Oxford University Press, 1991.

Powledge, Fred. *Free at Last? The Civil Rights Movement and the People Who Made It*. Boston: Little, Brown, 1991.

Salmond, John A. *"My Mind Set on Freedom": A History of the Civil Rights Movement, 1954-1968*. Chicago: Ivan R. Dee, 1997.

Shapiro, Ian, and Will Kymlicka, eds. *Ethnicity and Group Rights.* New York: New York University Press, 1997.

Weisbrot, Robert. *Freedom Bound: A History of America's Civil Rights Movement.* New York: Plume, 1991.

Wexler, Sanford. *The Civil Rights Movement: An Eyewitness History.* New York: Facts on File, 1993.

Williams, Cecil J. *Freedom and Justice: Four Decades of the Civil Rights Struggle as Seen by a Black Photographer of the Deep South.* Macon, Ga.: Mercer University Press, 1995.

Williams, Juan. *Eyes on the Prize: America's Civil Rights Years, 1954-1965.* New York: Penguin, 1988.

Young, Andrew. *An Easy Burden: The Civil Rights Movement and the Transformation of America.* New York: HarperCollins, 1996.

Civil Rights: Affirmative Action

Curry, George E., and Cornel West, eds. *The Affirmative Action Debate.* Reading, Mass.: Addison-Wesley, 1996.

Dreyfuss, Joel, and Charles Lawrence III. *The Bakke Case: The Politics of Inequality.* New York: Harcourt Brace Jovanovich, 1979.

Eastland, Terry. *Ending Affirmative Action: The Case for Colorblind Justice.* New York: Basic Books, 1996.

Eastland, Terry, and William J. Bennett. *Counting by Race: Equality from the Founding Fathers to Bakke and Weber.* New York: Basic Books, 1979.

Schwartz, Bernard. *Behind Bakke: Affirmative Action and the Supreme Court.* New York: New York University Press, 1988.

Sindler, Allan P. *Bakke, DeFunis, and Minority Admissions: The Quest for Equal Opportunity.* New York: Longman, 1978.

Weiss, Robert J. *"We Want Jobs": A History of Affirmative Action.* New York: Garland, 1997.

Civil Rights: Segregation

Atkinson, Pansye S. *Brown v. Topeka: An African American's View: Desegregation and Miseducation.* Chicago: African American Images, 1993.

Bolner, James. *Busing: The Political and Judicial Process.* New York: Praeger, 1974.

Davison, Douglas, ed. *School Busing: Constitutional and Political Development*. 2 vols. New York: Garland, 1994.

Kluger, Richard. *Simple Justice: The History of "Brown v. Board of Education" and Black America's Struggle for Equality*. New York: Alfred A. Knopf, 1976.

Lagemann, Ellen C., and LaMar Miller, eds. *Brown v. Board of Education: The Challenge for Today's Schools*. New York: Teacher's College Press, 1996.

Loevy, Robert D. *The Civil Rights Act of 1964: The Passage of the Law That Ended Racial Segregation*. Albany: State University of New York Press, 1997.

Olsen, Otto H., comp. *The Thin Disguise: Turning Point in Negro History: Plessy v. Ferguson; A Documentary Presentation, 1864-1896*. New York: Humanities Press, 1967.

Orfield, Gary, Susan E. Eaton, and the Harvard Project on School Desegregation. *Dismantling Desegregation: The Quiet Reversal of Brown v. Board of Education*. New York: New Press, 1996.

Rasmussen, R. Kent. *Farewell to Jim Crow: The Rise and Fall of Segregation in America*. New York: Facts on File, 1997.

Rosenfeld, Michael. *Affirmative Action and Justice: A Philosophical and Constitutional Inquiry*. New Haven, Conn.: Yale University Press, 1991.

Schwartz, Bernard. *Swann's Way: The School Busing Case and the Supreme Court*. New York: Oxford University Press, 1986.

Speer, Hugh W. *The Case of the Century: A Historical and Social Perspective on Brown v. Board of Education of Topeka, with Present and Future Implications*. Kansas City: University of Missouri Press, 1968.

Thomas, Brook. *Plessy v. Ferguson: A Brief History with Documents*. Boston: Bedford Books, 1997.

Wilkinson, J. Harvie, III. *From Brown to Bakke: The Supreme Court and School Integration, 1954-1978*. New York: Oxford University Press, 1979.

Wilson, Paul E. *A Time to Lose: Representing Kansas in Brown v. Board of Education*. Lawrence: University Press of Kansas, 1995.

Woodward, C. Vann. *The Strange Career of Jim Crow*. New York: Oxford University Press, 1974.

Civil Rights of Asian Americans

Chan, Sucheng, ed. *Entry Denied: Exclusion and the Chinese Community in America, 1882-1943.* Philadelphia: Temple University Press, 1991.

Commission on Wartime Relocation and Internment of Civilians. *Personal Justice Denied: Report of the Commission on Wartime Relocation and Internment of Civilians.* Washington, D.C.: Government Printing Office, 1982.

Daniels, Roger. *Prisoners Without Trial: Japanese Americans in World War II.* New York: Hill and Wang, 1993.

Foner, Philip S., and Daniel Rosenberg. *Racism, Dissent and Asian Americans from 1850 to the Present: A Documentary History.* Westport, Conn.: Greenwood Press, 1993.

Free, Marvin D. *African Americans and the Criminal Justice System.* New York: Garland, 1996.

Hatamiya, Leslie T. *Righting a Wrong: Japanese Americans and the Passage of the Civil Liberties Act of 1988.* Stanford, Calif.: Stanford University Press, 1993.

Kim, Hyung-chan, ed. *Asian Americans and the Supreme Court: A Documentary History.* New York: Greenwood Press, 1992.

Levine, Michael L. *African Americans and Civil Rights: From 1619 to the Present.* Phoenix, Ariz.: Oryx Press, 1996.

Ng, Franklin, ed. *The Asian American Encyclopedia.* 6 vols. New York: Marshall Cavendish, 1996.

Smith, Page. *Democracy on Trial: The Japanese-American Evacuation and Relocation in World War II.* New York: Simon & Schuster, 1995.

Tsuchida, Nobuya. *American Justice: Japanese American Evacuation and Redress Cases.* Minneapolis: University of Minnesota, 1988.

U.S. Commission on Civil Rights. *Civil Rights Issues Facing Asian Americans in the 1990's.* Washington, D.C.: Government Printing Office, 1992.

U.S. Court Cases

Index

F

Kiowa, 318
Klopfer v. North Carolina (1967), 56
Klutznick, Philip, 224
Korematsu v. United States (1944),
  307-309, 350
Kraemer, Louis, 464
Ku Klux Klan, 153
Kurtzman, David, 315

L

Labor law, 365-366
*Lassiter v. Department of Social
  Services* (1981), 240
Lau v. Nichols (1974), 309-314
Law, 12-20, 26; definitions of, 12;
  purposes and functions of, 13,
  15; sources of, 17; types of, 16-17
Legal realism, 27
Legal rights and duties,
  philosophy of, 28
Legion of Decency, 368
Lemon v. Kurtzman (1971), 117, 202,
  315-316, 364
Leon, United States v. (1984),
  298-299, 340
Libel, 377-379
Liberty clause, 399
Liberty interests, 186
Lincoln, Abraham, 198; and *habeas
  corpus*, 342, 344, 349
Lincoln-Douglas Debates, 198
Literacy test, 272
Little Rock school integration
  crisis, 182-183
Living will, 185
Local Public Works Capital
  Development and Investment
  Act (1976), 224
Lochner doctrine, 514
Lochner v. New York (1905), 316-318,
  366, 514
Locke, John, 15, 28, 42
Lone Wolf, 319
Lone Wolf v. Hitchcock (1902),
  318-320

Lopez, Dwight, 245
Lorance, Patricia, 321
Lorance v. AT&T Technologies
  (1989), 321
Loving, Richard, 322
Loving v. Virginia (1967), 322
*Lucas v. South Carolina Coastal
  Council* (1992), 323-324
Lynch v. Donnelly (1984), 324-326

M

Mabry v. Johnson (1984), 455
McCleskey, Warren, 326
McCleskey v. Kemp (1987), 326-328
McCorvey, Norma, 435
McCulloch v. Maryland (1819), 99
McGautha v. California (1971), 227
McGehee v. Casey (1983), 473
McJunkins v. State, 415
McRae, Nora, 281
McReynolds, James C., 399, 516
Madison, James, 21, 41, 51, 334
Maher v. Roe (1977), 281, 328-329,
  449
Malapportionment, 426
Malloy v. Hogan (1964), 54, 121,
  329-331, 355
Mandamus, writ of, 334
Mandatory sentencing laws,
  277-279; and cruel and unusual
  punishment, 446-447
Mapp v. Ohio (1961), 53, 175, 214,
  331-333, 433, 511, 525
Marbury v. Madison (1803), 36, 82,
  90, 98, 333-336
Marchetti, Victor, 473
Marchetti v. United States (1972), 473
Marriage, 23, 267, 269, 528;
  interracial, 322; polygamous,
  427, 429; and privacy, 436
Marsh v. Chambers (1983), 504
Marshall, John, 82, 89-90, 98-99,
  141, 171, 189, 334-335, 387; and
  judicial review, 98; and *Marbury
  v. Madison* (1803), 99

N